A Guide to North Carolina's Wineries

A Guide to North Carolina's Wineries

Second Edition

by Joseph Mills
and Danielle Tarmey

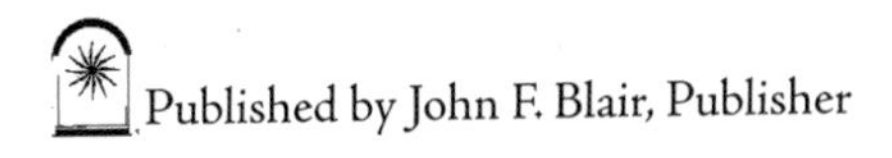

Published by John F. Blair, Publisher

*The paper in this book meets the guidelines
for permanence and durability of the Committee on Production
Guidelines for Book Longevity of the Council on Library Resources.*

*Unless otherwise noted, all photographs are by Danielle Tarmey
Design by Debra Long Hampton and Angela Harwood*

Library of Congress Cataloging-in-Publication Data
Mills, Joseph, 1965–
A guide to North Carolina's wineries / by Joseph Mills and Danielle Tarmey. —2nd ed.
p. cm.
Includes index.
ISBN 978-0-89587-342-2 (alk. paper)
ISBN 0-89587-342-7
1. Wineries—North Carolina—Guidebooks. 2. Wine and wine making—North Carolina—Guidebooks. 3. North Carolina—Guidebooks. I. Tarmey, Danielle. II. Title.
TP557.M545 2007
641.2'209756—dc22 2007009686

Contents

Wineries of the Yadkin Valley

Wineries of Piedmont North Carolina

Wineries of Eastern North Carolina

Wineries of Western North Carolina

1. Banner Elk Winery
2. Biltmore Estate Winery
3. Cerminaro Vineyard
4. Chateau Laurinda
5. Ginger Creek Vineyards
6. Green Creek Winery
7. Lake James Cellars
8. New River Winery
9. Rockhouse Vineyards
10. The Teensy Winery
11. Thistle Meadow Winery
12. Waldensian Heritage Wines
13. WoodMill Winery

Wineries of the Yadkin Valley

14. Black Wolf Vineyards
15. Brushy Mountain Winery
16. Buck Shoals Vineyard
17. Childress Vineyards
18. Elkin Creek Vineyard
19. Flint Hill Vineyards
20. Grassy Creek Vineyard and Winery
21. Hanover Park Vineyard
22. Laurel Gray Vineyards
23. McRitchie Wine Company
24. Old North State Winery
25. Raffaldini Vineyards
26. RagApple Lassie Vineyards
27. RayLen Vineyards and Winery
28. Round Peak Vineyards
29. Shelton Vineyards
30. Stony Knoll Vineyards
31. Weathervane Winery
32. Westbend Vineyards
33. Windy Gap Vineyards

Wineries of Piedmont North Carolina

34. Benjamin Vineyards and Winery
35. Chatham Hill Winery
36. Creek Side Winery
37. Dennis Vineyards
38. Desi's Dew Meadery
39. Garden Gate Vineyards
40. Germanton Art Gallery and Winery
41. GlenMarie Vineyards and Winery
42. Grove Winery
43. Horizon Cellars
44. Old Stone Vineyard and Winery
45. Rock of Ages Winery and Vineyard
46. SilkHope Winery
47. Stonefield Cellars
48. Stony Mountain Vineyards
49. Uwharrie Vineyards
50. The Winery at Iron Gate Farm

51. Bannerman Vineyard
52. Bennett Vineyards
53. Cypress Bend Vineyards
54. Duplin Winery
55. Grapefull Sisters Vineyard
56. Hinnant Family Vineyards
57. Lu Mil Vineyard
58. Lumina Winery
59. Martin Vineyards
60. Moonrise Bay Vineyard
61. Sanctuary Vineyards
62. A Secret Garden Winery
63. Silver Coast Winery
64. Somerset Cellars

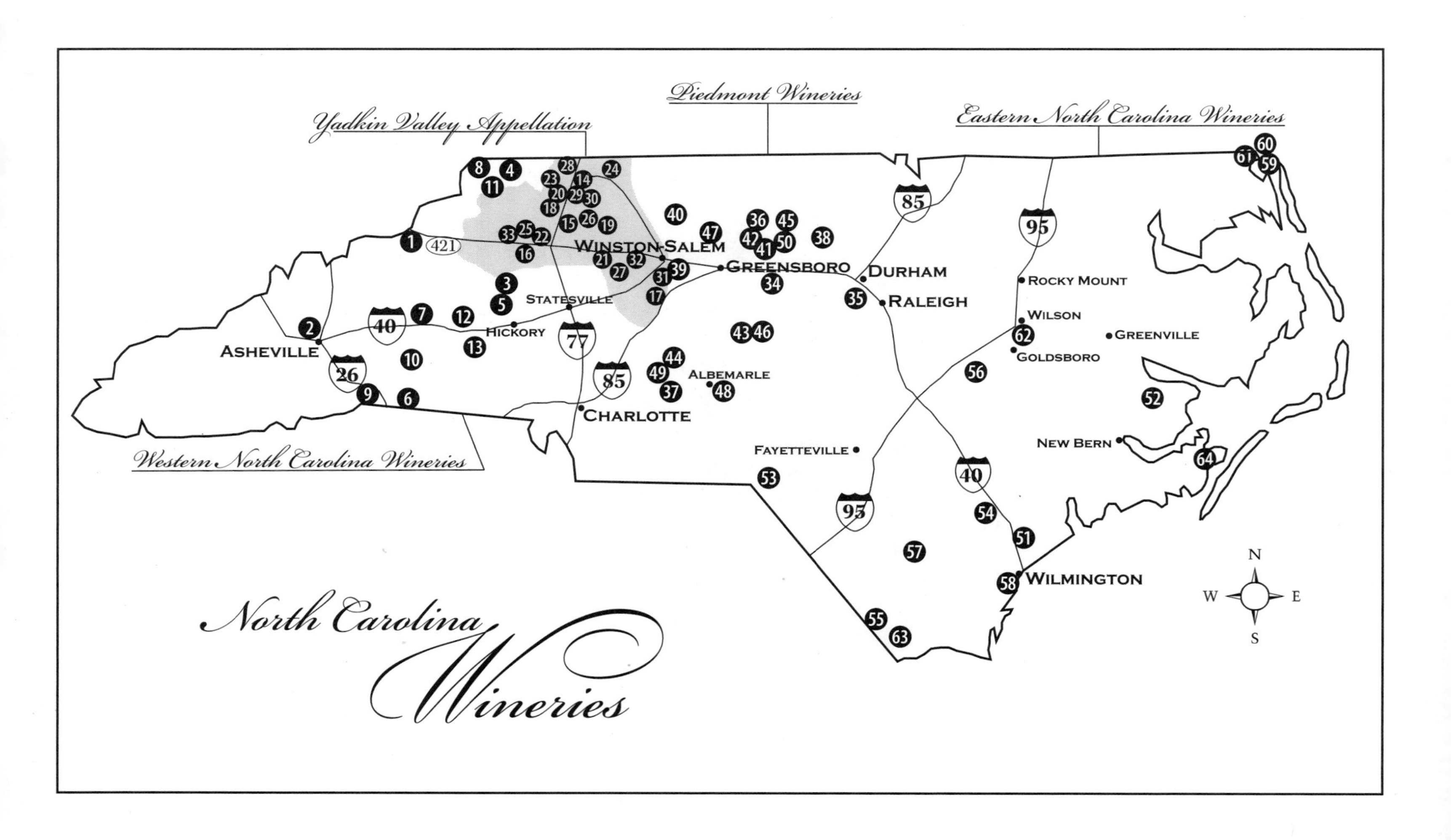
North Carolina Wineries
Yadkin Valley Appellation
Piedmont Wineries
Eastern North Carolina Wineries
Western North Carolina Wineries
Asheville
Hickory
Statesville
Winston-Salem
Greensboro
Durham
Raleigh
Charlotte
Albemarle
Fayetteville
Rocky Mount
Wilson
Goldsboro
Greenville
New Bern
Wilmington
N
S
E
W

Preface to the Second Edition

In the four years since the first edition of this book, the number of wineries in North Carolina has almost tripled. Consequently, for this edition, we have changed some of the format. To give as much space as possible to the histories of the wineries, we no longer include recipes, pairings, or individual profiles.

As with the first edition, we also do not offer tasting notes or critique wines. For one, many wines in the state are made in small batches and will be unavailable during the life span of this book. For another, the wine offerings in North Carolina are remarkably diverse, ranging from apple to Zinfandel, and they appeal to a wide variety of tastes. We believe this variety is one of the industry's strengths, and we have no interest in presenting our individual tastes as a standard for others to follow.

For us, wine is not about numbers and notes but about people and their stories. In this book, we give an overview—a taste—of each winery and the people involved in its founding and operation.

People in the North Carolina wine industry come from diverse backgrounds—art and accounting, teaching and textiles, manufacturing and medicine—but most of them share a number of characteristics. They tend to be stubborn, independent, strong-willed, opinionated, and unafraid to take risks. They don't like the word *no*, and they often ignore people who tell them that they can't or shouldn't do something. They also are forthright, hardworking, and optimistic. Most winery owners say that they must have been crazy to get into the business, yet most of them would do the same thing again.

Talk to people in the industry long enough and most will admit that the business is financially expensive, physically tiring, and emotionally draining. It's difficult work, and there are easier ways to make a living. In fact, many—perhaps most—of the winery owners are not making a living, although they hope to someday. So why do they do it? What drives people to commit so much time, energy, and money? There are many answers. For some, it's a hobby that grew to commercial proportions. For others, it's a way to preserve land from development. There are people who hated their previous jobs and felt this would offer a more satisfying lifestyle, and those who do it as a retirement activity. Some believe in wine's health benefits, and others simply relish the challenges involved. Regardless of the reason that they entered the field, they stay because, despite the difficulties, they find it rewarding. As Lillian Kroustalis of Westbend Vineyards says, "Wine is seductive. It gets you. It grabs you. It won't go away."

Acknowledgments

We would like to thank all of the babysitters, paid and volunteer, without whom we could not have researched this book.

Introduction

Although it took decades to recover from the "great national experiment" of Prohibition, America's wine industry is now flourishing. Every state has at least one winery, and there are more than 100 "appellations," or American Viticultural Areas (AVAs), including North Carolina's Yadkin Valley. Wine sales increase each year, visiting wineries has become a major tourist activity, and the agribusiness of grapes is an important part of states' economies.

Most of the development in the North Carolina wine industry has occurred in the last 15 years. In 1991, the state had a handful of bonded wineries and fewer than 70 commercial vineyards. As of this writing, there are 64 wineries (with several more planning to open soon) and over 350 vineyards. To anyone who has traveled the state's highways and interstates, the growth has been obvious. Department of Transportation directional signs and various billboards point out the presence of wineries from the mountains to the sea.

The industry has become visible in other ways as well. Groceries, wine shops, and restaurants are devoting more space and attention to North Carolina vintages. High-profile wineries such as Shelton Vineyards, Childress Vineyards, and Duplin Winery regularly attract the attention of the national media, and wines around the state have won awards in respected national and international competitions.

Almost everyone involved in the business applauds this expansion. Stephen Lyons of Raffaldini Vineyards points out, "The absolute best thing to happen to a winery is to have another winery open right next to it. Then it becomes a destination." In many parts of North Carolina, people can now tour multiple wineries in a day, and in the Yadkin Valley AVA, almost two dozen wineries are within a short drive of one another.

North Carolina's wineries are diverse. They range from Biltmore Estate Winery, which produces over 100,000 cases a year and bills itself as the most-visited winery in America, to The Teensy Winery, which some years produces a few hundred gallons of wine and most years produces none at all. There are wineries located in old farmhouses, basements, converted garages, and million-dollar showpiece buildings. There are wineries for art lovers, NASCAR fans, boccia players, picnickers, fine-diners, winemaking hobbyists, connoisseurs, and people who have never drunk wine before.

The wines are diverse as well. Vineyards in North Carolina grow every major type of grape, including European vinifera, French-American hybrids, Lambruscos, muscadines, and scuppernongs. Many wineries also offer fruit wines such as apple, blackberry, pear, plum, and strawberry.

An explosion of related ventures and businesses has paralleled the growth of the industry. Three colleges in the state now have oenology and viticulture programs, and there have been sociological studies of the Yadkin Valley wine industry. There are an industry newsletter (*On The Vine*), a North Carolina Wine of the Month Club, and dozens of wine-related festivals throughout the state. There are restaurants, B&Bs, hotels, and shops affiliated with wineries. People run equipment supply stores, offer their services as vineyard consultants, and focus their real-estate businesses on vineyards.

The industry's rapid growth has surprised even the most optimistic people, but there are several who urge caution. Stephen Rigby of Raffaldini Vineyards says, "It's a wonderful business, and everyone wants to get into it. I don't blame them, but you need to be careful." Like that for almost any agricultural product, the market for grapes involves risks. In 2006, a production glut drove prices down, and many growers suddenly found themselves unable to sell their crops. Among some people in the industry, there also are concerns about too much young wine on the market and too many inexperienced winemakers. Furthermore, winery owners face daunting competition from global markets. A person can buy a good, inexpensive bottle from Chile, Argentina, Australia, and other countries at their local grocery store. Finally, as the earth's overall temperature rises, the climate in the state is changing, which will make grape growing even more challenging.

Although in the future some wineries may close or change hands, it's likely the industry will continue to grow and develop. Dan Smith of Cypress Bend Vineyards even predicts that in a couple of years, North Carolina will surpass Virginia in its number of wineries. The wineries in several areas—including the Haw River region and Green Creek near Tryon—are considering applying for AVA appellations. Already, the Yadkin Valley is so well established that some wineries within the AVA are forming smaller designations, such as the Wineries of Swan Creek. This, as Stephen Lyons points out, is the logical progression that happened in places like California's Napa Valley.

Small changes also will continue to occur within the industry. For example, in the past few years, tasting fees have become standard, court decisions have dramatically altered shipping regulations, and wineries throughout the state have increased their posted hours.

The development of the state's wine industry has resulted in changes both to the landscape and to the culture. Traditionally, in many communities, alcohol has been regarded with suspicion. Now, however, wine has come to be regarded as the possible salvation of farmers and as a type of medical elixir. Many wineries have even been established by people whose families are teetotalers. It's a revealing shift. The state is changing, and there may be no better symbol of its transformation than a wine bottle with "North Carolina" on the label.

The History of Wine in North Carolina

Here's to the land of the cotton bloom white,
Where the scuppernong perfumes the breeze at night . . .
Second verse of the North Carolina state toast

In 1900, North Carolina wines won medals at the Paris Exposition. It wasn't a fluke. Four years later at the Louisiana Purchase Exposition in St. Louis, a champagne from the state took the grand prize for sparkling wines against competition from other states as well as France, Italy, and Argentina.

The maker of these medal winners was Paul Garrett, one of the most important figures in the history of American wine. Garrett built a business empire that spanned the nation. At one point, Paul Garrett & Co. was selling almost a million cases a year. His success owed as much to his flair for marketing as to the quality of his wines. In his promotional materials, he argued that wine should be considered a food, noted its medicinal properties, and insisted that if people drank wine regularly, it would "forever remove the vexatious problem of intemperance." Critical of those who insisted on drinking foreign wines, he emphasized both the heritage and patriotism of his products. For example, bottles of Garrett's American Wines prominently featured an eagle. His most popular brand, Virginia Dare, was named after the most famous woman of Roanoke's Lost Colony.

Garrett's advertising created an enduring North Carolina belief. The back of one pamphlet showed an old vine that Garrett claimed was "discovered in 1585" and was the source of the rootstock for many of the state's vineyards. This "Mother Vine" has become an important symbol for the state's wine industry, even though viticulture scholars such as Clarence Gohdes, author of the book *Scuppernong*, suggest the story is highly improbable.

The real history of North Carolina wine, however, is just as impressive as the one constructed by Garrett. It covers hundreds of years and consists of repeating cycles. Several times in the past two centuries, the industry has grown vigorously and then collapsed.

The first Europeans who came to the area commented on the wild grapes they saw. The earliest known account is by Giovanni da Verrazano, who explored the coast in 1524 and wrote about the "many vines growing naturally there." He thought that "without doubt they would yield excellent wines." Sixty years later, colleagues of Sir Walter Raleigh described the coast of North Carolina as "so full of grapes that the very beating and surge of the sea overflowed them. They covered every shrub and climbed the tops of high cedars. In all the world, a similar abundance was not to be found." In fact, Gohdes notes, "legend has it that Sir Walter Raleigh took back to England 'a white grape that was esteemed among the best ever seen' and it was cultivated by Queen Elizabeth's patronage."

These wild grapes—varieties of muscadines that grow only in the American South—were made into wine by a number of colonists. In 1737, Irish physician John Brickell noted of North Carolina, "There are but few Vineyards planted in this Colony at present, for I have seen but one small one at Bath-Town and another at Neus [New Bern], of the White Grape, the same with the Madera. I have drank the Wine it produced, which was exceeding good." The *1878 Guide Book of North-West-*

ern North Carolina noted that "in 1769, three settlements of Carolina Moravians made nineteen hogsheads from 'the great abundance of wild grapes.'" By the first decades of the 19th century, thousands of gallons of wine were being made throughout the state, and scuppernongs were beginning to be cultivated as a crop.

The first important figure in the history of North Carolina wine was Sidney Weller, who established vineyards in Halifax and wrote two groundbreaking articles—"The Southern System of Vine Culture and Wine Making" in 1835 and "Wine Making, as Practiced in North Carolina" in 1845. Weller sold not only grapes and wine but vine cuttings as well, and he systematically studied viticulture. He also invented a new trellising system. But his greatest influence was as a promoter, rather than a grower. He championed the scuppernong in every forum possible, believing that everyone should grow at least some of the grapes. In an 1832 article, he insisted, "If only as a pleasurable employment for hours of relaxation from business, attention to cultivation of vines would afford present compensation to a tasteful, virtuous mind. A number of vines, in regular order, is beautiful and agreeable to the sight especially in the season of leafing and bearing. Then becoming ripe, the Scuppernong and some other choice kinds of grapes, perfume the air around some distance with a delightful healthful fragrance. As an article of innocent luxury, no family of settled residence should dispense with rearing a few vines, at least." Weller's Vineyard eventually was renamed Medoc Vineyards. By 1840, it led the country in wine production.

Although many of those interested in making wine or having a vineyard first tried French vinifera, they had little success. In fact, Paul Lukacs points out in *American Vintage: The Rise of American Wine* that every colony planted vinifera, but no one could get the vines to survive. They were defenseless against pests and diseases to which native plants had a natural resistance. Consequently, farmers turned to scuppernongs. Easy to grow and flavorful, scuppernongs became known as "the Grape of Grapes" and "the Grape of the South."

Joseph Tongo, an enterprising viticulturist, chose North Carolina over Virginia and Kentucky because the land "flows with the milk of human kindness and Scuppernong wine." Intending to make Wilmington "the Bordeaux of America," he started the North Carolina Vine Dresser and Horticultural Model Practical School. In 1849, he advertised that students over 14 years of age would be taught "all the manipulations of the Vineyard, the orchard, and horticulture in general. The pupils will be taught besides all the practical and scientific details of grape and fruit raising &c, the art of making wine, and of taking care of it at all periods of ripening." The school was a failure, but the vineyard flourished.

The 1850s saw a national grape craze. During that time, North Carolina had at least 25 wineries and numerous vineyards. By the end of the decade, a doctor in Boston insisted that "with proper attention and care, Scuppernong wine may be made so fine as to excel all other wines made on this continent; and I would earnestly advise those interested to attend to the cultivation of this grape, in regions where the vine will grow, and make use of more skill in the manufacture."

The state's thriving industry was devastated, however, by the Civil War. David Fussell of Duplin Winery believes that "we were the leading wine state in the Union. When we seceded from the Union, the Southern winemakers no longer paid and maintained their federal bonded wine licenses. So when North Carolina lost, they were not licensed by the federal government to operate. Since North Carolina had dominated the wine market, like California is dominating it today, in the reconstruction of the South, the conquering forces decided that they didn't want us to make wine, so they would not renew these boys their federal wine licenses."

Eventually, the state's industry did rebuild. In fact, scuppernongs were championed as the best crop to grow because they required minimal labor. (Paul Garrett called a scuppernong vineyard "a literary man's Utopia and a lazy man's Paradise.") Farmers were encouraged to grow grapes as a solution to a depressed economy, and wine was seen as an important part of the future. By the end of the century, North Carolina was again at the forefront of the nation's industry. The Tryon area had a number of commercial vineyards. The Waldensian community in Valdese had brought a winemaking tradition with it from Europe.. The federal government was heavily promoting scuppernong grapes, and Paul Garrett had begun building his empire.

Although the industry thrived for several decades, the state's temperance movement succeeded in crushing it yet again. In 1909, North Carolina enacted a statewide prohibition on alcohol. Garrett moved his business to Virginia. In 1917, he had to move again—this time to New York—when Virginia went dry. Then, in 1919, the 18th Amendment enacted Prohibition throughout the country. In *Winegrowing in Eastern America,* Lucie T. Morton notes, "The eastern wine industry was so effectively ruined by Prohibition and its aftermath that today the region's vineyards and estate wineries are objects of surprise and curiosity in areas where local wines were once taken for granted."

A straw poll conducted in 1932 indicated that two states wanted to continue Prohibition: Kansas and North Carolina. In the following decade, many counties throughout the state voted to return to being dry. During the Depression, scuppernongs again were cited as a crop that would promote employment, but it was decades before making wine reemerged as a serious commercial endeavor.

Paul Garrett managed to shepherd his company through Prohibition, in part by offering such products as Virginia Dare Tonic, a "medicament" with beef extract and pepsin, and Virginia Dare Flavoring Secrets, which included 21 flavors such as fruit, peppermint, and vanilla. But in the 1930s, he couldn't convince Southern farmers to plant the grapes he needed for expansion. By the time of his death in 1940, Virginia Dare Wine, which had been known for its scuppernong flavor, was no longer made with any of the grape.

In the 1950s and 1960s, the federal government promoted the growing of scuppernong grapes. Many farmers sold their crops to Northern wineries. A few wineries tried to establish themselves in North Carolina, but none lasted long. Lucie T. Morton explains, "The thirty five years from Repeal to the 1968 passage of the Pennsylvania Limited Winery bill was for the most part a 'dark ages' for American wine in general and for that of eastern America in particular."

Of North Carolina's current wineries, only two date back as far as the late 1970s: Duplin and Biltmore. By the early 1980s, these were joined by two more: Germanton Art Gallery and Winery and Westbend Vineyards. These wineries did well until legislative changes in the mid-1980s again curtailed the industry.

Over the last 20 years, significant growth has occurred again. Not only are there hundreds of new vineyards, but a wide variety of grapes are being planted. After Biltmore and Westbend demonstrated that vinifera could be grown successfully in North Carolina, many followed their lead. Plantings of muscadine and scuppernong have also increased, in part because of the numerous studies citing the health benefits of antioxidants in wine. Consequently, grapes are once more being championed as an important part of the state's economy.

In 1935, Paul Garrett hailed grapes as "a new money crop for the farmer." It's a belief that sounds strikingly contemporary.

Basics of Winemaking

> How do you make a small fortune in the wine business?
> Start with a large fortune and buy a winery.
>
> A favorite joke of winery owners

What does it take to make wine?

The first requirement is patience. Larry Ehlers of Chateau Laurinda emphasizes, "It's a long-term thing. I think in the wine or grape-growing business, you have to think in terms of 10 years, rather than two or five years. . . . Most businesses, you think you should be turning a profit in two years. In this business, I think you would have to be considered crazy to think that you could turn a profit in two years. I don't see how you could."

A significant planting of vine stock needs to be ordered a year in advance, and then the vines usually require two to three years to produce grapes and five to 10 years to reach maturity. Consequently, as Lillian Kroustalis of Westbend Vineyards advises, "it's never too early to plant a vineyard. If you don't use the grapes, fine, but get them in the ground."

The second requirement is effort. Growing grapes, like most farming, is labor intensive. Dennis Wynne of Biltmore Estate Winery says, "Everybody thinks a job in the vineyards is so romantic. It's hard, hard work. It's hot in the summer and cold in the winter." Grapevines require constant attention, and they are susceptible to excessive cold, heat, dryness, and moisture and to dozens of diseases. In short, grapes are a fragile, temperamental crop.

The third requirement is money. Almost everyone in the wine industry emphasizes the expense of the overall process.

For those willing to make the commitment and put in the hours and the years, there are immense rewards, although at times these are more emotional than financial. At some point, almost every winemaker describes the process in religious, spiritual, or artistic terms. Consider Lucie T. Morton, who in *Winegrowing in Eastern America* says, "Harvest brings a kind of death to grapes, and destruction as they pass through the crusher-stemmer. But there is no doubt about the afterlife of grapes—they are reborn into wine—and there is a direct correlation between their life on a vine and their reincarnation on the palate. Wine can be heavenly, hellish, or somewhere in between. It is the job of all winegrowers to place at least some wines in the company of angels."

In more practical terms, making wine has two main parts: the growing of the grapes and the processing of the grapes.

Growing the Grapes: Viticulture

Most winemakers insist that wine is made in the vineyard. Some estimate that roughly 90 percent of a wine's quality comes from the grapes and 10 percent from the processing. Consequently, although good grapes can make a bad wine, an excellent wine can never be made from poor grapes.

Winemakers also are fond of talking about the terroir, or the distinctive environment in which their grapes are raised. Steve Shepard of RayLen Vineyards and Winery explains the concept of terroir by saying, "Every area is different. The growing season, and the soils, and the topography, and the climate—all that is different. It's even different 10 miles from here, where the amount of rainfall varies even when the temperatures are consistent." The terroir and the varietal contribute to the grapes' taste. The multitude of ways these elements can combine account for the diversity and complexity of wines.

Geography

Where vines are planted can determine the quality and quantity of grapes at harvest time. Certain varietals are suited to particular geographical areas. For example, Germany, which is known for its Rieslings, does not produce much red wine. The reason, according to wine expert Kevin Zraly, is that the country's northern latitude results in a growing season that is too short. Even though most German vineyards are on south-facing hills to try to capture as much sunlight as possible, it usually is insufficient to adequately ripen red-wine grapes. Because North Carolina's geography ranges from coastal islands to Mount Mitchell, the highest point east of the Mississippi, most varietals can be grown somewhere in the state.

Soil

The soil provides the vines with the water and mineral nutrients they need. In doing so, it affects the grapes' taste. For example, Marian Baldy, a viticulture scholar, explains that rich and heavy soils promote grassy flavors in Sauvignon Blanc. If, however, winegrowers want to increase the fruity flavors of this varietal, they might plant the vines in less fertile, shallower soil.

Vineyards throughout the state are planted in a wide variety of soils. The Teensy Winery has a vineyard in soil that is so rocky that holes cannot be dug manually. In the Piedmont region, the soil can be clayey or heavy. And Martin Vineyards is planted on a sand dune. Regardless of the type of soil, the key is good drainage. Where water collects, rot can develop. For vines that have life spans measured in decades, this can be devastating.

Climate

Grapes need sunshine, fairly warm temperatures, consistent rainfall, and a long growing season to flourish. A vineyard's optimal season is a mild winter, a wet spring to promote growth, and then a fairly dry ripening season—one with warm days and cool nights. This increases the grapes' sugars, which will turn into alcohol during fermentation.

The diversity of North Carolina's geography has created a variety of climate conditions. As writer Bill Lee notes, some places in the Appalachians have a climate similar to southern Canada, while areas south of Wilmington can be considered subtropical. Wineries in the mountains experience a great deal of rain. As a result, thin-skinned varietals like Chardonnay and Riesling are difficult to grow, and crops must be sprayed every two weeks to ensure that the grapes don't succumb to black rot and other moisture-related problems. Dennis Wynne explains that Riesling grapes grow in such tight clusters that "the problem is, once they start getting ripe and they get rain, they explode. There is nowhere to grow because the cluster is so tight. They expand and pop, and here come the bees, ants, rot, and everything. So then you have to pick them, and the sugar is too low for what the winemaker wants to make." In contrast, at wineries by the sea, such as Moonrise Bay Vineyard, the ocean breezes immediately dry any moisture, so growers don't have to spray and Chardonnay does well. Although coastal vineyards must deal with sea breezes that dry out the fields and create a need for irrigation, the stable climate provides a good environment for delicate white-wine grapes.

In general, North Carolina's humidity is greater than that in other wine-producing regions, which means there are more problems with disease. In certain areas of the state, dramatic temperature shifts also cause difficulties. This is because vines go into a dormant period after the first frost and acclimate as temperatures cool. If a sudden freeze occurs during this acclimation stage, it can damage the vines. A warm spring combined with a late frost can cause similar problems. Steve Shepard notes that on the East Coast, "April is a notoriously unpredictable month." Grapes, particularly European varietals, require a relatively short dormant cycle and are susceptible to budding out too early and becoming vulnerable to cold snaps. In the mountains, frosts can occur even in mid-May. "We've had years where basically we've lost everything," Dennis Wynne points out.

Grapes

Traditionally, the state has been known for its sweet wines made from muscadine grapes. These grapes flourish in part because their thick skins allow them to thrive in the Southern heat. They are also much more resistant to diseases than thin-skinned European varietals. Consequently, they are relatively easy to grow. However, beginning in the 1970s, European grapes such as Chardonnay, Merlot, and Cabernet Sauvignon were planted in significant numbers. By the 1990s, the acreage of these grapes surpassed that of muscadines for the first time. Because large-scale production of European varietals in North Carolina is relatively new, the wineries planting them are still determining which work best. In some cases, this takes years. Westbend planted Viognier in 1991, and the vines grew for eight years without significant grape production. The different varietals on nearby acres were producing well, and there were no frosts or obvious problems. Finally, after a change in the trellising system, the vines began producing enough fruit to make a vintage.

Trellising, the spacing of vines, pruning, and irrigation all play a part in the development of grapes. Proper pruning can protect grapes against disease and slow the growth of overly vigorous vines. Thinning a vine's grape bunches can lead the remaining ones to produce more plentiful fruit. Agricultural techniques in the vineyard affect vines' production and can alter the grapes' sugar content. Thus, quite literally, a wine can be shaped on the vine.

One of the most important decisions made in the vineyard is choosing when to pick the grapes. Harvest too soon and the grapes haven't reached their potential. Wait too long and the quality begins to decline, rot can set in, or the sugar content can change. For many reasons including financial considerations, using a combination of mechanical and manual pickers is common. However, because grapes are delicate, most vineyards would prefer to harvest entirely by hand if possible. Many small wineries rely on the volunteer help of relatives, friends, and colleagues.

Processing the Grapes: Vinification

When the harvest arrives at the winery, the winemaker analyzes the fruit and begins to decide how best to bring out its quality. Shepard insists, "You can basically look at the grapes as they're coming in and taste the grapes and know if you're going to have really good wine or not."

Changing grapes into wine is a five-step process of fermentation, clarification (which removes suspended solids—the lees—from the liquid), stabilization (which ensures that the bottled wine won't become hazy or deteriorate), aging, and bottling. Although every winery follows these steps, each one develops its own techniques. For example, Shelton Vineyards prides itself on a gravity-flow technique, which requires little reliance on mechanical pumps to move liquids.

The overall process for making red wine and white wine is fundamentally the same, but during each step, there are key differences.

Initially, grapes for red wines are destemmed, while white-wine grapes are left "whole berry." All grapes are pressed. Then, since the grape skins give red wine its color, they remain in the juice. For white wines, the skins must be removed.

The grape juice, which is now called "must," is pumped into holding tanks. There, the fermentation process begins, as yeasts convert sugars to alcohol. Although a few wineries use the grapes' natural wild yeast, such as Rockhouse Vineyards' Chardonnay Native Yeast, most add a commercial cultured yeast to ensure consistency. Some wineries introduce sulfur dioxide to kill the wild yeast before adding the industrial product. Others do not, relying on cold temperatures to stun the wild strain and introducing the cultured yeast to "overrun" it.

In the tanks, red wines are kept at a higher temperature than whites, which makes them ferment more quickly. After 10 to 15 days, the red wines are pressed and then transferred into oak casks for aging. Storage in wood allows for slow oxidation, thus creating a smoother, rounder wine. White wines, which are kept at temperatures as low as 45 degrees, take much longer to fully ferment. A white wine is kept in the vat for six to eight weeks, after which it can be aged in either stainless-steel tanks or wooden barrels. Many wineries offer "barrel-fermented" white wines, which are fermented and aged directly in oak casks. This can give them a smoother, often buttery, flavor.

After the wines are produced and aged, they can be bottled directly or blended. By law, to be labeled a varietal, a wine must have at least 75 percent of that particular grape. Thus, a Merlot can be one-fourth Cabernet Sauvignon and still be called a Merlot. Many wineries also develop special proprietary blends, such as RayLen's "Carolinius" and Martin Vineyards' "Atlantis Meritage."

As the winemaker continually monitors the fermentation and aging, he or she makes decisions to steer the wine in a certain direction. It's a constant process of fine-tuning. Shepard admits, "I sometimes wake up at 3 A.M. with an idea to change the wine." For example, fermentation may bring out a grape's citrus flavors, and he may decide to accent this. Or he may strive for a taste of vanilla, which often comes from oak barrels. A Sauvignon Blanc may have a grassy taste that needs to be countered. Shepard says, "The grape gives a wine its aroma. The winemaker gives it its bouquet." He estimates that a winemaker makes 600 to 700 decisions during the process, each one of which could have resulted in a different wine.

Since so many variables and so many small factors affect chemistry, no two wines are alike. Westbend, Hanover Park, and RayLen have all made Chardonnays from grapes from South Mountain Vineyard, yet each of their wines is distinctive. Marek Wojciechowski of Chatham Hill Winery says, "That's why this business is so interesting. With the same grapes, you can make wines that can taste so different." Even the water used to clean the equipment and rinse the grapes can affect the outcome. If one winery uses city water and a neighboring winery uses well water, their wines will differ.

Once a wine begins aging, the winemaker has only one more major decision: He or she must monitor the maturation and decide when to bottle. White wines are usually ready more quickly than red wines. Some can be bottled as soon as six months after the harvest date. Many red wines can be aged in wood for more than a year before being bottled. Although all wines will age further once bottled, this does not always improve them. Whites should usually be drunk within three years, while some reds, such as Merlot or Cabernet Sauvignon, will benefit from longer storage.

In trying to realize the grapes' potential, a winemaker must have a good palate, the ability to identify problems, an understanding of basic chemistry, and a feeling for terroir. He or she should have another quality as well. In talking about the process, Steve Shepard repeatedly returns to one word: creativity. He believes a winemaker must have a style, a flair, a creative sense. A person trained in chemistry who has a sense of timing can make a good wine, but making a great wine requires the skills of an artist.

Wineries of Western North Carolina

Wineries of Western North Carolina

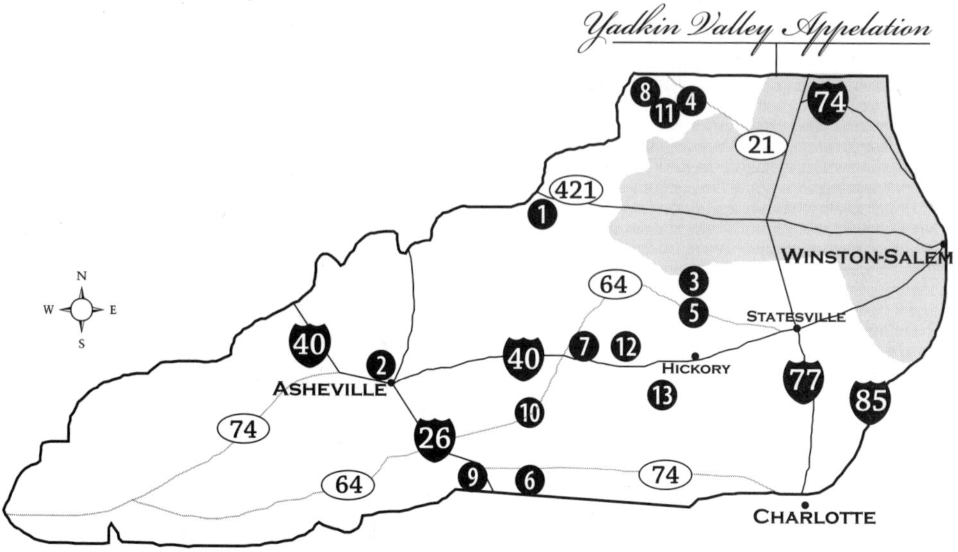

Yadkin Valley Appelation

1. Banner Elk Winery
2. Biltmore Estate Winery
3. Cerminaro Vineyard
4. Chateau Laurinda
5. Ginger Creek Vineyards
6. Green Creek Winery
7. Lake James Cellars
8. New River Winery
9. Rockhouse Vineyards
10. The Teensy Winery
11. Thistle Meadow Winery
12. Waldensian Heritage Wines
13. WoodMill Winery

Banner Elk Winery

135 Deer Run Lane
Banner Elk, N.C. 28604
Phone: 828-898-9090
Website: www.bannerelkwinery.com
E-mail: info@blueberryvilla.com
Hours: Wednesday–Sunday, noon–6 p.m.

Owners: Richard Wolfe and
Angelo Accetturo
Winemaker: Richard Wolfe
First year as bonded winery: 2006
Tasting fee: Yes
On-line ordering: No
Wine club: No

Wine List
Whites: Banner Elk White, Seyval Blanc, White Wolf (Golden Muscat)
Reds: Banner Elk Red, Cabernet Sauvignon, Villard Noir
Fruit: Blueberry

Directions: From Boone, take U.S. 221 to N.C. 105, then follow N.C. 105 to N.C. 184 at Tynecastle. Turn right on N.C. 184 and go approximately 4 miles to Banner Elk. Turn right onto N.C. 194 and go 1.5 miles. Turn left on Gualtney Road. The winery is on the right after 0.5 mile.

In Richard Wolfe's vision for North Carolina's High Country, he sees mountainsides full of grapes. Comparing the elevation around Boone to wine-producing regions in the European Alps, he insists,

"This area can be covered with vineyards all around here." Not only is it possible, but according to Richard, it makes good economic sense, particularly for farmers who are searching for alternative crops to tobacco and fir trees.

Although Richard, who has degrees in chemical and nuclear engineering, spent his career in the energy industry, his passion has always been wine. He says, "I've been making wine as a hobby all my life. I doubt there's been a year in 50 that I haven't made wine." His father was in the coal-mining business near Beckley, West Virginia, and Richard grew up among the Italians who worked the coal fields. In their free time, they tended vines, made wines, and showed him how to do both. He laughs that this winemaking ability made him popular in college. Years later, in the 1990s, it also led him to establish Wolf Creek Vineyards in Abingdon, Virginia.

Believing that the North Carolina mountains 50 miles away from Abingdon had untapped potential as a viticultural area, Richard approached Appalachian State University in 2001 about starting a program to help teach local farmers how to grow grapes. Intrigued by the idea, ASU hired Richard to be the director of the program of Applied Science and Research and began establishing test vineyards.

Tasting room at Banner Elk Winery

Richard Wolfe and Dede Walton

According to Richard, viticulture at higher elevations requires different choices than those made in the flatlands. Plantings must always be done on slopes with as much southern exposure as possible, and only some varietals, such as French-American hybrids, can withstand the cold temperatures. However, he insists that "we have advantages here." The area doesn't have the same disease issues as other parts of the state, and Richard also believes the climate makes for more flavorful, fruitier grapes.

Richard also began developing Banner Elk Winery because, as he notes, "if you're going to teach farmers to grow grapes, they need a place to sell them." Featuring a spacious tasting room including a bar that came from the historic Banner Elk Hotel, the 6,000-square-foot winery has a production capacity of 10,000 cases a year. Although he will continue to use fruit from Wolf Creek Vineyards and may eventually expand Banner Elk's vineyards to three acres, he hopes to buy mainly from local growers. His wife, Dede Walton, notes, "Farmers keep coming to the winery to talk with Dick about planting grapes." Like her husband, Dede believes that "our local farmers have land available, they understand the opportunities provided by new crops, and they are interested in being a part of this new venture."

Banner Elk Winery is part of a $3 million complex called the Villa at Blueberry Farm. The villa, which is run by Dede, contains eight bedrooms, 10 baths, and a full kitchen. The complex's size and amenities make it appealing for those who want to hold special events. In just the first 12 months after its June 2006 opening, Banner Elk Winery and the villa hosted 15 weddings, several corporate functions, and a photo shoot for a national retail clothing store.

The estate grounds have a putting green and a trout pond, but most importantly, the property includes 15 acres of 20-year-old blueberries. Richard believes the maturity of this fruit will result in superb wines. In fact, when the winery opened, the first blueberry wine he made sold out in two weeks.

Richard has other products in development that will help distinguish Banner Elk Winery. Because of the elevation, he believes "we'll be one of the first wineries in the state that will have the chance to make an ice wine." He also intends to make a blueberry port; he has planted thornless blackberries; and he has received a permit from the state to have a distillery. He notes with satisfaction, "We have the opportunity to do a lot of exciting things here."

Richard believes Banner Elk's growth will be "dictated by the response of the tourists," but since "this is the hottest corner for tourist growth in the state," he is very optimistic. Of course, the winery's future also depends on the development of the area's vineyards, and Richard is confident about that as well. He believes the High Country will become an important part of the state's wine industry. He insists, "The quality of the grapes we're growing here is going to be superb."

Biltmore Estate Winery

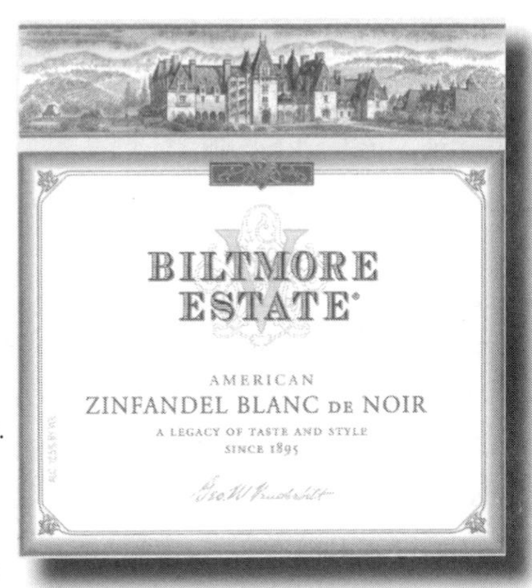

One North Pack Square
Asheville, N.C. 28801
Phone: 800-543-2961
or 828-274-6333
Website: www.biltmore.com
E-mail: info@biltmore.com
Hours: Monday–Saturday,
11 a.m.–7 p.m.; Sunday, noon–7 p.m.

Owner: The Biltmore Company
Winemaker: Bernard DeLille
First year as bonded winery: 1977
Tasting fee: Access to the winery is limited to those who buy tickets to Biltmore Estate. Once guests are inside the winery, the tasting of estate wines is free. There is a fee to taste premium wines.
On-line ordering: Yes
Wine club: Yes

Wine List
Whites: Century White (Riesling, Gewurztraminer, Muscat Canelli, Malvesia, and Chenin Blanc), Chardonnay, Chardonnay Sur Lies, Chenin Blanc, House White (Chenin Blanc and Chardonnay), Pinot Grigio, Riesling, Sauvignon Blanc, 75th Anniversary White (Viognier, Rousanne, Sauvignon Blanc, and Chardonnay), Viognier
Blushes: Cabernet Sauvignon Blanc de Noir, Grenache Rosé, Zinfandel Blanc de Noir
Reds: Cabernet Franc, Cabernet Sauvignon, Cardinal's Crest (Cabernet Franc, Cabernet Sauvignon, Merlot, Pinot Noir, Petite Sirah, Syrah, and Mourvedre), Century Red (Sangiovese, Zinfandel, Merlot, Syrah, and Malbec), Claret (Cabernet Sauvignon, Merlot, Cabernet Franc, and Syrah), Merlot, Pinot Noir, Sangiovese, Syrah, Zinfandel
Specialties: Brut, Methode Champenoise Blanc de Blanc (brut and sec), Methode Champenoise Blanc de Noir (brut and sec), Pas de Deux (Muscat Canelli and Riesling)

DIRECTIONS: THE WINERY IS ON THE GROUNDS OF BILTMORE ESTATE IN ASHEVILLE. TAKE INTERSTATE 40 TO EXIT 50A. GO NORTH ON U.S. 25 FOR 2 BLOCKS TO THE ESTATE ENTRANCE.

When George Washington Vanderbilt visited Asheville in 1888, he liked the area so much that he decided to build a home there. Its 250 rooms—including 33 bedrooms and 43 bathrooms—make Biltmore the largest private residence in America. Designed by Richard Morris Hunt, the French-style château required hundreds of builders and artisans. Construction lasted from 1890 to 1895. The estate's grounds, which originally covered 125,000 acres, were equally impressive. They included a timber farm, a dairy farm, and 250 acres of formal and natural gardens created by landscape architect Frederick Law Olmsted, the designer of New York's Central Park.

Since the estate was designed to be self-sufficient, George Vanderbilt's grandson, William Amherst Vanderbilt Cecil, decided in 1971 that vineyards would be a suitable addition. As an experiment, a few acres of vines, including French-American hybrids such as Marechal Foch, were planted. In 1977, when it became clear that grapes could be grown here, the estate increased its plantings, established a bonded winery, and hired Philippe Jourdain as a winemaking consultant. He later served as winemaker. In the following decade, the dairy barn, one of the estate's original buildings, was renovated to make a 90,000-square-foot state-of-the-art winery. This commitment of resources has paid off. In the last 30 years, Biltmore wines have won hundreds of awards in national and international competitions.

When Jourdain retired in 1995, Bernard DeLille became wine master. DeLille insists, however, that considering a single person responsible for a wine is a mistake. He points out that in France, people don't know the names of winemakers. Instead, they know the names of owners or estates. "What is good in winemaking is that it's not the work of one person, it's teamwork from the vineyards on," he says.

Biltmore vineyards
USED WITH PERMISSION FROM THE BILTMORE COMPANY, ASHEVILLE, NORTH CAROLINA

One crucial member of the "Biltmore team" is vineyard manager Dennis Wynne, who joined the estate after finishing his horticulture degree in 1981. Wynne has seen the vineyards go through a number of changes. When he arrived, there were 50 acres of vines. In the next few years, the estate not only doubled its plantings but built a 40-acre lake to irrigate them. At its largest, the vineyards encompassed 140 acres, but it became clear that some varietals, particularly thin-skinned white grapes, simply don't grow well in the Blue Ridge environment. Consequently, a process of contraction and regrouping took place. For example, the vineyards once included 35 acres of Sauvignon Blanc but now have none. The estate also greatly reduced its Reisling acreage.

Thanks to his more than 20 years of experience, Wynne has become an expert on the problems of growing grapes in the area. Geese, deer, and other wildlife destroy a certain percentage of each crop, but the vineyards' biggest enemy is fungus. The area usually gets a great deal of rain. "If we get thunderstorms in the afternoons, the vines will stay wet all night, and then we'll have fog in the morning," Wynne explains. "Sometimes, they can be wet 24 hours." Such weather makes the vines so susceptible to rot that regular spraying is crucial. Wynne insists, "We're trying to use everything as safely as we can. We've gotten sprays

Biltmore Estate winery
USED WITH PERMISSION FROM THE BILTMORE COMPANY, ASHEVILLE, NORTH CAROLINA

that are safer and safer." It's a matter of personal concern for him and his crew. After all, he points out, "we work here, and we want to be here 20 and 30 more years."

Although visitors to Biltmore Estate Winery aren't able to see its vineyards, which are located away from the estate, there is plenty to do. A self-guided visit includes a video presentation and a great deal of information about wine, the winery, and the estate. At various points on the route, windows offer views of the winery's working areas, such as the barrel room and the champagne room. After guests go through the enormous tasting room, where they can sample estate wines, the visit ends at a gift shop that sells wines, gourmet food, Biltmore souvenirs, and other products. One area of the shop is devoted to cooking displays by chefs from Biltmore's restaurants. If visitors are hungry, they can picnic at one of the covered tables outside or eat at the next-door bistro.

Biltmore Estate Winery has established three labels: Biltmore Estate Wines, Biltmore Estate Château Reserves, and George Washington Vanderbilt Premium Vintages. The winery has been expanded several times and now has a tank capacity of 250,000 gallons. Because it produces over 100,000 cases a year, it buys a large quantity of grapes in addition to using the harvests from its own vineyards. Although it has usually relied on California fruit, the winery has begun working more with regional growers as vinifera plantings in the Southeast have increased. In fact, DeLille believes that in North Carolina, "we have the soil to make some wines with great personality."

As the state's industry develops, DeLille hopes it will establish its own identity. He suggests, "You have to forget about French wine. You have to forget about California wine." With North Carolina grapes, a winemaker should make wine that will be unique to the region. To do this, DeLille says, "you must discover and find out what is working and what is not working." Regardless of a person's desires, he or she must pay attention to the grape. The number-one mistake a winemaker can make, according to DeLille, is "overestimating the quality of the grapes. Some years, you have to say, 'Oh, with that, I cannot make a good red wine. I'll have to do a blush.' " DeLille insists, "You have a grape, and your role is to interpret the potential of the grape and try to do the best you can with it. As winemakers, we don't create, we interpret. That's the fun part."

Cerminaro Vineyard

4399 Wilkesboro Boulevard
Boomer, N.C. 28606
Phone: 828-754-9306
Fax: 828-757-3958
Website:
www.cerminarovineyard.com
E-mail: cerminaro@charter.net
Hours: Saturday, noon–6 p.m., and by appointment

Owners: Joe and Deborah Cerminaro
Winemaker: Joe Cerminaro
First year as bonded winery: 2001
Tasting fee: No
On-line ordering: No
Wine club: No

Wine List
Whites: Cayuga White, Riesling, Seyval Blanc, Vidal Blanc, Vignoles, Vino d'Oro (Seyval Blanc and Vignoles)
Reds: Cabernet Sauvignon, Chancellor, DeChaunac, Leon Millot, Merlot, Sangiovese

Directions: Take U.S. 421 to the N.C. 18 exit (Lenoir/Taylorsville). Drive north on N.C. 18 into Caldwell County. From the county line, go 2 miles. The winery is on the right on top of the hill.

Joe and Deborah Cerminaro

To support his family, Joe Cerminaro spent 20 years in the navy and then 15 more as a mechanical engineer. What he really wanted to be, however, was a farmer. Having been raised in an Italian-American culture that valued wine, he "always had this dream of growing grapes." After moving with his wife, Deborah, to a 50-acre farm in the rolling hills of Caldwell County, he had his chance. Joe says, "I kept looking at the sun and the soil, and I thought, 'Grapes can grow here. I'm sure they can.'" In 1995, he planted vines on three-quarters of an acre as an experiment. They did so well that he and Deborah began to consider growing more, both for fun and "as something to subsidize our retirement." After three years of research, they made the decision to establish a commercial vineyard and winery.

Although they are self-described "country people," the Cerminaros knew little about viticulture when they started. Deborah comes from a North Dakota farm, but her family grew wheat, a much different crop than grapes. Consequently, after reading books and talking to experts, the couple still had to learn about practical matters. Joe recalls their experience putting in holes for hundreds of posts. He drove a tractor

Cerminaro vineyard

with an auger while Deborah walked behind and indicated where he should drill by yelling, "Drop it. Drop it!" Joe says, "If anybody saw us, they must have thought, 'What a bunch of idiots.'" After a while, the auger no longer worked. Joe recalls, "I went to the farm implement place and asked, 'What's wrong with my auger? It quit drilling.' The man said, 'There's two teeth on the bottom to help you get started.' I said I didn't see those. They had worn out. We had worn out the drill bit and were trying to punch holes without it." Joe laughs. "It was funny."

In their conversation, the Cerminaros frequently use the word *fun*, even as they talk about the difficulties of the winery's first years. "We made some mistakes," Joe acknowledges, "but we've had a lot of good experiences, and we've had fun. About killed ourselves, though," he admits after a moment. Deborah agrees, saying that it was almost "a slow, happy death." She remembers one electrical storm when their new crusher/destemmer was outside but hadn't been grounded. She wanted to move it but was "shocked all to pieces" every time she came near. "Yeah," Joe laughs, "that was a learning experience."

Originally, the Cerminaros planted hybrids such as Leon Millot and Chancellor because these tend to be hardy and able to survive frosts and cold snaps. "We're a small vineyard," Joe explains. "We can't afford to lose any grapes. If we lost three acres of grapes, we'd be wiped out." In recent years, however, they have begun to experiment with vinifera, and their five planted acres now include Cabernet Sauvignon, Merlot, and Sangiovese. Although in the future these may result in the creation of some full-bodied wines, so far the winery has specialized in what Joe calls "fresh wines" or "early wines." He says, "We try to produce a soft wine with no heavy tannins." They want to produce "nice, easy-drinking wines" that appeal to "experimental wine drinkers" and even to people who believe they don't like red wines.

Cerminaro Vineyard produces about 600 cases a year. For the most part, Joe and Deborah do the work themselves. Joe admits being surprised at the effort required to crush their first harvest using a 125-year-old hand press. He remembers thinking, "Boy, this is a lot of work for a little bit of juice." Deborah points out, "Like any agricultural thing, it is a lot of work, but you feel so good about the final product. Maybe it wouldn't be quite as rewarding otherwise." The winery occasionally gets volunteers. When two Mormon missionaries came by and admitted that they wouldn't mind something to do, Joe said, "Come on out. You can help us put in posts and grapes." Each year, friends, neighbors, and even church groups help with the harvest. They pick in the morning, stopping before the grapes get too hot. Then Joe cooks a big Italian meal for lunch and puts out wines made the previous year. He says with satisfaction, "They have a good day. We have a good day."

Currently, the winery offers private tastings that include cheeses and olive oils. Because Joe loves to cook, he and Deborah may at some point consider hosting small dinners outside, where guests would have views of the vineyard, the woods, and the surrounding hills. The Cerminaros talk about future plans with caution, however. Joe's "hobby gone wild" has already taken over their basement, and they know that if they're not careful, it could take over their lives. Deborah speaks with pride about what they've accomplished. "You just only meet so many people who are so driven," she says of Joe. "That's how we know it's a passion, because he keeps going and going." She notes, however, that "because he is so passionate about it, you can end up doing nothing but that. You have to be careful to find a balance." Joe agrees. "There's more to life than wine," he says. If any of their 10 children become interested in the business, they might consider expanding. The winery could be moved from the basement to the barn, and additional acreage could be planted. But since the kids still, as Joe puts it, "think we're crazy," they intend to stay small.

Whatever the future holds, for now the Cerminaros enjoy having a vineyard in their backyard. Besides its beauty and the satisfaction of drinking their own wine with meals, there are other benefits. Deborah says, "Having fresh grapes to walk out and pick is so luxurious." As for Joe, he simply likes his life as a farmer: "It's a nice feeling when you get out there early in the morning and the sun's coming up. It's just a nice feeling."

Chateau Laurinda

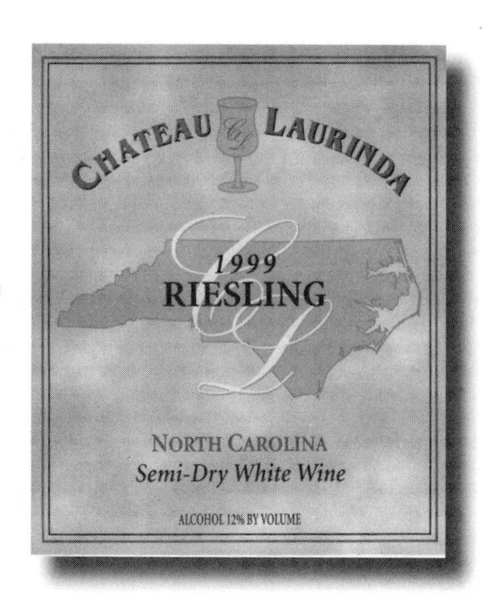

690 Reeves Ridge Road
Sparta, N.C. 28675
Phone: 800-650-3236 or
336-372-2562
Fax: 336-372-5529
Website:
www.chateaulaurindawinery.com
E-mail: clwinery@gmail.com
Hours: Tuesday–Friday,
11 a.m.–6 p.m.;
Saturday, 10 a.m.–6 p.m.;
Sunday, noon–5 p.m.
Call for winter hours.

Owners: Linda and Larry Ehlers
Winemaker: Larry Ehlers
First year as bonded winery: 1997
Tasting fee: No
On-line ordering: No
Wine club: Yes

Wine List
Whites: Alleghany White, Captain's Choice (Concord), Chardonnay, Magnolia, Scuppernong, Seyval Blanc, Vidal Blanc
Reds: Alleghany Red, Blackberry Merlot, Cabernet Franc, Chambourcin, Crimson Passion (scuppernong), Dry Noble, Merlot, Muscadine
Fruits: Apple, Blackberry, Cherry, Heavenly Citrus (orange and tangerine), Mango, Pear, Pineapple, Plum, Raspberry, Strawberry
Specialties and Desserts: Christmas Wine, Cranberry Delight, New River White

Directions: From Interstate 77, take Exit 83 and follow U.S. 21 toward Sparta; from the Blue Ridge Parkway, take the U.S. 21 exit toward Sparta. Follow U.S. 21 through Sparta to U.S. 221 South. Turn right on N.C. 93. Go 1.5 miles to the second road on the left. The winery is on the right at the end of the paved road.

When Larry and Linda were young, they met, fell in love, and wanted to wed. Because they were underage, they needed the permission of their parents. Larry's father refused to give it, so, following the advice of Linda's father, the couple eloped. They drove across the New Jersey state line, headed south, and ended up getting married in North Carolina. It was a sign of things to come.

Years later, Larry and Linda Ehlers were making regular trips to North Carolina to buy special tires for cars that they raced as a hobby. The tire salesman kept urging them to move, saying, "You don't know what you're missing. This is God's country. You've got to get out of that rat race up there." Eventually, they decided he might be right. So they quit their jobs, sold their house, took their kids out of school, and formed "a caravan down the road." Now, more than 20 years later, they maintain that they could never return to the stress that comes with living in the Northeast.

Larry and Linda first moved to China Grove, where they began renovating an old house. They became friends with a neighbor, Pete Faggart, a butcher who made muscadine wine from grapes on his property. Pete's hobby reignited an interest in Larry, who had grown up in a "European-style household" where wine was "considered a food." As a child, Larry had often helped his grandfather make German Riesling and fruit wines until, as he puts it, "I became more interested in girls than grapes." When Pete Faggart died in 1990, Larry was unwilling to let the grapes rot, so he arranged with Pete's family to take over the winemaking.

Larry became a "happy hobbyist," but his avocation sometimes caused problems. Linda remembers, "We had an old house, and the floor wasn't level, and [the juice] would kind of ferment all over the place while we were at work. I'd come home, and it would be running across the kitchen. I said, 'This has got to go.'"

Encouraged by enthusiastic responses to Larry's wine, they began to consider commercial winemaking. This time, it was Linda's father who

Chateau Laurinda wine bottles

advised against it, insisting they were too old. "It's going to kill you," he said. Again undeterred, they founded Chateau Laurinda, a name that combines their first names.

Initially, they used Pete's old meat shop for the winery. Larry recalls, "That was happiness, having all these different coolers." Zoning issues, however, forced them to move. They relocated to Spencer. While Larry and Linda worked day jobs, their son, Steve, and his wife, Melissa, ran the winery's tasting room. Eventually, Larry and Linda began searching for land to establish a larger winery. They were intrigued when they heard about an old homestead in Alleghany County. Their realtor looked at the property and advised them against it, saying, "You don't want to come see this. It's in terrible shape. There's so much work that would have to be done." As usual, they resisted such conventional advice. Reminding the realtor about their talents as builders, Linda said, "Do me a favor. Go back to the house. Open your eyes and look at it for the potential that it could become." Soon, they received a call asking, "When are you coming?" In addition to the house, the property had room for a winery, land to grow grapes, and beautiful views of the countryside. They bought it immediately.

Built by some of the area's original settlers, the Reeves homestead dates to the late 1800s. Larry and Linda attempted to restore the structure to its original state, as far as possible. They put in claw-foot tubs

Linda and Larry Ehlers

and pedestal sinks. They had the original oak floors sanded. They took down the wood paneling in a bedroom, planed the boards, and put them back up. While acknowledging that such work took a great deal of time, Linda claims it was worth it. Now, she says, "the room is absolutely gorgeous." When the house was finished, Linda was able to realize a longtime dream of running a bed-and-breakfast.

People who stay at the Laurinda House have a variety of Chateau Laurinda wines to drink with their meals. Catering to different tastes, Larry and Linda make around 26 different types of wine, from Merlot to muscadine. These include 12 to 14 regular wines and 12 to 14 specialty wines such as blueberry, raspberry, and plum. Because they make small batches throughout the year, the wine list continually changes.

Larry notes that when they started, there weren't many vinifera grapes available, but there were plenty of scuppernongs, cherries, berries, and other fruits. Consequently, "we sort of cut our eyeteeth in business on alternate fruits, or what are called alternate fruits, and we still specialize in those type of wines," he says. They use only North Carolina fruit. Larry speaks with enthusiasm about the state's crops: "We can go to different areas within an hour of here at different times of year and get superb fruit, which for a winemaker is almost a dream come true." He insists that many fruit wines—cherry, for example—have a complexity and richness that can rival those made from grapes. "We treat apple the same way we treat the best Merlot," he says. "We don't show partiality just because it is vinifera or American hybrid."

According to Larry, "people who drink Chardonnay and Cabernet do the most writing and make the most noise," but they don't actually buy the most wine. Those who enjoy sweet and semisweet wines comprise the largest market segment, and they should not be ignored. Larry learned this the hard way. He ruefully remembers Chateau Laurinda's first show: "We went with 12 dry wines, and they wanted to show me the bus and send me back home." In those first years, Linda used to go to Château Morrisette in Virginia to buy cases of sweet wine for herself. "Boy," Larry says, "that hit home with me." Consequently, he began making sweet wines. "It's quite complex compared to making a dry wine," he says. "Making dry wine is a simple process. You can go to Florida on vacation and come back, and your wine will be ready. You cannot do a sweet wine like that." He was dubious of his early efforts, refusing to sell his blackberry wine. He thought it was "too earthy" and a "family wine." But Linda convinced him to take it to the Southern Christmas Show in Charlotte, and they sold every bottle. Today, the winery sells all it makes, a fact that Larry says Linda doesn't let him forget.

Chateau Laurinda, which was designed and built by Larry and Linda, encompasses 5,300 square feet and sits on a small hill. In addition to a large tasting room that includes a "hobbyist's corner" with products for amateur winemakers, it has a conference room for meetings and a long porch with rocking chairs. The winery also has a "glass room," where rows of jugs with wines in various stages of fermentation can be seen. As a hobbyist, Larry developed this technique for monitoring wines. At first, he kept his carboys out of sight: "At our Spencer winery,

I thought it was kind of seedy, so we generally didn't show people. It was a personal thing where I could tell what my wines were doing. It was like a worktable. Then the Salisbury Women's Club got loose in there one day, and they thought that we should 'make sure everyone sees this because it's so pretty.' So we do."

People said Larry and Linda's relationship wouldn't last. That was in 1965. In 2005, they celebrated their 40th wedding anniversary. In 2007, they will celebrate the 10-year anniversary of Chateau Laurinda, another commitment people advised them against making. But the winery, like the relationship its name celebrates, promises to have a long, productive, happy life.

Ginger Creek Vineyards

858 John Cline Road
Taylorsville, N.C. 28681
Mailing address: P.O. Box 6237
Hickory, N.C. 28603-6237
Phone: 828-635-0327
Fax: 704-658-0868
Website: www.gingercreekvineyards.net
E-mail: gingercreek@bellsouth.net
Hours: Thursday–Saturday,
noon–6 p.m.; Sunday, 1–5 p.m.

Owners: Dwight and Sharon Austin
Winemaker: Dwight Austin
First year as bonded winery: 2004
Tasting fee: No
On-line ordering: Yes
Wine club: No

Wine List
Whites: Chardonnay, Jeh'n Cheel (scuppernong in sweet and dry versions), Riesling
Reds: American Classic (muscadine in sweet and dry versions), Beaujolais, Cabernet Sauvignon
Fruits: Baya Silvestre, Blackberry Mystique, Delicia de Verano (scuppernong and citrus), Fresa de Pasion (scuppernong and strawberry), Gabrielle (cranberry, cinnamon, and red muscadine), Salida del Sol (Alberta peaches), Sugar Plum, Sweetheart (scuppernong and cherry)

Directions: From Interstate 40 West, take Exit 125 and head north on Lenoir-Rhyne Boulevard to N.C. 127. Go north on N.C. 127 to Antioch Church Road. Turn left on Antioch Church Road, then right at Caldwell Pond Road. Turn left on John Cline Road. At the end of the road, turn left. At the first fork, bear right. At the second fork, bear right again. The vineyards are on the left.

Several years ago, Dwight and Sharon Austin became convinced of muscadines' health properties, and they began to consider planting vines on their historic family farm in Alexander County. To explore viticulture's commercial possibilities, Dwight and Sharon toured Shelton Vineyards. Although they were impressed with the winery's large operation, they thought there was no way they could start such a venture. However, Sharon suggested that before they rejected the idea entirely, they visit other, smaller places. Tours of Dennis Vineyards and Waldensian Heritage Wines renewed their enthusiasm and helped convince them that they could establish their own place. Eventually, they invested the family's life savings and, as Dwight puts it, "everything we could scrape together" to found Ginger Creek Vineyards. After they had done so, Dwight remembers calling one of his best friends and saying, "Do you remember that passage out of Luke about the certain man who planted a vineyard?" The friend said yes, and Dwight admitted, "I've become that certain man."

Overall, people have been supportive about the venture. Even Dwight's 90-year-old mother, who is a teetotaler, is enthused about the business. She loves to bring friends and relatives to the winery. During the bottling process, she likes to help put the caps on. Dwight laughs that if a cap doesn't align with the label, you know "somebody other than Mom did it." His mother is particularly happy that the land is again being cultivated after decades of lying fallow. The property has been in the family since 1770 and was part of an original land grant from Governor William Tryon to Benjamin Austin. Dwight points out that the property's designation as a "Century Farm" is misleading because "if they had the designation, we could be listed as a Two-Century Farm."

The Austins have planted two of the property's 47 acres. They built the winery a quarter-mile from Ginger Creek, which is also called Middle Little River. Someday, they hope to construct a tasting room and visitor center next to the creek itself. Sharon says, "It's a beautiful setting. In five years, we hope it's going to be a destination place."

The Austin family

For the Austins, one of the major benefits of having a winery is the ability to be together. Dwight explains that while researching the idea, "I saw families working together and being together, and I thought that was something I wanted for my family." In fact, Ginger Creek's first release was called Jeh'n Cheel, which is Gaelic for "Of the Family." Each label has the initials of every family member.

Eventually, Dwight hopes that he can pass the winery on to his children, and he jokes that he constantly tells them about Internet cruise deals he wants to book. For now, however, Ginger Creek requires all his time. It's a situation he knows well. Dwight used to be a minister and often had to put vacation plans on hold. Once, he postponed a trip four times. The fifth time, as the family got ready, the organist said to Dwight's son, "So, you're going on a vacation," and the son said, "Yes, ma'am, if no one gets sick, no one dies, and no one needs my daddy."

Although the shift from minister to winery owner may seem drastic, Dwight feels that they require similar people skills. He still listens to people to find out what they need and desire. He still reaches out, making it a point that, at wine festivals, "nobody walks by us without getting spoken to." Most importantly, he feels that Ginger Creek is continuing a family tradition of hospitality. Dwight says with pride that people know "they're always welcome at 'the Creek.'"

Green Creek Winery

413 Gilbert Road
Columbus, N.C. 28722
Phone: 828-863-2182
Website: www.greencreekwinery.com
E-mail: Contact form is on website.
Hours: Thursday–Sunday, 1–5 p.m.

Owner: Alvin Pack et al
First year as bonded winery: 2005
Tasting fee: Yes
On-line ordering: No
Wine club: No

Wine List
White: Chardonnay
Blushes: Cabernet Franc Rosé, Chambourcin Rosé
Red: Merlot

Directions: From U.S. 74, take Exit 167, go south on N.C. 9 for 3 miles to Landrum Road, and turn right. Go 1 mile to Gilbert Road and turn right. The winery is on the left after approximately 0.5 mile. From Interstate 26, take Exit 1 at Landrum, South Carolina. Go northeast on Landrum Road (S.C. 14) for 5 miles. Turn left on Gilbert Road. The winery is on the left after approximately 0.5 mile.

Alvin Pack was born and raised in Tryon, North Carolina. Then, as he puts it, he "took a vacation to California for 29 years." Because his wife, Loretta, was a third-generation San Franciscan, Alvin lived

Green Creek Winery entrance

there, and he jokes that "it took 25 years to get her out of the city and get her to Sonoma." For three years, the Packs lived in the California wine country, where they dreamed of establishing their own vineyard, but the land was simply too expensive. Rather than abandon the idea, however, the Packs decided to relocate. In 2000, they said goodbye to the San Francisco Bay area, moved across the country to Alvin's home state, and, with partners, bought a 10-acre apple orchard on which to establish Green Creek Winery.

Alvin knew the Tryon area was good for grapes in part because his sister, Anna Pack Conner, had written a book about the region's long history of viticulture. From the late 1800s until the 1940s, there were almost two dozen thriving local vineyards and at least two wineries. Farmers took their grapes to the train depot and sold them to passengers who were traveling the East Coast between Florida and Canada. The industry was devastated, however, by Prohibition and World War II.

Thanks to wineries like Green Creek, Tryon is again experiencing a grape-growing boom. Over 100 acres of vines have been planted throughout the area, and 11 vineyards are located within a five-mile radius, including one owned by Alvin's brother, Marvin, who grows the grapes for Green Creek. In anticipation of more wineries opening, Alvin has helped initiate a feasibility study to explore establishing a

Green Creek Winery patio

Green Creek American Viticultural Area (AVA) designation.

According to Alvin, Green Creek Winery is western North Carolina's first "purpose-built" winery; others such as nearby Rockhouse Vineyards are in renovated spaces. Alvin designed his winery on the model of two buildings he liked in California—the short-lived Sonoma Mountain Brewery and the Paloma Vineyard in St. Helena. He tried to incorporate elements he admired in other wineries as well, including a barrel-racking system designed to withstand earthquakes. He points out that most winemakers and owners are happy to share information: "I probably went to 200 wineries in two years in Napa and Sonoma. People will tell you their successes and, if you talk to them long enough, they'll tell you their failures."

Alvin designed the winery with expansion in mind. Eventually, he would like Green Creek Winery to reach a production of around 4,000 cases. In its first year, Green Creek sold 1,000 cases of wine, including a dry Chambourcin Rosé and a Cabernet Franc Rosé. Alvin says of these, "They were very, very popular, and soon they were very, very gone." Noting that rosé is making a comeback in California, he says, "I hope that's a trend because we make dynamite rosé here."

To help set the winery apart, Alvin uses a variety of marketing strategies. Green Creek is one of the first wineries in the state to run television ads, and its wines will be offered in various sizes, including splits and 500-milliliter bottles. Alvin explains, "We know there's a new market for wine—21- to 30-year-olds—and they're looking for different containers." Green Creek also has vigorously targeted tour bus companies and large groups. Alvin estimates that in the neighboring states, there are over 100 tour bus companies, and he would like them to be aware of the advantages of stopping at Green Creek. To be tour friendly, Alvin made sure to include a loop driveway at the winery, since the number-one criteria for bus drivers is "they don't want to back up." This, of course, also makes Green Creek traffic friendly for RVs and other large vehicles.

Alvin welcomes tours in part because he believes "our mission here is to educate people." For those who are interested, Alvin explains such practices as grafting in the vineyard and filtering in the winery. He also champions the economic value of grape growing, pointing out that when people hold weddings, receptions, and events at Green Creek Winery, it benefits the local hotels and restaurants: "Agribusiness is probably the best thing you can do for a community—and that's wine and vineyards."

Although it took him years to get his wife to move away from San Francisco, Alvin says that "she loves [the winery]. She thought I was crazy to start with. Now, she thinks, like myself, that we should have done it earlier."

Lake James Cellars

204 East Main Street
Glen Alpine, N.C. 28628
Mailing address: P.O. Box 359
Glen Alpine, N.C. 28628
Phone: 828-584-4551
Fax: 828-584-6893
Website: www.lakejamescellars.com
E-mail: wineworx@bellsouth.net
Hours: Tuesday–Friday, 11 a.m.–6 p.m.;
Saturday, 10 a.m.–5 p.m.; Sunday, 1–5 p.m.

Lake James Cellars
Bridgewater Bramble
Red Wine
8% Alc by vol 750 ml

Owners: Mike and Betty Fowler
Winemaker: Josh Fowler
First year as bonded winery: 2005
Tasting fee: Yes
On-line ordering: Yes
Wine club: Yes

Wine List

Whites: Chardonnay, Gewurztraminer, Luna Blanc (Libfraumilch), Pinot Grigio, Riesling Ice Wine, Symphony (Muscat and Alexandria), Turkey Tail (White Merlot), Turkey Tail White (Riesling)

Blushes: Indian River (pink grapefruit blush), Raspberry Blush, Wild Blueberry Blush

Reds: Cabernet Franc, Cabernet Sauvignon, Corvina Classico Di Veneto, Italian Villa (Valpolicella), Shiraz, Shortoff Red (Pinot Noir), Vino Classico (Chianti)

Fruits: Bridgewater Bramble (blackberry and Cabernet Sauvignon), Caribbean Mist (mango and Symphony), Fonta Flora Blush (cranberry and Shiraz), Linville Mist (green apple Riesling), Southern Magnolia (peach Chardonnay), Table Rock Red (black cherry and Pinot Noir), Tropical Fruit Mist (Pinot Grigio)

Directions: From the east, take Interstate 40 West to Exit 100. Turn left on Jamestown Road, go 0.7 mile, turn right on Conley Road, and go 1.5 miles. Turn right on U.S. 70 (Main Street). The winery is on the left.

Betty Fowler warns that visiting wineries is a dangerous hobby. If people aren't careful, they can get more and more involved in the business until they even end up owning one. She speaks from experience; it happened to her family.

For years, Betty and her husband, Mike, enjoyed exploring the countryside and seeking out wineries. Some of these were in remote areas, and Betty still remembers the sound of tree branches scraping the side of their RV as they slowly drove dirt roads. At each place, they would taste and talk and learn people's stories. Then, around 2001, they visited Thistle Meadow Winery, and their son Josh bought a winemaking kit for "something to do." Since Josh had degrees in chemistry and biology and enjoyed brewing beer, it wasn't surprising for him to become interested in winemaking. Soon, he was making batches for family and friends. A few years later, when Mike began looking for a business to start after he

Betty Fowler

retired from his job at Bell South, people kept suggesting, "Why not a winery?" After all, it was the family's hobby and passion. The Fowlers thought, "Well, why not?" As they talked over the idea, Mike asked his son, "Do you want to be the winemaker?" Josh said, "Sure," and a family winery began to take shape.

The Fowlers knew that trying to establish their own vineyard would be expensive and would require a tremendous amount of labor, but they decided it was unnecessary. They were willing to follow the model of Thistle Meadow and work with concentrates, and they knew they could buy high-quality grapes from growers such as Larry Kehoe of South Mountain Vineyard. So, instead of farmland, Betty and Mike searched for business property around Glen Alpine, where they had grown up. Eventually, they decided to lease an old textile mill built in 1915. In half of the building, they put Lake James Cellars. In the other half, they opened The Old Mill Antiques and rented space to antique dealers. Betty points out, "Antiques and wine are a good combination. People can shop with a glass of wine." In fact, it's appealing not only to customers but to dealers as well. Betty has a waiting list of people who would like to rent space in the building.

Although Glen Alpine is a dry town, the Fowlers had little trouble with the permit process. At one town meeting, an alderman said, "I don't

Josh Fowler

know why we'd have a problem with it. Half the people in Glen Alpine make wine." The area has so many hobbyists that, in conjunction with Lake James Cellars, the Fowlers also run Foothills Wineworx, a supply store for home winemakers. Josh says, "We help them out as best we can"—for example, by offering advice and special-ordering equipment.

Lake James Cellars opened in August 2005 and was immediately successful, according to Betty. She believes this was due in part to the appeal of the old building, which was "like a magnet," and in part to the almost two dozen offerings in the tasting room. As a result, "we have something that somebody is going to love," she says. In 2006, the winery made approximately 800 cases of wine, and the Fowlers hope to double that production in the near future. Josh notes, however, that it's important to find a balance. He would like production to increase so that he can become a full-time winemaker, but "I don't want to get too big because I like the family atmosphere."

For Josh, the key to making a consistently good product is going slowly. He says of wine, "If it's not ready for the next step, leave it alone." He laughs that sometimes it's hard to get his parents to understand this. They keep asking him when a wine will be ready, and he responds, "Don't rush things."

In the future, the Fowlers may develop the building's downstairs, add a deck, or even put in a bistro. They might expand the winery or even buy a vineyard someday. The future seems full of possibilities. For now, they're happy to have established what they consider one of the more unique wineries in the state. It's taken hard work and the effort of the entire family to turn their hobby into a business, but Betty insists, "We feel blessed."

New River Winery

9316 N.C. 194 North
Lansing, N.C. 28643
Mailing address:
106 North Jefferson Avenue
West Jefferson, N.C. 28694
Phone: 336-846-1498
Fax: 336-846-7900
Website: www.newriverwineries.com
E-mail: info@newriverwinery.com
Hours: The winery is not open to the public. It may be in 2008.

Owners: New River Wineries, Inc.
Winemaker: Dan Strickland
First year as bonded winery: 2006
Tasting fee: Yes
On-line ordering: No
Wine club: No

Wine List
Whites: Bohemia White, Pinot Blanc, Viognier
Reds: Bohemia Red, Hellbender Red
Fruits: Apple-Blueberry, Back Porch Blueberry

Directions: The New River tasting outlet is in the Bohemia Gallery in downtown West Jefferson at 106 North Jefferson Avenue. West Jefferson is located at the junction of U.S. 221 Business and N.C. 194 in Ashe County.

If you spend much time in Ashe County or the surrounding area, there's a good chance you will run into a winery owner. At first, this may seem unusual, since the county has only one winery, but it has a unique business model. New River Winery is a corporation owned and run by its 70 shareholders, who also provide all its labor. Its president, Haskell McGuire, points out, "The winery business is usually either a family business or it's a millionaires' club or multimillionaires' club. That's the only way you can get into it. We have a different way, one which allows a lot of people to participate."

The idea for the winery originated with Dan Strickland, who is New River's chief winemaker, the chairman of its board, and the publisher of *Small Winery Magazine*. Dan made his first batch of wine over 30 years ago using grapes from his mother's backyard, and he has been making wine ever since, even while living in places like Saudi Arabia. In 1995, he bought land in the Blue Ridge Mountains and decided to try growing his own grapes. After he began experimenting with various varietals, he discovered that because of the area's high altitude and short growing season, hybrids such as Seyval Blanc and Marechal Foch grow best. "Hybrid wines are different from vinifera wines," Dan says. "They're not necessarily worse, just different." They tend to be fruitier, and because they lack tannins, they're meant to be drunk young.

Dan would give friends much of the wine he made, and they would praise it and urge him to start a winery. Although Dan suggests a person should be wary of compliments about a free product, he also notes

Haskell McGuire
COURTESY OF NEW RIVER WINERY

wryly that after a while, "like everything else, you start to believe the publicity." So he decided to explore the possibilities of commercial winemaking. With Tom Burgiss, the owner of Grapestompers, a winemaking supply company, he attended a Wineries Unlimited trade show. By the end of the trip, both Dan and Tom had become convinced they should start wineries, but neither had money for the kind of equipment they had seen displayed. Consequently, Dan delayed acting, but when he heard that Tom had opened Thistle Meadow Winery, he thought, "If Tom can do it, then I can do it."

As Dan began to seriously pursue the idea, he kept in mind advice he had once heard from Virginia winemaker Dennis Horton: "Don't go into debt. Debt will kill you." But when he "sat down and did some numbers," Dan didn't see how he could pay for employees, equipment, supplies, and overhead. Then he realized that a type of equity financing might offer a solution. With shareholders, he could not only raise capital to buy equipment, but he might be able to develop a work force as well. He started having conversations with people to see who might be interested, and the response surprised him: "Talking to people locally, the idea took off like a snowball downhill. People would talk to their friends, and their friends would talk to their friends." After filing the necessary paperwork, he began to offer shares. Soon, New River Winery had 27 shareholders, enough funds to finance the winery for a year, and a volunteer labor pool. The second year, the winery did another stock offering, and there was even greater interest. Dan says, "It was amazing. We had to cut it off at 70."

Shareholders invest with the understanding that they can volunteer as little or as much as they want. Some people work one day a year, and others contribute several weekends a month. According to Dan, there is never any shortage of help, and as a result, the winery doesn't place an undue time burden on any one person. Furthermore, because the shareholders are a diverse group, they bring a variety of talents to the business. Haskell McGuire says, "I don't think if you tried to find the right people with the right interests, personalities, and so forth to do this, you could have done it as well as this came together."

Display at Bohemia Gallery

The people involved insist that the social interactions are a key aspect of the project. Haskell explains, "We've been clear with all potential new investors that if your only interest is to make money, then this may not be for you because it is a social thing. We are doing it because it's fun. We are not adverse to making money—we hope someday we'll be profitable—but that is not the primary goal." Darlene Massey, who is on the board of directors, agrees: "Our business plan explicitly says that it will be an enjoyable business to operate." Darlene says that her husband, Ben, compares the investment to buying a set of golf clubs: "You are going to enjoy playing with them, and you are going to enjoy the people you socialize with when you use them, but you're never going to resell them, and you're never going to get your money out of them. It's an expense for an indefinite future good time."

Not only are people enthused about making New River wine, they're also enthused about drinking it. The winery has a tasting outlet in the Bohemia Gallery in West Jefferson. Dan says of its opening in August 2006, "Without exaggeration, it was incredible." The gallery had wall-to-wall people, and they stayed for hours. Since then, interest has remained high. "We're getting such good local reaction," Haskell says. "It's been phenomenal."

The popularity of New River wines is gratifying. "It's great. It's absolutely wonderful," Dan says. "Winemakers love to have people enjoy their wines." However, it has also caused the winery an unforeseen problem. New River has trouble producing enough to meet demand. In its first year, the winery made 1,000 gallons, and it did so in a 500-square-foot space. The area was barely large enough for three people to work in, and winery tours were out of the question. In 2007, the winery plans to move to a much larger building in Lansing, a historic 1930s schoolhouse that is being renovated by Jim McGuire and Dorne Pentes. There, the winery will be part of a complex that will include apartments, artists' studios, and other related businesses. Eventually, it will be open to visitors.

In the future, even as it increases production, New River Winery would like to make all of its wines using Ashe County grapes and fruit. Dan believes it can be done. He also believes that there are great opportunities for other wineries in the region: "I would like to see a High Country wine trail." He insists that this could happen in the next five or 10 years. If it does, people will encounter even more winery owners in the area. In fact, Dan says, "maybe someday there can be a whole book on the High Country wineries."

Rockhouse Vineyards

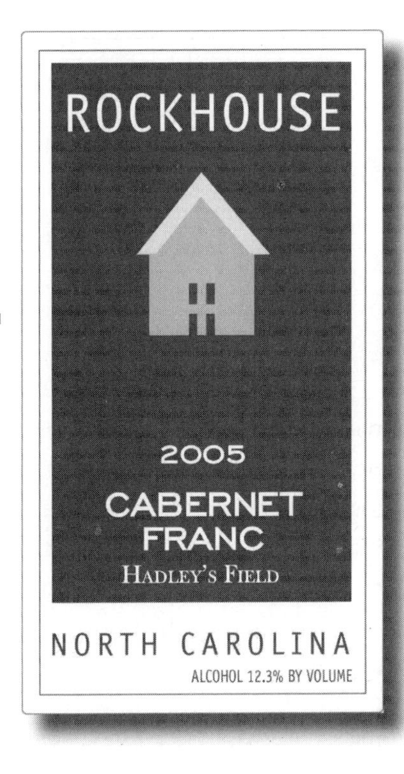

ROCKHOUSE
2005
CABERNET
FRANC
HADLEY'S FIELD
NORTH CAROLINA
ALCOHOL 12.3% BY VOLUME

1525 Turner Road
Tryon, N.C. 28782
Phone: 828-863-2784
Website:
www.rockhousevineyards.com
E-mail: mail@rockhousevineyards.com
Hours: Thursday–Sunday, 1–5 p.m., or by appointment. The winery is closed January, February, and major holidays.

Owners: Lee Griffin and Marsha Cassedy
Winemaker: Lee Griffin
First year as bonded winery: 1998
Tasting fee: Yes
On-line ordering: Yes
Wine club: Yes

Wine List
Whites: Chardonnay, Chardonnay Native Yeast, Viognier
Blush: Liason (dry rosé)
Reds: Cabernet Franc, Cabernet Sauvignon, Meritage, Merlot, Petit Verdot

Directions: From U.S. 74, take Exit 167 (N.C. 9/Mill Spring/New Prospect). Travel south 2.2 miles to Turner Road, turn left, and drive 1.5 miles to the entrance to the vineyards. From Spartanburg and Greenville, South Carolina, take Interstate 26 West to Exit 1 (S.C. 14/Landrum Highway). Turn right and travel east for 6 miles to N.C. 9. Turn left, go 1 mile to Turner Road, turn right, and drive 1.5 miles to the entrance.

Rockhouse Vineyards entrance

At first, the stone farmhouse that gives Rockhouse Vineyards its name seems ordinary. As you look at its walls, however, you begin to notice much more. Embedded in the mortar is an amazing array of geologic specimens: huge chunks of quartz and silica, fossils and shells, odd bits of modern-day glass shards, and various found objects. Built over the course of 10 years, the house contains rocks from at least 14 states.

Attracted to the house's unique design and its beautiful location in the foothills of the Blue Ridge Mountains, Marsha Cassedy and Lee Griffin bought the property in 1989. Since they lived and worked in Charlotte, the farm provided a relaxing weekend retreat. Marsha remembers, "We would come and sit on the porch and read. Our daughter was young, and she would dig in the dirt, climb trees, and just play. It was wonderful." Then, in 1991, with their daughter and her cousins helping, the couple planted four dozen vines by hand with a posthole digger. Although for years they had toured vineyards all over the world and toyed with the idea of one day having their own, they "started off thinking we were just going to have enough grapes for a hobby," according to Lee. Marsha adds, "It was a lark at that point, and it mushroomed bit by bit. As soon as we got a crop, the whole 'weekend retreat'

Marsha Cassedy and Lee Griffin
COURTESY OF ROCKHOUSE VINEYARDS

thing changed." They discovered they had a far larger harvest than they could realistically keep for themselves: "We looked at all those grapes and said, 'Oh, my God, what are we going to do? We might as well see if we can make wine that other people will want to drink.'" That was the beginning of Rockhouse Vineyards.

The success of the grapes wasn't altogether surprising, considering the area's history. There have been commercial vineyards in Tryon since the late 1800s, when the region was known for table grapes such as Niagaras and Delawares. During the summers, local farmers would take their crops to the train station and sell them to people traveling to the mountains to escape the Southern heat. For decades, the area also had a substantial peach and apple industry. Fruit grows well here because of a thermal belt that protects crops from extremes of heat and cold. The hills and the soil, a mixture of clay and loam, offer good drainage, while the 1,100-foot elevation ensures a combination of warm days and cool nights. In fact, according to Lee, a survey map charting the state's winegrowing areas has "a line along the foothills of the Blue Ridge Mountains showing where the best place for grapes would be." Rockhouse Vineyards is on that line.

Prior to buying the land, Lee and Marsha "hadn't grown a tomato." Consequently, in the winery's early years, they had to educate themselves about viticulture. They read, talked to people, and continued to tour vineyards, now with a professional interest, taking reams of notes and hundreds of slides. Before proceeding, however, they had to solve some key problems, such as a lack of water. Initially, the family couldn't even shower without the farmhouse's well running dry. Lee and Marsha hired a company to dig a new well. On the first try, the workers discovered "so much water, you couldn't even measure it," Marsha recalls. "It was unbelievable. That was a sign: 'Okay, we are supposed to do this because we now have water.' It really was amazing."

Each year as they planted more vines, Marsha says, "I kept looking at Lee and asking, 'What are we doing? What is the plan here?' " They didn't have one. The winery "just sort of evolved." Lee admits, "Initially, we did it the wrong way. We planted just a few vines of several varieties as an experiment to see what would grow. The problem with doing it that way is that you can't produce enough wine of any single variety to make it economically worthwhile." Although they found that almost every varietal would grow, they decided to concentrate on vinifera grapes. They dedicated the vineyards' 10 acres to Cabernet Sauvignon, Merlot, Chardonnay, Viognier, Cabernet Franc, and Petit Verdot. The choice was dictated in part by personal tastes. They say of their wine, "We make it the way we like it."

In Rockhouse's first decade, a key figure in its development was Javier Calderon, who helped establish several of the state's vineyards. When he began assisting Lee and Marsha in 1993, the vineyards grew dramatically. In their first year, Lee and Marsha had planted 48 vines in two days; with Javier, they planted 2,000 in a day. He taught them a great deal and became, according to Marsha, "so much a part of this place. A huge part." Tragically, he was killed in 2001. It's a loss that still affects Lee and Marsha on both a professional and a personal level. "Losing Javier was very sad, for a lot of reasons," Marsha says. "He was so trusted, so competent, and, above all, such a great friend."

Since opening Rockhouse to the public in the summer of 2001, the couple has relied on local retiree Jay Adams to run the tasting room. A noted beer maker with a Ph.D. in genetics, Adams provides a wealth of scientific expertise. He laughs that his wife, Arlene, volunteered him for the job. According to Adams, when she heard that Lee and Marsha needed help, she said, "Boy, do I have the guy for you." He enjoys the work and notes that the building's unique construction helps him: "When we're in the tasting room and people come in here who are younger, I tell them that there is a DeSoto horn button in the wall outside the barrel room. When they say, 'What's a DeSoto?' I ask them for their ID."

Thanks to the tourism signs on the highway and an increasing public awareness of North Carolina's wineries, Lee and Marsha find themselves having to guard against becoming too commercialized. What many people value about the winery, Lee says, is "the smallness of it, the intimacy." After all, the wood-paneled tasting room used to be a living room, and to get there, you must walk by a kitchen with mint 1940s appliances. Lee and Marsha want to retain this personal quality. Their attitude shows in their marketing approach, which is understated, the majority of their time and effort being focused on winemaking.

Since they live in Charlotte—where their "paying" jobs are—and commute to the vineyards, they don't have time for a lot of extras. According to Lee, the pressure they feel is "the pressure to make good wines." Their approach seems to work. Rockhouse's first releases in 1999 received enthusiastic responses. Soon, Rockhouse wines began winning medals in prestigious competitions across the country. Lee and Marsha laugh that these awards were not only gratifying but also helped reassure their now college-age daughter, Hadley. Skeptical about the merits of her parents' endeavors, she was less than thrilled to see a local newspaper article that featured a photograph of Lee and Marsha in bib overalls "looking like the *American Gothic* couple." Now, however, she appreciates what her parents have accomplished.

Though Rockhouse Vineyards is small, it rewards repeat visitors because there is always something new to contemplate. Guests enjoy the splendid views of rolling hills, old orchards, and the vineyards. In

the tasting room, Lee, Marsha, and Jay Adams offer an easygoing hospitality that complements the tranquil location. Although Rockhouse doesn't sell food, people are encouraged to bring picnics and linger. Adams remembers one couple who chose to celebrate their 50th wedding anniversary at the winery. They bought a bottle of Chardonnay, then spread a cloth on the porch table and took Spam sandwiches out of their picnic hamper. He recalls, "I went out and said, 'Spam sandwiches for your 50th anniversary?' And they said, 'That's all we could afford 50 years ago, so that's what we're celebrating with.'" Jay laughs, "Rockhouse wines go with everything. Even Spam."

The Teensy Winery

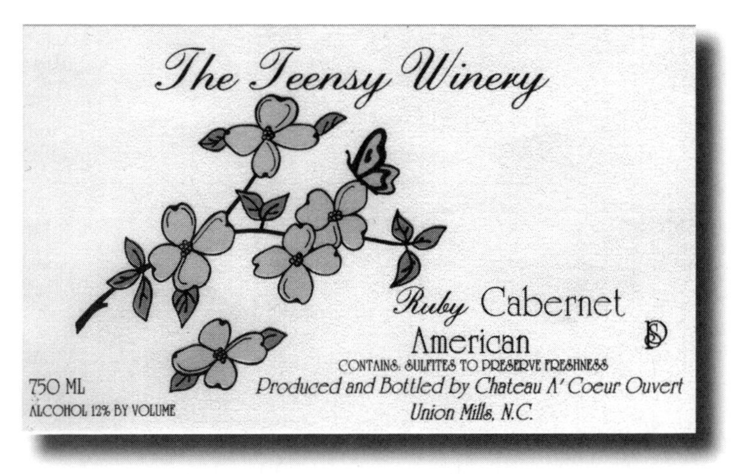

3661 Painters Gap Road
Union Mills, N.C. 28167
Phone: 828-287-7763
Hours: By appointment

Owner: Bob Howard
Winemaker: Bob Howard
First year as bonded winery: 1986
Tasting fee: No
On-line ordering: No
Wine club: No

Wine List
White: Chardonnay
Reds: Cabernet Sauvignon, Merlot

Directions: Take Interstate 40 to U.S. 221 South (the Rutherfordton exit). Follow U.S. 221 South to Thermal City. Turn right on Gilkey School Road. Take the left fork onto Painters Gap Road and drive approximately 8 miles. The winery is on the left.

Bob Howard and friend

Located in the basement of Bob Howard's house, The Teensy Winery is true to its name. Bob points out that he has the same equipment as a "normal" winery, only most of it is smaller. He says, "We're the Mini-Me of wineries in North Carolina." When he gets a harvest from his vines, the winery produces around 300 gallons, and whatever he makes "just doesn't stick around." He doesn't, however, always have a harvest. For the past five years, black rot has infected the vines and prevented the grapes from ripening. After experimenting with different pruning and spraying programs, Bob believes he has finally turned the corner and figured out how to control the disease.

Bob's winemaking career started in Florida. A friend had an orange grove, so "just for the fun of it," they taught themselves how to make orange wine. He insists that it wasn't bad, sweet with a high alcohol content—"kind of like a Muscatel," Bob says. "You just didn't sit down and drink a lot of it. You drank a small amount and said, 'Yeah, that's pretty good.' " When he and his family moved to the mountains of North Carolina, he decided to plant a small vineyard and to try making European-style wines.

Bob laughs at the memory of getting his vines in the mail: "It's really depressing when you order these five-dollar vines, and they send you a box that's got nothing but a bunch of twigs and sticks. You think, 'My word, I've been had.'" After weeks of digging holes in the rocky soil and carefully planting 500 cuttings of Cabernet, Merlot, and Chardonnay, he went on a trip with his wife, only to realize "there's something wrong. These pants don't fit." He weighed himself and discovered he had lost 11 pounds putting in the vineyard. The work paid off. The next year, the vines "exploded out of the ground, and the following year, it was all I could do to keep up with them. They literally were begging to grow here."

Bob's wife advised him, "If you're going to do this, really do it." So when he ordered his vines, he also got the government application to become a bonded winery. But he didn't fill it out right away. Then, "after two years walking around the table, I decided, 'Yeah, let's go ahead and do this for real.' When I sent the forms in [to the Bureau of Alcohol, Tobacco and Firearms], they were shocked. They said, 'These are obsolete forms. Where did you get these?' I said, 'I got them from you, where else?'" After receiving new forms, Bob started the process again. When the application was finally approved, he became the only legal maker of alcoholic beverages in Rutherford County.

To prepare himself for his first crush, Bob bought book after book. He insists that if you want to learn, "you just keep reading. Knowledge is power. Those are the three most important words in the world." He says that, as a winemaker, "a nice quality Cabernet is what I'm always shooting for," but really, "the goal is to have a good time." So far, he has been pleased with the results, which have received "good compliments from pretty intelligent wine people." He laughs that no one has ever complained except to say, "You mean you don't have any more?"

Although he does most of the work himself, Bob gets friends to help during harvests. He points out that most people "normally don't ever get a chance to do something like this, so it's a great enjoyment and fellowship when folks come out and get together." His friends have been surprised by the effort involved. They think it's going to be a lark, something like a Lucille Ball episode. Instead, they find themselves working hard and sweating heavily.

For Bob, the winery's small size makes it manageable. There is, he believes, an economy of scale. He and his wife own the equipment and operate with relatively low expenses. "If we don't make it, it doesn't hurt us at all," he says. "Some people are financed to the hilt, and they've got to produce. We're not in that position." If Teensy were to increase production to thousands of gallons, Bob would have to borrow money, and then "it becomes my master, instead of me being its master." And he has only a limited amount of time to invest in the work. In addition to owning Teensy, Bob is a commercial pilot, a flight instructor, an insurance agent, and the president of an Internet service provider. All of these jobs make him appreciate working in the vineyard because "it's a good chance to concentrate on something else besides the other multiple things I do. It's a time to contemplate."

Bob enjoys what he calls "a unique business," one that he feels is an art form. Even his battle with black rot hasn't dampened his enthusiasm. In fact, he has never considered quitting. For one, when he has a batch of wine fermenting downstairs, "the whole house smells so good, just so good, when it's cooking." Plus, "when you factor in the time and you factor in the taxes" and, most importantly, "when you factor in the joy," he figures he always comes out ahead.

Thistle Meadow Winery

102 Thistle Meadow
Laurel Springs, N.C. 28644
Phone: 800-233-1505
Fax: 413-803-9850
Website:
www.thistlemeadow.com
E-mail:
info@thistlemeadowwinery.com
Hours: Monday–Saturday,
noon–5 p.m.; Sunday, 2–5 p.m.

Owner: Tom Burgiss
Winemaker: Tom Burgiss and
the Thistle Meadow staff
First year as bonded winery: 2002
Tasting fee: Yes
On-line ordering: No
Wine club: No

Wine List
The winery offers over 40 different selections, including European and American varieties.

Directions: From Sparta, go south on N.C. 18 for 12 miles to the intersection of N.C. 113 and Elk Knob Road. Turn left on Elk Knob Road. The winery is the first drive on the right. From Milepost 246 on the Blue Ridge Parkway, follow Elk Knob Road for 3 miles to the winery, on the left.

Thistle Meadow Winery and Grapestompers

Tom Burgiss has a mission. As someone who loves wine so much he claims that, while in France, "I brushed my teeth with Beaujolais," he wants to share his passion with others. However, he wants to get people not only to drink wine, but to make it themselves. Talk with Tom and it quickly becomes clear that he considers himself primarily a teacher. Even though he's the owner of Thistle Meadow Winery, he insists, "I get more pleasure out of showing you how to make wine than having you buy mine." In fact, he established his winery in part to showcase the types of products that people can buy from Grapestompers, his wine-kit and equipment supply store.

Like many educators, Tom speaks from his personal engagement with his subject. He says, "I've chased wine all my life. I was considered a nerd in college. I drank wine instead of beer." In his "chase," he has traveled to all the major wine-producing regions of the world except for Argentina and South Africa; however, it was a visit to Canada that may have had the greatest effect on him. There, he was presented with a bottle he liked. When Tom asked where he could buy it, the host explained that he had made it himself. After returning home, Tom decided to try winemaking, and he made a batch in his dining room. He soon realized, "I can make three as well as one." As the batches increased in size and number, he eventually moved his equipment to a tractor shed,

Tom Burgiss

and he started showing other people how to do it. In 1996, he founded Grapestompers, which Tom believes was for a while the second-largest wine equipment supplier east of the Mississippi.

The popularity of the business has surprised some, but Tom points out with a smile that "winemaking products really take off in dry counties. You never know what goes on behind closed doors." For several years, he offered Grapestompers customers samples from the various kits, but people kept asking if they could buy the finished product as well. Eventually, he decided to open Thistle Meadow "to stop folks from complaining," as his website puts it. Now, the winery makes 40 of the approximately 75 kits and concentrates that Grapestompers sells.

As a teacher, Tom wants to help people learn good practices and principles of winemaking. These include the development of high standards. He insists that people need to "put the product above themselves." He says, "If it's not good, I don't want to expose it to anybody." He has hired interns from Appalachian State University, trying to offer as many opportunities to students as possible.

In addition to teaching about wine, Tom sees himself as a promoter of the state's industry. He says, "Our main purpose is to promote North Carolina and North Carolina wine that everyone will go home and talk about." He once had an intern from France who criticized everything at first, but by the end of three months, "I won him over to North Carolina wine," Tom says proudly. Thistle Meadow's tasting room displays bottles from the state's different wineries, and Tom visits these places as well. He laughs, "They say apple farmers don't buy apples. I'm not like that. I'm a little strange. I go to other wineries and buy their wines."

Almost everyone who knows Tom describes him as a character, and he acknowledges, "I'm a wild man. I'm old. I get to act however I wish." He often speaks bluntly about his likes and dislikes. For example, he says, "People in a hurry shouldn't be tasting wine." He does not allow bus tours. "I despise herding people like cattle. We are not in the cattle business." And if someone calls the winery, "you're going to get a person, not an answering service!"

Tom's personal approach isn't surprising, since Thistle Meadow Winery and Grapestompers are located on 140 acres of land that have been in his family for generations. His grandfather built the nearby house where Tom and his wife live and run a bed-and-breakfast. Next to the Grapestompers store—which, in addition to winemaking equipment, sells beer- and soda-making supplies, T-shirts, and artwork—is a barn that has a dance floor, a music stage, a kitchen, and the capacity to seat 250 people. For years, the Burgisses held Saturday-night dances that were so popular the dance floor had to be replaced. Now, the building serves as a reception area for weddings and a place to hold business meetings and other events.

Tom admits to being surprised by Thistle Meadow's popularity: "It amazes me. We are in the boonies. I'm not ashamed to say it, it *is* the boonies." And yet people from all over the United States and almost two dozen countries have visited. He laughs that the enthusiasm for his wine "wrecked" his business plan: "I thought people would buy a bottle as a courtesy, but instead they buy cases." Consequently, even though he doesn't ship wine or sell it anywhere but on the premises, "we can't keep it around."

As for the future, Tom says his plan is simple: "To enjoy what I'm doing." Right now, he believes that "of all the wineries around, we have the most fun." But he insists, "When this gets to feel like a job, I'll quit."

Waldensian Heritage Wines

4940 Villar Lane
Valdese, N.C. 28690
Phone: 828-879-3202
Website:
www.waldensianheritagewines.com
E-mail:
info@waldensianheritagewines.com
Hours: Thursday–Sunday, 1–6 p.m.;
Monday–Wednesday, by appointment

Owners: John Bounous, Joel Dalmas, Roger Heavner, Joe Jacumin, Freddy Leger, Blenda Leger, Dennis Powell, Julie Zimmerman, and Eddie Zimmerman
First year as bonded winery: 1989
Tasting fee: No
On-line ordering: Pending
Wine club: No

Wine List
Whites: Blanc Royal, Waldensian White Sweet
Blushes: Blush Regal, Piedmont Rosé
Reds: Burgundy Valdese, Heritage Burgundy Valdese, Villar Rouge Sweet
Specialty: Millennium Deux (a blend of all Waldensian Heritage wines)

Directions: From Interstate 40, take Exit 112 and drive north to Valdese. Go north on Eldred Street to North Laurel Street. Follow North Laurel to Villar Lane. Turn left and follow the signs to the winery.

Waldensian Heritage Wines

Waldensian Heritage Wines is a tinkerer's dream. Walk inside and you enter, as co-owner Joel Dalmas says, "a great big, overgrown, homemade operation." You won't see expanses of chrome, glass, and oak. Rather than being a showcase winery displaying what money can buy, Waldensian Heritage Wines is a tribute to what ingenuity and resourcefulness can fashion.

Throughout the winery's history, the people involved have built most of the necessary equipment. For example, when they needed a filter, instead of buying a stainless-steel Italian one from a catalog for $3,000, they built one out of recycled equipment and odd parts, including an old typewriter stand, for a total cost of $106. When they needed a bottle washer, they built one using donated PVC piping, rather than paying $7,000. Although the winery's official motto is "Life is too short to drink bad wine," its unofficial slogan is "Plastic makes it possible."

Resourcefulness at the winery is a matter of practicality as well as a point of pride. The owners want to keep the wine as inexpensive as possible. They refuse to use oak barrels that cost between $500 and $800 each because, according to Joel, doing so would mean "we couldn't sell our wine for less than $20 a bottle." Instead, they age the wine in recycled plastic containers that a beverage company gives them for free. (In fact, the only place wooden barrels are used are as tables in the picnic area.) For labor, the winery relies entirely on volunteers and "Waldensian work parties." This cost-effectiveness guarantees the success of Waldensian Heritage Wines. Because profits are put back into the business, the owners don't get rich. Instead, they have the satisfac-

Joel Dalmas

tion of fulfilling part of the winery's mission, which, as its name implies, is to preserve Waldensian heritage.

The Waldensian Church dates to medieval times, when, to escape religious persecution, its followers moved to high valleys in the Cottian Alps of Europe. There, they developed a culture that combined their evangelical faith, their Italian heritage, and the French language. By the 1890s, population growth forced many to emigrate to America in search of land and better livelihoods. Moving from the western Piedmont of Italy to the western Piedmont of North Carolina, a group of Waldensians established the town of Valdese in 1893.

The community attracted immigrants for several decades. Joel Dalmas's parents, for example, came to the United States from Italy in the early 1900s. They married in New York City but didn't want to raise a family there because they felt the city was too enclosed, too dirty, and, as Joel puts it, "the sky isn't blue and the people have no manners." In 1913, they moved to the Valdese area and started a dairy farm. Born and raised on the farm, Joel has lived there his entire life except during World War II. He says of the war, "It took me four years to get back home." When he did, he found that "the cows were gone, but the buildings were still here."

Decades later, Joel and a group of Waldensian men converted one of those buildings—the 4,000-square-foot barn, built of stone and 30-foot timbers—into a winery. Pooling their resources, they formed the Villar Vintners of Valdese, a name that would later be changed to Waldensian Heritage Wines. They referred to themselves as the "Buonvino family"—the "Good Wine family." Although the winery officially opened in 1989, everyone involved had been making wine for much longer. In fact, the owners claim over 250 years of collective experience and see themselves as part of a tradition that goes back centuries. The winemakers work mainly with Lambrusca-type grapes such as Concord and Niagara, which they buy from growers in New York's Finger Lakes region. They make both a traditional red and a traditional white wine, Heritage Burgundy Valdese and Blanc Royale, and they also offer successively sweeter versions of these. In recent years, the winery has made an effort to buy North Carolina grapes and local crops of Cabernet Franc and Cabernet Sauvignon. Using vinifera grapes, however, can mean an increase in the wines' price, which makes the Waldensians uneasy. They want a quality inexpensive product.

The Waldensians' European heritage is evident not only in the wines but also at the winery itself, where the restroom doors say *Signiori* and *Signore* and where a boccia (Italian bowling) court runs the length of the building. A boccia tournament is held every June. Winners have their names engraved on a plaque displayed in the tasting room. Next to the court is a row of tables where people can picnic, sip glasses of wine, or simply enjoy the view of woods, a small planting of vines, and nearby hills.

Because of the popularity of the wines and the winery, the owners decided in 2003 to expand. They renovated the interior of a nearby building and built a deck around the exterior. When they finished the project in 2005, they were able to both increase wine production and host larger functions, yet the expansion also remained true to their frugal heritage. This "new" building was constructed in 1939 and for years had been used as a toolshed and workshop. Its renovation was another example of Waldensian recycling.

1350 WoodMill Winery Lane
Vale, N.C. 28168
Phone: 704-276-9911
Website: www.woodmillwinery.com
E-mail: lcagle@woodmillwinery.com
Hours: Thursday, Friday,
and Sunday, 1–6 p.m.;
Saturday, 10 a.m.–6 p.m.

Owner: Larry Cagle, Jr.
Winemaker: Larry Cagle, Jr.
First year as bonded winery: 2006
Tasting fee: Yes
On-line ordering: Yes
Wine club: No

Wine List
Whites: Scuppernong (dry, semidry, semisweet, sweet)
Reds: Muscadine (dry, semidry, semisweet, sweet)
Fruits: Blueberry (dry, semidry, semisweet, sweet)
Specialties: Carolina Christmas (muscadine and scuppernong), Carolina Jubilee (muscadine and blueberry), Red White and Blue (muscadine, scuppernong, and blueberry)

Directions: From Interstate 85, take Exit 17 onto U.S. 321 North. Follow U.S. 321 to N.C. 27, then drive west on N.C. 27 to Lincolnton. Continue north on N.C. 27 for another 8 miles, turn right on Cat Square Road, drive 2 miles, turn left on Beam Lumber Road, go approximately 0.5 mile, and turn right on John Beam Road. The winery is on the right.

Larry Cagle insists that he became involved in grape growing and winemaking in an effort to improve his father's health. Throughout much of his life, Larry Cagle, Sr., has suffered from arthritis. He also has had heart trouble, having undergone a quadruple bypass at age 50. A doctor suggested red wine might help, so Larry, who had traveled frequently in France, bought his father a bottle of good French wine. It was not a hit. In fact, Larry remembers, "he said he'd rather drink vinegar."

Larry, who is a research engineer, began reading studies about wine's health benefits and the "French paradox." (The French eat relatively high-fat diets yet suffer a low incidence of heart disease.) He also began examining claims about wine's antioxidants and resveratrol. His research convinced him that wine could benefit his father if only he could get him to drink it. Several years earlier, Larry had bought a dairy farm; now, he decided to put a vineyard on the land because, he reasoned, "we need to grow grapes and make our own wine and make it taste differently because Dad won't drink wine."

Larry Cagle, Jr., and daughter

As he chose varietals to plant, Larry decided to concentrate on native American grapes instead of European ones. He knew there was a stigma attached to muscadine wine, and he discovered that people in a wine association he joined "looked down their noses at me." But he also knew that such grapes would be easier to grow, and the research suggested that they had the highest levels of antioxidants. Most importantly, he had figured out that his father would drink muscadine wine.

Initially, in 2000, Larry planted an acre. Half of the vines died, and when he replanted them, half of them died again. He discovered that because the land's clay held so much water, he was drowning them. When he figured out a drainage system, the vines began to thrive, and he increased the vineyard's acreage.

Larry had similar struggles on the winemaking end. He tried to educate himself by reading books, but he discovered that all of the instructions were for vinifera wines and were inappropriate for muscadine ones. As a result, "the first three years we made wine, we couldn't drink it," Larry says. "The first one was like vinegar, and the second year it may as well have been." The fourth year, Larry scrapped what he had been doing and started over. The secret he discovered was to "take what you normally would do in a vinifera winery and do the opposite." After approximately 120 tests, he finally made a wine that led his father to say, "That's perfect. That's what I want." At that point, Larry decided he was ready to open WoodMill Winery.

Besides the family's personal reasons for focusing on muscadine wines, Larry believes the choice made smart business sense, particularly considering a discussion he had with a winery owner who was making excellent vinifera wines. The wines had won awards, and Larry regarded them as superb. He was shocked when the owner told him that only about 5 to 10 percent of visitors bought them. People in the South, the owner explained, prefer sweeter wines. To Larry, it made sense to offer selections that the majority of wine drinkers in the area prefer, instead of competing with the majority of wineries for 10 percent of the market.

Immediately upon opening, Larry realized he had made a good

WoodMill vineyard
COURTESY OF WOODMILL WINERY

decision. In the first eight weekends, WoodMill exceeded its six-month goal, and after 12 weeks, Larry knew he would have to immediately expand. He says that "99 percent of the people that walk in this door walk out with a bottle of wine. I'm pleased beyond my dreams and my imagination the way people have supported us." Ironically, the wines' popularity has meant a reconsideration of the plan that gave the winery its name. Larry intended to have the tasting room in the building's basement and to put a woodworking shop for his cabinet-making hobby on the first floor. The reception the wines received, however, and the number of people who want to have events at the vineyard have meant that the entire building will be dedicated to the winery's business.

Larry believes one reason for the community support is because "they know we didn't buy this place. They know we built it. They see us struggle. They see us pruning in 30-degree temperatures. We're here doing it ourselves." People also know that it's a family business, and Larry emphasizes this in the marketing. For the wines' labels, Larry commissioned a local artist, Bud Ramseur, to paint scenes of Larry's childhood memories. The first four labels include a representation of the house where he grew up and scenes of fishing, cutting wood, bringing a Christmas tree home, and a picnic. Eventually, these paintings will hang in the winery.

In marketing and promoting its products, WoodMill emphasizes their heart-healthy nature. Larry insists that he doesn't believe in miracle drugs and that he would never say muscadines have a guaranteed health benefit; however, his enthusiasm for the grapes is clear, and considering his father's experience, it's understandable. In 2001, Larry Cagle, Sr., became allergic to his arthritis medicine and had to stop taking it. Larry remembers that "it was extremely bad. He could not pick up a glass of water. All he could do was sit in the house." Now, his father takes one Advil each morning, drinks six ounces of wine before going to sleep, and spends his days tending vines and mowing in the vineyard. It's incredible, according to Larry, and the Cagles believe, "It's the wine."

WoodMill vineyard
COURTESY OF WOODMILL WINERY

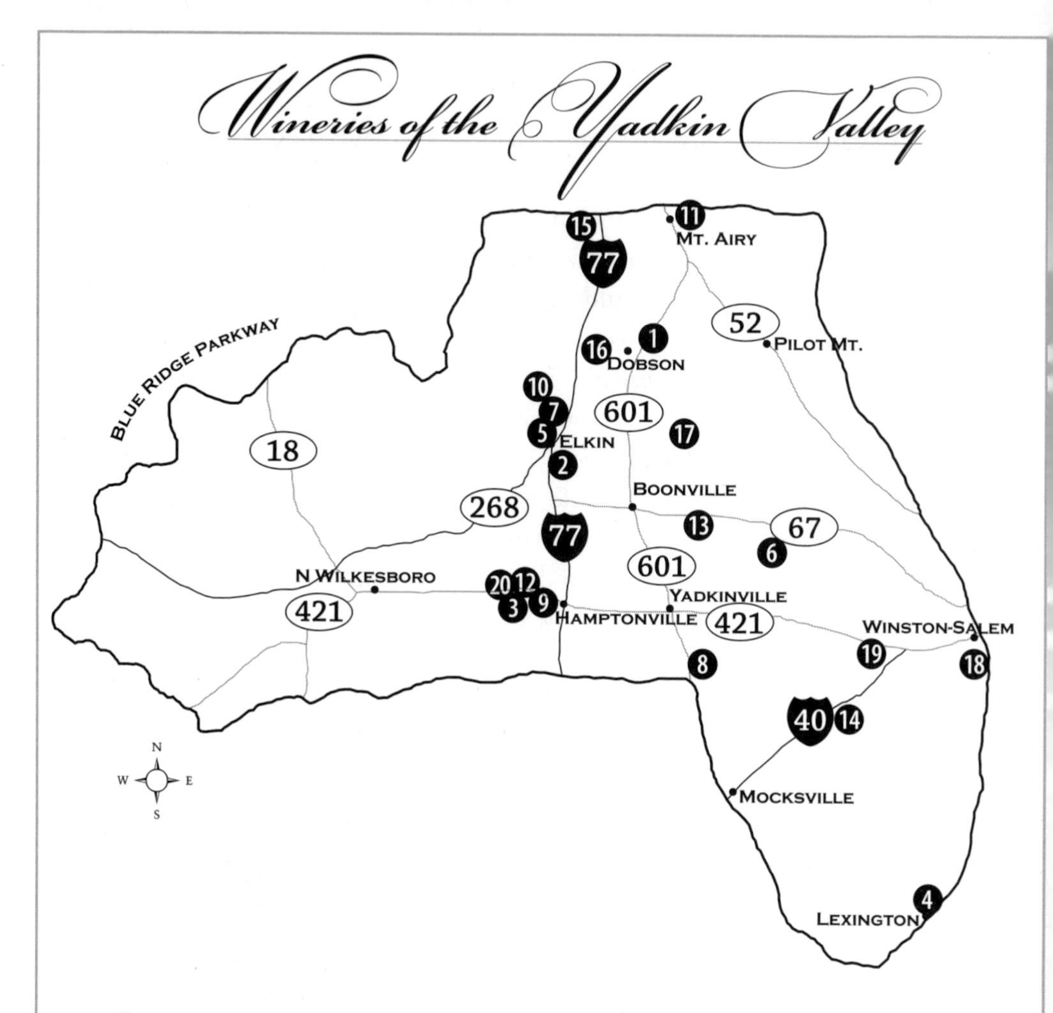

1. Black Wolf Vineyards
2. Brushy Mountain Winery
3. Buck Shoals Vineyard
4. Childress Vineyards
5. Elkin Creek Vineyard
6. Flint Hill Vineyards
7. Grassy Creek Vineyard and Winery
8. Hanover Park Vineyard
9. Laurel Gray Vineyards
10. McRitchie Wine Company
11. Old North State Winery
12. Raffaldini Vineyards
13. RagApple Lassie Vineyards
14. RayLen Vineyards and Winery
15. Round Peak Vineyards
16. Shelton Vineyards
17. Stony Knoll Vineyards
18. Weathervane Winery
19. Westbend Vineyards
20. Windy Gap Vineyards

Wineries of the Yadkin Valley

Black Wolf Vineyards fountain

Black Wolf Vineyards

283 Vineyard Lane
Dobson, N.C. 27017
Phone: 336-374-2532
Fax: 336-374-3496
Website:
www.blackwolfvineyards.com
E-mail: info@blackwolfvineyards.com
Hours: Monday–Wednesday,
11 a.m.–2:30 p.m.; Thursday–Saturday,
11 a.m.–2:30 p.m. and 5–10 p.m.;
Sunday, noon–8 p.m.

Owner: Dana Theis
Winemaker: Joyce Rigby
First year as bonded winery: 2005
Tasting fee: Yes
On-line ordering: Yes
Wine club: No

Black Wolf Vineyards
Yadkin Valley
Semi-Sweet White Wine
Blue Moon White
12.1% ALC/VOL

Wine List
Whites: Blue Moon White, Chardonnay, Moonlight White, Sauvignon Blanc, Seyval Blanc
Reds: Cabernet Sauvignon, Chambourcin, Pinot Noir, Sweet Wolf Red, Wolf's Lair Red

Directions: From Interstate 77, take Exit 93 and follow Zephyr Road into Dobson to the second traffic light (Main Street). Turn right, go 1 block on Main Street to the traffic light, and turn left on East Atkins Street. Cross U.S. 601, take the U.S. 601 North ramp, and continue to Vineyard Lane, on the right.

Running a winery can be a risky proposition, but Dana Theis is used to difficult ventures. For years, he raised and bred wolves with huskies and sold the animals to clients around the world. Although in retrospect he says, "I wouldn't do it again. They're dangerous. They're not tame pets," his business introduced him to "some very interesting characters," including a Malaysian general and a Saudi Arabian prince. Dana no longer raises wolves, but his love of them can be seen throughout Black Wolf Vineyards, from the name to the wine labels to the bronze animal head in the tasting room.

When Dana bought the Surry County property from a retired dentist in 1991, he had no intention of building a winery; he simply wanted some land in the country. At the time, the 55 acres had no electricity or water, and the only building was a shed that was "full of crates and rats." There were, however, a number of vinifera vines. While traveling in Europe, the dentist had become interested in viticulture, and on his return, he had planted several European varietals. "Rather than plow them under," Dana says, "I decided to learn about them." He started gathering information and visiting area vineyards. "It took me six or seven years to learn to grow grapes," Dana remembers. "It's a difficult crop that can change fast. The grapes can be underripe one week and go over the next. And if you don't lose the grapes to mildew or hail, and you get them all done right, then the birds come by, or the deer."

Dana began selling his crops to regional wineries, including Biltmore Estate and Château Morrisette in Virginia. However, after a couple of years, he realized "there's no money in grapes. The money is in the wine." Consequently, he made a deal with Marek Wojciechowski of Chatham Hill Winery. Marek agreed to make wine from a crop in exchange for keeping a portion of the fruit for his own use. The first year of this agreement, Dana discovered that with no alcohol license and no winery, "I had all this wine, and I couldn't sell it, so I had to put it in cold storage." At that point, he decided to open a restaurant on the property as an outlet for his wine.

Because of its location, the Wolf's Liar restaurant could not rely on walk-in traffic, so Dana wanted something that would help make the place unique. First, he built a large, two-story log cabin in the middle of the vineyard. Complete with stone fireplace, it provides an atmosphere

Joyce Rigby and Dana Theis

that is "cozy, fun, and romantic." Next, Dana explains, "I wanted something that if people couldn't remember the restaurant, they would remember the dish. And that was elk." The kitchen has also served wild boar, rattlesnake, and other exotic dishes. However, Dana believes that "you can't just have good food," so he began to bring in entertainment. In addition to music, readings, and dramatic productions, he even hired a psychic who had worked with the Charlotte police. (She didn't work out, since the people who came to see her weren't always interested in fine dining or fine wine.) Dana also instituted an annual festival—The Grape Jam. He admits, "I tried just about everything to get people in from the cities." Ultimately, the most helpful event for the restaurant was the opening of Shelton Vineyards. Dana says, "It changed everything for the town and the area. I wondered what would happen, if they would take away my business, but the opposite happened."

With the restaurant on firm footing, Dana decided in 2005 to build his own winery. He hired Joyce Rigby as a consultant to help with the design. In 2006, he asked her to be the winemaker as well. Joyce laughs that when she told friends she was becoming the winemaker at Black Wolf, they said, "You've got to be kidding." They knew of her lifelong love affair with wolves. Twenty years ago, Joyce's first dog seemed to be part wolf, and ever since, she has collected jewelry, pictures, and other items featuring the animal. There were, however, other good reasons for taking the position. Joyce had already developed a good working relationship with Dana—one, she says, "based on trust and an understanding of each other." She also was excited to be working with such old vines. In fact, Joyce, who has helped develop vineyards and wineries across the state, believes there is something special about Black Wolf's location. Although the Yadkin Valley has "great places to grow grapes," Black Wolf's site is cooler than most of the valley, which means it is able to grow varietals such as Pinot Noir, Riesling, and Sauvignon Blanc, which are difficult or even impossible to grow elsewhere.

In designing Black Wolf's winery, the decision was made to build a separate facility behind the vineyard, so the focus would remain on the Wolf's Lair Restaurant. The winery is functional, rather than aesthetic. In contrast, Black Wolf's tasting room—located above the restaurant—is atmospheric. Dana likes to light candelabras and quote poetry sometimes. He admits that he has even been known to howl on occasion.

Over the years, Dana has tried to create a mysterious, romantic place that offers a memorable experience. People celebrate birthdays, anniversaries, engagements, and other events at Black Wolf, and Dana and his staff strive to make these occasions special. He believes that "they will remember this place 30 years from now because of what we do for them. They will always remember the time they had here." He's proud of his wines and his vineyards, and he's proud of the effect Black Wolf has on visitors: "When people leave the restaurant, I see them holding hands and sometimes kissing, and I know the environment led to that."

Brushy Mountain Winery

125 West Main Street
Elkin, N.C. 28621
Phone: 336-835-1313
Fax: 336-835-3713
Website:
www.brushymountainwine.com
E-mail:
info@brushymountainwine.com
Hours: Thursday–Saturday,
noon–4 p.m.; Sunday–Wednesday,
by appointment

Owners: The Mayberry family
Winemaker: Sean McRitchie (consultant)
First year as bonded winery: 2006
Tasting fee: Yes
On-line ordering: Pending
Wine club: No

Wine List
Whites: Booger Swamp (blend), Chardonnay
Reds: Bugaboo Creek (blend), Merlot
Fruits: Blackberry, Raspberry

Directions: Elkin is on U.S. 21 in Surry County. The winery is located at 125 West Main Street in downtown Elkin.

In January 2005, Matthew Mayberry had a vision: "I was in my car late afternoon, driving home, and I had a kind of epiphany. This concept came in. *Shazam!*—there it was. It just kind of exploded in my mind. People think I'm crazy, but I saw every aspect of this winery in a matter of seconds. It came in totally unexpected and totally complete."

His wife, Ann, and her family owned a building in downtown Elkin, and in this moment of clarity, Matthew saw how it "would make a perfect setup" for a winery. He envisioned a small winery that could produce high-quality wines by buying the best grapes available from local growers.

Matthew was familiar with the state's industry. In 1998, on hearing of the Shelton Vineyards concept, he was convinced that viticulture was "the future of northwest North Carolina." He started developing vineyard properties and eventually set up his own real-estate brokerage to do so. For his own winery, however, he didn't want to be tied to the land. Although the Mayberrys owned a 155-acre farm, Matthew wanted to concentrate the financial capital on the making of wines, rather than the growing of vines.

Despite the intensity of his vision, Matthew had a hard time convincing his wife and family to invest in the project. The family had just celebrated Matthew and Ann's 55th wedding anniversary and what

Ribbon cutting with the Mayberry family
COURTESY OF BRUSHY MOUNTAIN WINERY

would have been Ann's father's 100th birthday, and Ann is straightforward about her reaction to the idea. She says, "I thought he was out of his mind." Matthew arranged a series of presentations to convince her, their sons, and his mother. He had the family meet Elkin's mayor, town manager, and head of downtown development. He took them around to different vineyards and had them talk to people in the industry, including Stephen Lyons of Raffaldini Vineyards. By the end of the tour, the family was impressed and, according to Ann, "everyone was on board." Subsequently, the Mayberrys began working closely with Sean and Patricia McRitchie of McRitchie Associates, Inc., to establish a winery. Sean is responsible for the winemaking at Brushy Mountain, Patricia completes the various necessary applications, and they both help with the ongoing business of the winery.

The family decided to call the winery "Brushy Mountain" because it was the only one of "around 400 names" that everyone could agree on. And, Ann explains, "as a geologist, Matthew has always loved the Brushy Mountains," which are some of the oldest in the United States.

Brushy Mountain Winery storefront
COURTESY OF BRUSHY MOUNTAIN WINERY

In fact, it was during his career as a geologist that Matthew discovered wine. He worked for the Occidental Minerals Corporation and was sent all over the world on a first-class expense account. He even traveled in Europe with a member of the Frescobaldi family, who own one of Italy's oldest and most prestigious estates. It was a fine opportunity to sample a variety of international wines.

Matthew makes no claims to being a connoisseur or wine expert, but his passion is obvious, and he is convinced that Brushy Mountain Winery will be a boon to Elkin. He believes, "This winery is a big shot in the arm to start bringing tourists in." If Brushy Mountain is successful, he anticipates other wineries will open nearby.

Although the selections that Brushy Mountain offers will change each year according to the available grapes, the Mayberrys plan to always offer a blackberry wine. Decades ago, family members ran the Elkin Canning Company, a business where people would pick fruit and the company would can it for them and ship it to customers. When orders from West Virginia totaling thousands of cans kept arriving, someone from the company went north to find out why. It turned out that coal miners believed that blackberries in their lunchpails brought good luck and would keep them from harm. The Mayberrys hope the fruit will be lucky for them as well. For their wine label, they have incorporated the label from the old canning company.

Establishing Brushy Mountain has taken a great deal of work, and Matthew knows that some people might consider him foolish. However, he insists of his epiphany, "I consider what happened to me like a gift and a grace. For someone my age who is watching TV and getting fatter and fatter and drifting slowly toward the end of his time here, to have something like that happen is miraculous. I'm more excited about this than anything that's happened in the last 20 years in my life, since exploring for gold in central Borneo."

Buck Shoals Vineyard

6121 Vintner Way
Hamptonville, N.C. 27020
Phone: 336-468-9274
Fax: 336-924-2720
Website:
www.buckshoalsvineyard.com
E-mail: info@buckshoalsvineyard.com
Hours: Wednesday and Thursday, 11 a.m.–5 p.m.; Friday and Saturday, 11 a.m.–6 p.m.; Sunday, 1–5 p.m.

Owners: Terry and Joanne Crater
Winemaker: Dana Acker
First year as bonded winery: 2004
Tasting fee: Yes
On-line ordering: Via e-mail
Wine club: Yes

Wine List
Whites: Bryan's Legacy (white blend), Chardonnay, Pinot Grigio, Shoals Creek Sweet White, Viognier
Reds: Rocco Red (red blend), Shoals Creek Red (semisweet), Vito's Pride (red blend)

Directions: From U.S. 421 in Yadkin County, take Exit 267 (Windsor Road) and follow the signs south for approximately 2.5 miles. The vineyard is on the right.

A self-described "salty character" with "a crazy sense of humor," Joanne Crater is frank about the fact that she has never been "a country

Buck Shoals patio

girl." Growing up in suburban New Jersey, she fantasized about living in Manhattan. She didn't care if that meant she wouldn't be able to have a lawn or garden because she also wasn't "a flower person." In fact, when she saw other people mowing their yards, she thought, "What are they, nuts?" Consequently, she recognizes the irony of not only running a winery in rural North Carolina but also being a graduate of the viticulture program at Surry Community College.

Establishing Buck Shoals Vineyard was the idea of her husband, Terry, and Joanne jokes that in the preliminary stages, she was "in denial." She says that had she realized how serious Terry was, "I would have hightailed it out of here." Then, because Terry works full time at Wachovia, it fell to Joanne to take many of the necessary viticulture courses. She laughs that after starting these classes, she finally realized how big an acre was. She came home to try to talk her husband into reducing his plans, but it was too late. He had already begun planting five acres.

Eventually, Joanne learned to appreciate working in the vineyard. It was peaceful and "gave me time to think." She also discovered something magical in watching the plants grow and understanding what was happening to them. That was the turnaround in her attitude.

Unlike his wife, Terry did grow up in the country. Five generations of his family have raised crops in the Yadkin County area, and he wants to enable future generations to do so as well. A collector of wine since the 1980s, Terry began following the developments in the state's industry in the 1990s, when he became convinced that growing grapes offered a way to keep the family farm in production. He also saw vineyards as a way to help strengthen the local economy.

To emphasize their commitment to the land, the Craters named the winery after a local creek. They also chose an old waterwheel gristmill, the Buck Shoals Mills, for their logo. Although the 1880s mill was destroyed in the 1960s, the Craters feel the image honors the area's heritage.

The Craters opened Buck Shoals in 2004, and it is a family winery. They and their relatives, including Terry's parents, staff the tasting room. During the winery's development, Joanne's brother, Victor, who is passionate about wine, offered a great deal of help and advice. The wines themselves honor Joanne's family. Rocco Red is named after her father, and Vito's Pride is named after a grandfather who made wine in his basement.

Relatives and friends also help in the vineyard, which has been expanded significantly since Terry and Joanne put in the first vines. Plantings now cover seven acres and include 11 different varietals. Because Terry loves Italian wines, he is growing several Italian varietals, such as Sangiovese, Traminette, Barbera, and Nebbiolo, in addition to the standard Merlot, Cabernet, and Chardonnay. He believes the Italian varietals will do well, since the elevation and soil at Buck Shoals are similar to areas in Italy.

Although the Craters intend to keep Bucks Shoals' production at around 5,000 cases, they have built a large winery with a 20,000-case capacity. At the moment, Buck Shoals shares the building as part of a business venture with Raffaldini Vineyards. The Craters own the land and the facility, and Raffaldini owns the equipment. In the future, Raffaldini plans on opening a winery on its own estate, and at that point,

Joanne and Terry Crater

the Craters hope to use the extra production capacity to develop a custom crush operation for other vineyards.

Next to the 15,000-square-foot winery, the Craters have built a modified log-cabin vacation home to serve as their tasting room. In addition to wines, Buck Shoals sells a variety of gift items, including wine jellies and other products created by local artisans and the Amish community. During a visit, people can relax in chairs on the front porch or use tables on the shaded back deck.

After the years of work, the Craters are proud of what they have accomplished, and they are hopeful about the winery's future. Although Joanne's father and grandfather never got to see Buck Shoals or taste the wines that bear their names, Joanne says, "you kind of hope that they're looking down favorably on what they see."

Childress Vineyards

1000 Childress Vineyards Road
Lexington, N.C. 27295
Mailing address: P.O. Box 847
Lexington, N.C. 27293-0847
Phone: 336-236-9463
Website:
www.childressvineyards.com
E-mail: info@childressvineyards.com
Hours: Monday–Saturday,
10 a.m.–6 p.m.; Sunday, noon–6 p.m.

Owners: Richard Childress and
Greg Johns
Winemaker: Mark Friszolowski
First year as bonded winery: 2004
Tasting fee: Yes
On-line ordering: Yes
Wine club: Yes

Wine List
Whites: Chardonnay, Classic White, Pinot Gris, Sauvignon Blanc, Serendipity White (Carlos), Viognier
Blushes: Classic Blush, Rosé
Reds: Cabernet Franc, Cabernet Sauvignon, Classic Red, Meritage, Merlot, Pinnacle (Cabernet Franc, Cabernet Sauvignon, and Merlot), Sangiovese, Serendipity Red (Noble), Syrah
Fruit: Blueberry Port
Specialty: Late Harvest Dessert

Directions: From U.S. 52, take the U.S. 64 exit. Go west on U.S. 64. The winery is on the immediate right.

Mark Friszolowski

Mark Friszolowski remembers the day he received "the call." As the winemaker of Pindar Vineyards on Long Island, he was examining rows of grapes when his cell phone rang one day and displayed the unfamiliar 336 area code. Out of curiosity, he answered. It was Richard Childress making a personal request that Mark consider joining the staff of Childress Vineyards.

Mark was aware that a North Carolina "celebrity" was developing a new winery, but he knew nothing about NASCAR, the sport in which Richard became famous. "All I knew," Mark admits, "was the cars went counter-clockwise." Consequently, he was not as impressed by the call as others might have been, and he had little interest in moving south. After 18 years at Pindar, he had established himself in the industry. He was making high-quality wines that were earning significant awards. One Viognier alone had won 14 gold medals. He had a crew that was so well trained he could work as a consultant around the world and even spend time sailing his boat. As he puts it, "Life was good."

After initially rejecting the invitation, Mark began to consider the "what if" possibilities. He recognized that it might be time for him to make a change and find a situation with new challenges and new opportunities. He had been following the development in the North Carolina industry for years and knew many of the people involved, including Jack Kroustalis of Westbend Vineyards and Steve Shepard of RayLen. "I had tasted all the wines, and I knew there was potential," he says. But he also knew that if he came, it would be to stay for a while. He explains, "I'm not one of those musical-chairs winemakers." He believes a person must remain in one place because it takes years to understand an area's climate, geography, and grapes. Each harvest is different, and "you may not see the same pattern again in seven years." He likes to quote his father, who would say, "A winemaker is like a baker who bakes one cake a year."

Mark decided to take the job in part because of the passion and involvement of Richard Childress. He insists, "My agreement with Richard is that he would be hands-on. I didn't want to have an absentee owner." Richard convinced Mark of his seriousness, as he has convinced many others. He may be a NASCAR "celebrity," but he is passionate about wine. In fact, his love of wine began decades ago and is intertwined with his involvement in auto racing.

In the 1970s, while racing at Riverside and Sears Point in California, Richard began spending time at small wineries. When NASCAR expanded to Watkins Glen in New York, he explored vineyards in the Finger Lakes area. Wherever he went, he made friends with winemakers and winery owners. He developed a passion for drinking and collecting wines and even began to think, "It would be cool to reach a point in life where I might start a vineyard."

In the 1990s, Richard decided he had reached that point. As he sought advice, he says, "the more people I talked to, the more excited I became." He bought land, began planting vines, and by 1999 was having grapes custom-crushed and giving the wine to friends. He still keeps a bottle from each of these vintages displayed in his office, and he points

Richard Childress

out, "Most people don't realize we've been making wine for many years." Finally, in 2003, ground was broken for a 35,000-square-foot winery. The next year, Childress Vineyards opened to the public.

Richard says of Childress Vineyards, "A lot of people thought it was crazy. They didn't realize how big my vision was of it." He didn't intend to grow a few grapes but, according to the business's mission statement, "to create the prestigious winery of the East coast." In addition to creating a showpiece, he foresaw the winery anchoring an entire retail development including specialty stores and a hotel. He explains, "If we were going to do it, we were going to do it right."

Childress Vineyards tries to appeal to the entire range of wine drinkers from novices to connoisseurs, which has proven a successful strategy. Kathleen Watson, the winery's director of marketing and public relations, says, "In our first year, we exceeded everyone's expectations." And she insists that, despite the winery's size, "it's truly too small already." It cannot accommodate all the requests for weddings and events, and the wine club has over 1,300 members. Consequently, soon after opening, discussions began about expanding event space. For example, The Bistro, a café in the winery, may be turned into a larger restaurant in the future, and the grounds may eventually include a freestanding banquet hall.

Kathleen estimates about half of the people who visit the winery are NASCAR fans, and Childress Vineyards certainly caters to them with checkered-flag labels, a collector's edition of five wines featuring Richard's race teams, and a wine club called "The Fast Track." The NASCAR demographic may be as large as 70 million people (including Mark, who now follows the races on television in the winery), and this huge potential market hasn't escaped people's attention. Even chefs of four-star restaurants are interested. Kathleen remembers a conversation she had with her boss in 2005. Richard told her, "This guy from the Food Network is calling me," but he couldn't remember the man's name. She asked if it was Bobby Flay or Emeril. "No," he replied. Then she asked, "Is it Mario Batali?" Richard nodded. "Yeah. He wants me to have dinner, but I don't know . . ." Kathleen laughs. "I said, 'Richard, if you have an appointment with God, you don't go, but otherwise, you're going.' " Soon afterward, the two had dinner and hit it off. Batali later featured Childress Vineyards wine in his book *Mario Tailgates NASCAR Style,* and he has singled out for praise the winery's port, which is made from North Carolina blueberries.

Childress Vineyards

Richard feels an obligation not only to his NASCAR fans but also to his home state: "We want to promote Childress Vineyards, but we're always talking about North Carolina wines. You wouldn't believe the people that we have drinking them." He knows the history of viticulture in the state and is quick to praise the pioneering and inspirational work of people like Jack Kroustalis. In fact, he hopes Childress Vineyards will one day inspire people in a similar way and that he will be regarded as "a plus" for the state's industry.

Mark is pleased with how quickly Childress has been able to make quality wines, but he insists that "the real progress will be in 10 years. We'll be doing great things. We're doing some great things now, but we'll be doing some unique things by then." Richard agrees, saying, "We'll just get better year after year." Nevertheless, he already finds owning a winery rewarding. For one, he believes that it has brought him closer to his daughter Tina, who runs its operations, and he also sees Childress Vineyards as a type of legacy. He says, "The wine business is made to be passed down through the generations. I'd love to see my grandchildren take over."

Elkin Creek Vineyard

318 Elkin Creek Mill Road
Elkin, N.C. 28621
Phone: 336-526-5119
Fax: 336-526-7950
Website:
www.elkincreekvineyard.com
E-mail: elkincreekwinery@aol.com
Hours: Thursday–Saturday,
lunch and dinner;
Sunday, brunch (11 a.m.–3 p.m.)

Owners: The Greene family
Winemaker: Mark Greene
First year as bonded winery: 2005
Tasting fee: Yes
On-line ordering: No
Wine club: No

Wine List
Whites: Chardonnay, Pinot Grigio
Reds: Barbera, Merlot, Rossa, Sangiovese

Directions: From Interstate 77 in Surry County, take Exit 85. Go west for 1.9 miles on N.C. 268 Bypass to U.S. 21. Turn right on U.S. 21

NORTH, GO 0.8 MILE, AND TURN LEFT ON CARTER MILL ROAD. GO 1 MILE, THEN TURN LEFT ON ELKIN CREEK MILL ROAD.

Mark Greene doesn't allow himself to be intimidated, discouraged, or dissuaded by others. He laughs, "If I had a dollar every time someone told me I couldn't do things, I'd be rich." If he had listened to some people, he might never have planted a vineyard on the steep slopes along Elkin Creek or built a post-and-beam winery of his own design. However, instead of being guided by those who caution restraint or inaction, he usually follows the advice he once heard from an old man: "You can do everything an expert can do, it just takes longer."

When Mark bought a historic mill and 25 acres of land along Elkin Creek, he didn't intend to establish a winery. In fact, he wasn't sure exactly what he was going to do with the property, but having been raised in the area, he "had fallen in love with it 34 years before." Then he visited Shelton Vineyards and was impressed by the beauty of the vines.

Mark began educating himself about viticulture. He took classes at Surry Community College. He read new and old books. He talked to people in the industry and to local farmers. Finally, despite the advice of some experts, he planted five acres of vinifera in 2000. He was deter-

Mark Greene

mined to grow the grapes as organically as possible. For the trellising, he used old-fashioned locust wood posts instead of pressurized wood ones. "It didn't make sense to me to put in a post that they wouldn't accept in a landfill," he explains. Pressurized posts may be considered more durable, but when he asked a farmer how long a locust post would last, he was told, "Two years longer than a rock."

To irrigate his grapes, Mark and his daughter built a windmill. It took them several days, and as they finished, his son expressed skepticism. Just as he was saying, "I don't know, Dad. What if something goes wrong 175 feet down?" water began gushing along the pipes. Mark says, "That's probably the most satisfied I've ever been, to see that water come out." The windmill has worked exactly as he envisioned, pumping water to the top of the hill, where gravity then distributes it throughout the property.

The steepness of the terrain makes working the vines difficult. Mark once looked up to find his tractor sliding sideways down the hill. He remembers thinking, "That's kind of cool. That's something you don't see every day." He believes, however, that the difficulties are worth it, and he felt vindicated when one person who had advised against the vineyard brought out an expert from the University of California at Davis. The visitor looked over the Elkin Creek property and said, "I like his site better than any in the valley."

In May 2005, Mark opened the winery. He had constructed a scale model of the building a few winters earlier and hadn't been dissuaded from the design by an engineer who suggested it was unsound. When Mark insisted that he put all his weight on the structure, the engineer was surprised to discover that the model supported him easily. "Post-and-beam is the simplest kind of construction," Mark explains.

The winery is made of wood, including 48-foot ridgepoles and a 23-foot center beam. It took Mark two years to build the structure, and he and his family did most of the work themselves. They laid the puncheon floors. He did the ironwork. He even mortised the doors. When he asked an old carpenter for advice on how to do this, he was told, "Boy, ain't you heard of Lowe's? There ain't a door that's been mortised

Elkin Creek winery

around here in 40 years." Mark still went ahead and did it himself. He admits that his passion for DIY isn't always efficient because "when you do things yourself, you overdo them. You want them to be as safe as possible." However, even though there may be easier and faster options, the process wouldn't be as satisfying.

In addition to the physical help of his family, Mark insists that the vineyard and winery could never have been completed without their emotional support as well, especially that of his wife, Elizabeth. Although he notes that he can be difficult to work with, Elizabeth "was always there to encourage, lend invaluable advice, and hold the other end of the board if necessary." She never questioned his motives, discouraged him from dreaming, or complained, and "she was always insistent that what I was doing would be a great success."

In his initial plans for the winery, Mark had no intention of including a fine-dining restaurant. For one, he didn't want it to be constantly compared to the Jolly Mill, an excellent restaurant formerly on the property. And since he had run half a dozen restaurants in his life, including three that he had constructed from scratch, he knew how time consuming they could be. However, as Elkin Creek began doing special events and receptions, Mark was approached by chef Jesse Williams about establishing a kitchen. They talked about the possibilities and eventually decided to open The Kitchen at Elkin Creek.

The restaurant seats 40, and the menu changes each week, but it always includes fresh bread. Mark designed the winery building to include a large European stone oven. The Kitchen at Elkin Creek uses the oven in baking a hearth bread whose only ingredients are flour, salt, and water. It's a time-intensive process, taking 48 hours. Mark learned it during a three-week internship at Gran Forno Bakery in Florida. He remembers that experience fondly. Once, when his daughter asked him what he would do if he had only a week to live, he replied, "I'd go work at Gran Forno."

Because of his Italian heritage—his grandfather was a winemaker in Sicily—Mark concentrates on varietals such as Barbera and Sangiovese. He also looks to Europe for his distribution model. Mark points out that there are certain wines you can get only in small Italian towns,

Elkin Creek vineyard

and this makes them special. Similarly, Elkin Creek doesn't distribute its 700-case production in retail outlets: "This is the only place that you can get it." Mark insists, "Wine to me is but one part of the whole process. I believe when you come and have a good experience when you're here, every time you open a bottle of our wine, you'll relive that experience."

In the future, Mark may develop the property further. He's thinking of putting a picnic area along the creek. He might eventually construct a bed-and-breakfast, put in a conference center, or establish an antiques business in the mill. Whatever he does, however, he is sure to keep building. He explains, "It's in every man's nature to want to create something."

Flint Hill Vineyards

2133 Flint Hill Road
East Bend, N.C. 27018
Phone: 336-699-4455
Website:
www.flinthillvineyards.com
E-mail: fhvineyards@yadtel.net
Hours: Friday, noon–6 p.m.;
Saturday, noon–5 p.m.;
Sunday, 1–5 p.m.

Owners: Brenda and Tim Doub
Winemaker:
Sean McRitchie (consultant)
First year as bonded winery: 2005
Tasting fee: Yes
On-line ordering: Via e-mail
Wine club: Pending

Wine List
Whites: Chardonnay, Olde Yattken (sweet white), Viognier
Reds: Cabernet Sauvignon, Chambourcin, Crushed Velvet (sweet Chambourcin), Syrah

Directions: From U.S. 421 in Yadkin County, take the Baltimore/Dinkins Bottom exit. Turn left and drive to Old U.S. 421 (Yadkinville Highway). Turn right on Old U.S. 421, then turn left on Flint Hill Road. The vineyard is on the left after 2 miles.

Flint Hill Vineyards is located in a country house that Tim Doub knows well. He grew up in it, his grandfather was born in it, and his

Flint Hill Vineyards

great-grandfather William Renigar built it. There is, Tim says, "a lot of history here." Nevertheless, he laughs, "if you told me 10 years ago I'd be selling wine out of it, I would have said, 'You're crazy.'" But then, 10 years ago, Tim didn't have children.

According to the Doubs, the birth of Flint Hill Vineyards is tied to the birth of their first daughter. Like her husband, Brenda Doub was raised on a farm, and even though they lived in the city after they married, they wanted their children to grow up in the country. Consequently, they moved from a six-year-old home to an 80-year-old one only two houses away from the Renigar farm.

Tim's family grows corn and soybeans throughout the area, but the Doubs have friends in the vineyard business, and as Tim puts it, "the bug called." After taking an introductory viticulture course at Surry Community College, they decided to experiment with growing grapes. In 2002, they planted five acres, one each of Cabernet Sauvignon, Syrah, Viognier, Chambourcin, and Chardonnay. They quickly realized that they couldn't keep two full-time jobs, raise kids, and tend a vineyard, so Brenda left her position with an insurance company and became the vineyard manager.

Grape growing can be difficult work. In addition to the constant daily tasks, there can be unexpected emergencies. One night, a windstorm spawned by Hurricane Cindy whipped through the area. The next morning, the Doubs found downed vines and trellises. Tim remembers that as they surveyed the damage, Brenda "was in tears and I was in pieces." However, after the initial shock, they called people to help, brought in equipment, and had the vines back up within hours. Brenda notes that since Tim has run his own company, Quality Steel Fabricators, for over 20 years, he understands the struggles, setbacks, and anxieties involved in building a small business. She says, "That's good because he can reassure me."

In the vineyards' first years, Flint Hill was a member of the Old North State Co-op. Twice, the co-op awarded Brenda silver medals for "Grower of the Year." Encouraged by this recognition, the Doubs expanded their involvement in the industry. They agreed to be the guinea pigs for the co-op's first custom crush operation, and since this meant they would have their own wine to sell, they decided to establish a tasting room at the Renigar House.

Built in the 1870s, the five-bedroom home had been empty for almost 20 years, but it was fundamentally in good shape. After putting on a new roof, buying "an incredible amount" of paint for the weathered exterior, and renovating the first floor, Tim and Brenda began to serve Flint Hill Vineyards wine to customers in October 2005.

Tim and Brenda Doub
COURTESY OF FLINT HILL VINEYARDS

In a way, the selling of alcohol at the house is a return to its origins. In the late 1800s, William Renigar ran Riverside Distillery, which sold jugs of whiskey and alcohol. Many of his neighbors operated similar businesses, and when the federal government decreed that a distillery had to be in an incorporated area, they formed Shore, North Carolina. (Later, part of that area became Flint Hill.) Tim collects Shore jugs, and he points out that although his ancestor sold them full for three dollars, it costs him $300 to buy an empty one. In a nod toward this heritage, the Doubs display a jug in the tasting room, and they call one of their wines "Olde Yattken," which was the name of one of Riverside Distillery's products. The house also contains a "generation room" with various portraits of the Renigars and other ancestors.

Although the Doubs understand how difficult it can be to make farming viable on a small scale, they insist there are important concerns besides economic ones. Tim likes to say, "The phone doesn't ring when you're working in the vineyards," and Brenda notes that when they staff the tasting room, one of them can watch the kids. In fact, the tasting room has become a second home. Brenda laughs, "We hold birthday parties a lot here now. This place is usually cleaner, and the flowers are definitely prettier."

Someday, the Doubs might construct a winery on the property and perhaps have Brenda serve as winemaker. Eventually, they may increase production from the current 1,300 cases to 3,000. For now, however, Tim and Brenda are satisfied to grow grapes, to sell a product about which they can say, "What's in the bottle is grown right here," and to raise their children to appreciate an agricultural way of life.

Grassy Creek Vineyard and Winery

235 Chatham Cottage Circle
Elkin, N.C. 28621
Phone: 336-835-4230
or 336-835-2458
Website:
www.grassycreekvineyard.com
E-mail:
derrill.rice@grassycreekvineyard.com
Hours: Thursday–Saturday, noon–6 p.m.;
Sunday, 1–5 p.m.

Owners: Derrill and Lori Rice and
Jim and Cynthia Douthit
Winemaker: Jim Douthit
First year as bonded winery: 2004
Tasting fee: Yes
On-line ordering: Yes
Wine club: Yes

Wine List
White: Chardonnay
Reds: Guernsey Red (sweet), Merlot, Red Barn Blend

Directions: From Interstate 77 in Surry County, take Exit 83 to U.S. 21 Bypass North. Turn left after the first traffic light onto Klondike Road and go approximately 0.5 mile. The vineyard entrance is on the left.

In the 1920s, John Hanes of the Hanes clothing company built a hunting cabin in the Blue Ridge foothills. When his sister, Lucy, married Thurmond Chatham, the two families began to add to the rural retreat, which came to include a dairy barn and creamery called Klondike Farms, a horse barn, a sawmill, and even a turbine dam modeled after the Hoover Dam to provide power. It was a self-contained community, and for years the families used it for vacations. Eventually, however, the complex became part of Chatham Manufacturing and a country resort for clients and executives of the textile company.

In 2000, Chatham Manufacturing was sold, and the property, then known as Klondike Cabins, was put up for sale. Derrill Rice, a former Chatham employee, and his wife, Lori, decided to buy it. Not only did they think it would be a good investment, they didn't want the buildings to be torn down and the complex's history to be lost.

In addition to renting the cabins, Derrill wanted to devote part of the property to a vineyard and winery. Lori admits that when she heard this idea, she thought, "He's crazy. He's lost his mind. It's a midlife crisis." But she became convinced about the merits of the project, and they approached a former colleague of Derrill's, Jim Douthit, who had already begun to develop a vineyard in Troutman. Both Jim and his wife, Cynthia, were interested in the idea, and the two couples agreed to work together. They began planting vines in 2002. Four years later, in 2006, they officially opened Grassy Creek Vineyard and Winery.

Lori acknowledges that everyone wanted to open the winery more quickly, but they experienced "setbacks after setbacks." For example, the initial plan called for having the winery and tasting room in the same

Jim Douthit and Lori Rice

Grassy Creek tasting room

building, but right before the contractor was about to start, they decided to move the winery to another building. Doing so, however, crossed a county boundary, which created new zoning issues. There were also difficulties in the vineyard, including the disappearance of grapes. Jim remembers that during the second year, he walked the rows on a Thursday, and the fruit looked great. He went to work in the Troutman vineyard for a couple of days, and while he was there, Derrill called and asked, "What happened to our Chardonnay grapes?" "What are you talking about?" Jim replied. Derrill said, "I'm walking the vineyard right now. There are no grapes." Birds and deer had stripped away all the fruit.

Despite the inevitable stress and tension of such an endeavor, the couples' friendship has deepened. Lori explains, "We're all strong enough personalities to deal with it." Jim agrees: "We have a close understanding, and we work things out, probably more smoothly than brothers and sisters do." He also points out that the two couples represent "four unique talents brought together." Derrill provides business and marketing expertise, Jim has a technical and chemistry background, Cynthia runs a design group out of New York and is responsible for the winery's "look," and Lori, a former teacher, has the organizational and social skills to "keep everyone in line."

Wherever possible, the couples have tried to utilize existing structures and to emphasize the property's heritage. The tasting room is in the old horse barn, which originally contained 12 stalls and had dirt floors and solid oak and metal doors. In her design, Cynthia emphasized an equestrian theme. For the renovation, she kept the bars on the windows and the iron tie rings on the walls. She also selected earth tones throughout, and as part of the color scheme, she chose to have the floor acid-stained. Jim laughs that the contractor doing this warned them that he couldn't guarantee consistency. When Jim told him, "I want you to screw it up as much as possible," he replied, "No one has ever said that to me."

Jim serves as Grassy Creek's winemaker. In addition to his background in chemistry, he comes from a winemaking family. He says, "My father made wine most of his life out of about any kind of juice he could get his hands on—muscadine, scuppernong, watermelon, peach. I grew up with wine in the bathroom and basement and wherever he could find a place, since we moved so much." At Grassy Creek, Jim has much more room than his father ever had. The couples are converting the property's 10,000-square-foot cow barn into the winery. In the building's renovation, they again are trying to retain as much of the original structure as possible, including its concrete troughs and signs above each stall that state the name, birth date, and lineage of each cow that was housed there.

In its first years, Grassy Creek Vineyard and Winery has produced approximately 3,000 cases annually. Eventually, the Rices and Douthits would like to increase production to 10,000 cases. They also would like for all four of them to be able to work for the winery full time. They know, however, that this may take awhile, and they recognize that they have already accomplished a great deal. They have had the satisfaction of watching vines they planted grow and seeing people enjoy wines they've made and bottled themselves. There is another unique reward to running the winery. Although Grassy Creek is new, the property has a long history, and when local people visit, they often tell stories about its past. These are fun to hear, but they symbolize something more. Lori points out, "For so many years when the Haneses and Chathams had the property, it was private, and no one could come. Now, it's open for people to see, enjoy, and even stay here. That's very satisfying."

Hanover Park Vineyard

1927 Courtney-Huntsville Road
Yadkinville, N.C. 27055
Phone and fax: 336-463-2875
Website: www.hanoverparkwines.com
E-mail:
hanoverp@hanoverparkwines.com
Hours: Thursday–Saturday, noon–6 p.m.;
Sunday, 1–5 p.m.

Owners: Michael and Amy Helton
Winemaker: Michael Helton
First year as bonded winery: 1999
Tasting fee: Yes
On-line ordering: No
Wine club: Yes

Wine List
Whites: Chardonnay, Early Twilight (Niagara, Viognier, and Chardonnay), Viognier
Blush: Rosé
Reds: Cabernet Franc, Cabernet Sauvignon, Chambourcin, Michael's Blend (traditional Bordeaux blend), Mourvèdre

Directions: From Interstate 40, take Exit 170, drive north for 9.8 miles on U.S. 601, and turn right on Courtney-Huntsville Road. The vineyard is on the left after 1 mile. From U.S. 421, exit at U.S. 601 and go south for 4 miles. At the second blinking light, turn onto Courtney-Huntsville Road. The vineyard is on the left after 1 mile.

Hanover Park Vineyard began with a trip to southern France in 1996. Amy and Michael Helton were on their honeymoon, touring the

Hanover Park Vineyard

countryside. Michael notes, "Before that trip, I had no opinion about wine one way or the other. I knew very little about wine." In France, however, "water was very expensive, and wine was very cheap. We had 23 days, and at the end of that period of time, I had a very definite opinion about wine. I loved it very much."

Noticing that the rolling hills of France were similar to those of the North Carolina Piedmont, the Heltons began considering growing grapes and getting into the wine business. As Amy puts it, "You start to wonder what you'd like to do with your life." They spent weekends driving around the Yadkin Valley looking at property. Michael explains, "It was still part of the romance of continuing our honeymoon from France—taking leisurely drives and having a wonderful time." Most of the available tracts were either too large or too expensive—until they found a farmhouse on an affordable 23 acres. According to Michael, "At that moment, we both . . . hesitated. We thought, 'Wait a minute. Up to this point, it's been sort of a fantasy of speculation, without any thought of reality.' So we had to step back for a couple of days and really think about it." They talked it over with people. Amy says, "Some of our friends thought we were crazy. Other friends said, 'Go for it.' And obviously, we listened to those people."

Michael and Amy Helton

Since they knew very little about growing grapes or making wine, the Heltons sought help. They took classes, searched the Internet, and talked to everyone they could. They contacted a grower in Virginia, Ed Schwab of Autumn Hill Vineyards, who immediately invited them to spend the weekend. Amy remembers, "When we were there that first time, he had to replace a few vines. He took us out in the vineyards. He did one, he had Michael do one, and he looked at me and said, 'You're getting into this, too.' So we each planted a vine. The first of many vines I've planted." Since then, Ed has become "a wonderful mentor and friend." They return to his vineyards every year.

Michael also went to Westbend Vineyards and said, "I want to volunteer." After talking with Steve Shepard, who was the winemaker at the time, he was put to work. Michael recalls that "for three solid days, I scrubbed tanks, I scrubbed gaskets, I scrubbed this and that. My first reaction was, 'He just wants to see if I'm serious. This weeds out the people that aren't.' I thought, 'I can handle that.' At the end of the third day, I realized that what he was actually doing was teaching me the golden rule of winemaking: Absolute fanaticism to cleanliness is the only way to be."

Initially, the Heltons planted two acres of vines. Later, they learned that their neighbors had been watching them with curiosity. No one had ever grown grapes in the area, and people didn't know what to make of these two schoolteachers who got their tractor stuck. Michael says, "I didn't know anything about farming. I thought [the tractor] could go down through that stream and right up the other side. . . . I was out plowing in the rain." What they lacked in experience, however, they made up for in energy. A friend later told the Heltons that people "couldn't figure out what you were doing or why you were doing it, but anybody that was working as hard as you do impressed the older people very much."

The neighbors were curious not only about the grapes, but about the restoration of the buildings as well. Constructed in 1897, the house had been abandoned since 1963. When the Heltons bought the property, the brambles and briars were so overgrown that it took a half-hour to walk the short distance from the barn to the house. Having made the decision to renovate, they spent 1999 working on the buildings. They took the barn apart and put it back together. As much as possible, they tried to stay true to the house's design and to reuse materials. When they ripped out the original flooring on the porch, they used the wood for shutters. The bar top in the tasting room was a shelf in the barn that they dried and restored. Michael and Amy admit that it's strange to look at photographs of the renovations. They can't believe the changes they've made and the amount of work they've done. Others can't either. Once the winery opened, people who once lived in the house began visiting and marveling at the restoration.

Hanover Park became the first bonded winery in Yadkin County since Prohibition. Local response was immediately positive. The chamber of commerce honored the Heltons for their contributions to the community. Equally important to them were the informal tributes. Michael was working on a ladder one day when a group of bicyclists sped past and one shouted to another, "Have you tried this wine? It's

Hanover Park, and it's excellent." Amy remembers one evening during the first year when they were walking through the fields. A father and daughter went by, and they couldn't see the Heltons in the vines. The daughter said, "Daddy, that's a lot of grapes," to which the father agreed. The child noted, "That's really pretty, isn't it?" and he answered, "Yes, dear, it's going to be beautiful."

Both Amy and Michael are artists, and it shows in their conversation. Amy often talks about the winery in terms of light and space. She believes that "there are many chemists that are winemakers, and yes, there's a science to it, but there is that something else. There is a certain art to doing it." Michael speaks of winemaking as problem solving: "On one level, it's alchemy. You're taking something of little value and making it of value. And you do the same with canvas. But it's also the process. When you're making art, you are discovering. . . . You're simultaneously discovering how to do the project. So discovery and knowledge are simultaneous as you're working your way through the project." The Heltons believe that, as with art, a person should make wine because he or she loves it. Michael insists, "You better have a passion for this because there are easier ways to make money."

The first years were financially difficult. Michael admits that "there were many times in the beginning that I was really worried, and [Amy] was just as calm as could be. Several times, she would say, 'Relax, relax.' At one point, she just had a conversation with me. She said, 'You make good wine. Don't worry about it. Stop driving yourself crazy.' " Amy knew they had a good product because, as she says, "I'm the one who watches people's faces in the tasting room." She came up with another method of reassuring her husband. As part of Michael's development as a winemaker, the Heltons regularly conduct blind tastings. Amy would put a bottle in a brown bag, and he would try a glass and then tell her everything he could about the wine. One night, she offered him "the mystery wine." Michael remembers, "I took a sip of it, and it was delightful, and I said, 'I hope someday I can make a wine this good. This would be all I want in life is to make something this good.'" They went into the kitchen, and Amy showed him the label: Hanover Park. Michael recalls,

"I was shocked and elated. That's why I'm in this business. I get joy from it." In their first year, the Heltons produced 375 cases. That amount has now grown to 2,000 cases a year, and Hanover Park wines have garnered acclaim both nationally and internationally. But perhaps the most rewarding honor came in the spring of 2005, when Amy and Michael returned to France. This time, they ate at a Michelin-starred restaurant in Paris called Violon d'Ingres. The meal prepared by chef Christian Constant was excellent. In fact, it had been created especially to go with a group of wines the chef admired, those from Hanover Park.

Laurel Gray Vineyards

5726 Old U.S. 421 West
Hamptonville, N.C. 27020
Phone: 336-468-9463 (336-GOT WINE)
Fax: 336-468-4326
Website: www.laurelgray.com
E-mail: laurelgray@triad.rr.com
Hours: Wednesday, 1–6 p.m.;
Thursday and Friday,
10 a.m.–6 p.m.; Saturday,
10 a.m.–5 p.m.; Sunday, 1–5 p.m.
The winery is closed during January.

Owners: Kim and Benny Myers
Winemaker: Stephen Rigby (consultant)
First year as bonded winery: 2007
Tasting fee: Yes
On-line ordering: Yes
Wine club: Yes

Wine List
Whites: Chardonnay, Circa 1773 (sweet blend of Chardonnay, Viognier, and Syrah), Viognier
Reds: Cabernet Sauvignon, Scarlet Mountain (red blend), Sultry (red blend)

Directions: Take U.S. 421 to Exit 267, which is located 1.5 miles north of Interstate 77. Turn onto Windsor Road, go north to Old U.S. 421, and turn right. The vineyard is just ahead on the left.

Kim Myers jokes that running a winery is a good way to stay out of trouble: "I'm a very good girl because I don't have time to do anything else." In addition to managing Laurel Gray's vineyards, doing tasks like designing the labels, and serving on various wine industry organizations, she oversees the tasting room and makes sure the area stays "manicured." Juggling these various responsibilities means that she has to switch roles quickly. People tease her about driving a tractor in a dress, but she says she wants to be ready to come in from the fields to serve customers, and she wants to be presentable.

Kim prides herself on how comfortable Laurel Gray's tasting room is. Visitors come in, relax, and tell her, "Oh, my gosh, you're living the dream." They imagine that she sits around all day chatting and sipping wine. The reality is far different. Kim works, as she puts it, "eight days a week until dark-thirty." She may be up at 4:30 in the morning to spray the vines because the wind is right, or she may be bottling a vintage long after dark. She laughs, "If I could just quit dreaming about it, so I could have a break when I'm sleeping."

Kim knew the hard work that was ahead when she and her husband, Benny, planted their first vines in 2001: "We really thought this

Laurel Gray patio

Laurel Gray vineyards
COURTESY OF LAUREL GRAY VINEYARDS

thing through. We studied hard. We knew what we were getting into." In the early 1990s, the Myerses had noticed the similarities between their farmland and wine-growing regions in California, but it was the example of others in the Yadkin Valley that inspired them to seriously consider grape growing. As they watched Shelton Vineyards develop, they talked to people in the industry, such as Amy and Michael Helton at Hanover Park Vineyard, and Kim began taking classes at Surry Community College. Eventually, they became convinced that their 84-acre family farm would be a good place for grapes, and they established Laurel Gray Vineyards, named after their two children, Ashley Laurel and Taylor Gray.

Benny Myers's family has farmed in the area for over 200 years. Consequently, Kim is committed to explaining not only Laurel Gray's wines to people, but also the area's history and agricultural heritage. She takes visitors along rows of grapes just outside the tasting room and describes the plants' seasonal cycle. She explains the nature of farming and the composition of the soil. She offers a quick lesson on how vineyards are oriented, what makes them productive, and the need for grafting and pruning.

During her tours of the vineyards, Kim insists that each varietal has a personality. To her, Cabernet Sauvignon vines are unruly teenage boys: "We discipline them, but when you turn your back, they're going to do what they're going to do." Over time, however, they settle down. Merlot and Cabernet Franc are "baby boomers" because "with a good health-care program, they produce and produce." Kim has discovered that even if people don't remember a varietal's name, they will remember the personality. For example, in the tasting room, they might say, "I want to try the young lady [Chardonnay]."

After establishing the vineyards, the Myerses renovated a 1930s milking parlor to serve as a tasting room. The room also contains handmade crafts and gifts, including artwork painted by Kim herself. Tables outside have views of the vineyards, a farm pond, and, depending on the season, displays of roses. Kim laughs that she started with a few roses in the front and just kept planting them. There is now such a wide variety that gardening clubs hold special events at the vineyards when the flowers are in bloom.

During its first years, Laurel Gray operated with a wine producer's permit, which allowed the Myerses to make the wine at a different facility and to operate the tasting room. When they began quickly selling out their wines, they had to make a decision about growth. They decided to build their own winery. They are excited about this expansion because they believe it will help increase their production while allowing them to maintain a high standard of quality.

Even as Laurel Gray grows, the Myerses are committed to maintaining close relationships with their customers. For example, Kim says that she wants to limit their wine club to 100 members. By keeping events intimate, she believes she can make them feel like "reunions." When Kim talks about the winery, she frequently uses the word *family*, and she wants people to feel special. Although she admits that the winery "ties us down so much," she also knows that people come not only to taste the wine, but to enjoy the atmosphere. She says, "I really believe what people love about coming here is the personal experience."

For the Myerses, running Laurel Gray may not be as easy as people imagine, but the hard work is worth it: "When the fruit is on the vine, it's beautiful, and it just gives you peace in your soul to walk in the vineyards in the evening."

McRitchie Wine Company

315 Thurmond PO Road
Thurmond, N.C. 28683
Phone: 336-874-3003
Website: www.mcritchiewine.com
E-mail: info@mcritchiewine.com
Hours: Thursday–Saturday,
noon–6 p.m.; Sunday, 1–5 p.m.

Owners: Sean and Patricia McRitchie
Winemaker: Sean McRitchie
First year as bonded winery: 2006
Tasting fee: No
On-line ordering: No
Wine club: Yes

Wine List
The winery offers European varietals and blends, as well as sparkling wines.

Directions: From Interstate 77, take Exit 83 or Exit 85 to U.S. 21 heading north toward Sparta. After about 8 miles, turn right on Thurmond PO Road (not Thurmond Road). The winery is on the left after approximately 0.1 mile.

Most teenagers get jobs at fast-food restaurants or shopping malls. When Sean McRitchie was 13, he was pruning vines and rolling oak barrels as he worked at wineries on weekends and in the summers. He remembers, "I liked doing it. It was fun." He also liked getting paid for doing something he enjoyed.

It was easy for Sean to get these jobs because his father, Dr. Robert McRitchie, was a winemaker; consequently, Sean has been hanging out in vineyards and cellars since he was nine. In fact, growing up, he and his sister Robin worked together in several places, and they often behaved like the kids they were. They would race each other on pallet jacks and play practical jokes. One winery had big wooden tanks that had to be sealed with beeswax, and the siblings would make wax balls and hurl them at the ceiling so hard they would stick. Sean has been told that many of the balls remain there, and that one will occasionally fall. He laughs at these memories and admits, "We got fired several times by my dad."

In his 20s, Sean notes, "I got to be a wine bum." He went around the world helping with harvests. Because the Northern and Southern hemispheres have opposite seasons, Sean often could make two or three vintages in a single year by traveling between Australia and Europe or the United States. He laughs that his career has given him a variety of contrasting experiences. He has worked in a moldy cave under German streets as he watched a centrifuge for hours at a time. To get there, he had to walk through bat-filled tunnels. Much of the equipment had brass fittings that were 200 years old. He also has been the cellar foreman at Domaine Chandon in Napa, where everything is new, high-tech, spacious, and bat-free.

For several years, Sean worked at Benton Lane, a prestigious Willamette Valley winery that specializes in Pinot Noir. But as he and his wife, Patricia, began raising kids, they started to consider moving again, in part because the winery was remote. "It took 20 minutes to go get a gallon of milk," Sean explains. Consequently, in 1998, the McRitchies decided to move to North Carolina to help develop Shelton Vineyards.

Sean says of his work at Shelton, "It was really fun. It was a good organization. It is a beautiful property with rolling hills." He designed the vineyards and infrastructure. Sean admires the operation—"It's a great

Sean McRitchie and friends

flagship winery"—but he says, "Running it wasn't my thing." Instead, he and his wife decided to set up a winery and viticulture consulting business. As a result, the McRitchies have played a key role in the expansion of the North Carolina wine industry. In addition to helping develop numerous vineyards and wineries throughout the state, Sean currently serves as a winemaking consultant for several wineries. With Mark Greene of Elkin Creek Vineyard and Frank Hannah of Owl's Eye Vineyard, the McRitchies also own Artisan Bottlers, a mobile bottling line. Patricia, who is a lawyer, was instrumental in getting the Yadkin Valley AVA designation, and she is helping other groups—including ones for the Haw River and Swan Creek areas—make AVA applications. She also helps individual wineries with the permit process, which, as Sean puts it, is "heavily regulated." (And to further detail the influence of the family, Robert McRitchie followed his son to the state and not only served as a consulting winemaker for a number of wineries but helped establish the viticulture program at Surry Community College.)

Although they love helping others make wine, Sean and Patricia decided in 2005 to start making their own. They founded the McRitchie Wine Company on 28 acres in the Blue Ridge Mountains. Sean says, "We had it in our heads for a long time. I've been doing this for almost 30 years. It's time." And they decided that North Carolina was a good place for their venture. In California, the land is "outrageously expensive and unavailable," and in Oregon, 500 brands compete for recognition. Here, it's possible for a small winery to create an identity. Sean says, "I have a good vibe about the market."

Sean recognizes that the state can be a difficult place to grow grapes, but he insists, "I like to get around the challenges of this North Carolina weather. It makes it fun for me." With his own vineyard, he has more freedom to address these challenges and grow grapes the way he wants. For example, he can experiment with environmentally beneficial and sustainable low-input techniques, such as having horses graze between the rows or spraying only with sulfur. Or he can try growing "field blends," which involves planting rows of various varietals—such as Merlot, Petite Verdot, Cabernet, and Malbec—in a group, and then picking them all at once and putting them together. Sean admits it's "a crazy, creative way to farm," but with his own vineyard, "I can choose to gamble."

The winery itself is small and features a number of mobile 550-gallon stainless-steel tanks, rather than vats. These can be stacked, moved, wheeled outside if it's cold, or even taken into the fields. They give Sean the ability to make various small batches according to the quality and availability of grapes. This flexibility is crucial because, as Sean points out, "anyone can make wine. It's difficult to make a good wine." Doing so requires constantly adjusting to conditions.

Ultimately, the McRitchie Wine Company will produce 1,500 to 2,000 cases a year. Rather than work with a distributor, Sean and Patricia would like to sell most of the wine in the tasting room, which they have put in a renovated house on the property. They believe the space offers a tasting experience that's "intimate, calm, and relaxed." The winery will produce sparkling wines and even carbonated hard cider, in addition to European varietals and blends. Sean also would like to offer selections from all the wineries where he has worked and from the one that his sister Robin has built on the West Coast with her husband.

Even with the establishment of the McRitchie Wine Company, Sean says he'd "like to be able to work some vintages elsewhere." He believes that you have to keep learning, seeing what others are doing, and challenging yourself. Nevertheless, he recognizes that he's no longer a "wine bum." In fact, as he and Patricia built the winery, their oldest child, Aidan, helped. Sean says, "I got a real kick watching him washing out a tank. And then I realized he's the third generation making wine. That's scary. And it happened so fast."

Old North State Winery

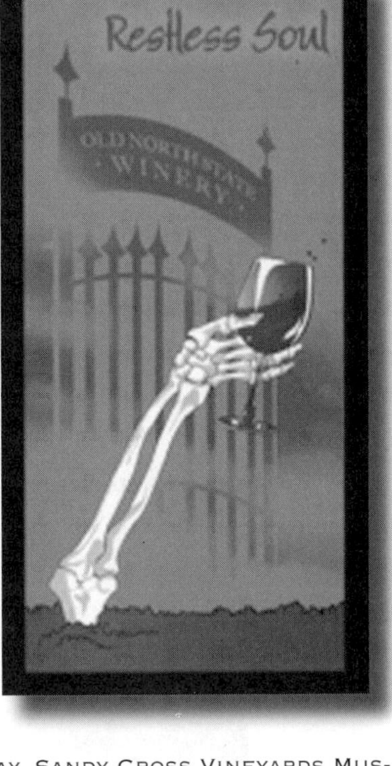

308 North Main Street
Mount Airy, N.C. 27030
Phone: 336-789-9463 (336-789-WINE)
Fax: 336-789-9060
Website:
www.oldnorthstatewinery.com
E-mail: sales@onswinery.com
Hours:
Monday–Wednesday, 11 a.m.–9 p.m.;
Thursday–Saturday, 11 a.m.–10 p.m.;
Sunday, noon–6 p.m.

Owners: Ben and Tom Webb and
Michael Thomas
Winemaker: Ben Webb
First year as bonded winery: 2003
Tasting fee: Yes
On-line ordering: Yes
Wine club: Yes

Wine List
Whites: Autumn Leaf Gold, Chardonnay, Sandy Cross Vineyards Muscadine, Spring House, Starlight White
Blushes: Autumn Leaf, Rosé
Reds: Afternoon Delight (muscadine), Autumn Leaf Red, Cabernet Franc, Merlot, Prelude (Merlot and Cabernet Sauvignon), Restless Soul

Directions: From U.S. 52 North in Mount Airy, take the N.C. 89/West Pine Street exit, to the right. At the light off the exit ramp, go straight onto Independence Boulevard. Go about 1 mile to the third stoplight and turn right on Main Street. The winery is on the left at 308 North Main, across from the museum clock tower. Visitors may park beside the building.

Old North State Winery began as a cooperative in 2001. Several people who were interested in growing grapes and becoming involved in the wine industry decided to overcome a lack of financial capital and experience by putting their resources together. As word spread about the idea and the charter was developed, there was a great deal of enthusiasm. The first day, 21 members signed up; within a week, there were 27. Membership eventually grew to 50, including growers from all over the state.

The organizers of the co-op believed, as one member stated, that it could be "the largest winery in the South." Aided by grants from the United States Department of Agriculture's Rural Development Program and the Appalachian Regional Commission, the co-op bought a building in downtown Mount Airy and converted it into a winery. The intention was to have the winery provide a market for the grapes of co-op members, to have it train people for the industry, and to have it act as a type of business incubator. At one point, the president, Fred Jones, estimated that at least 15 to 20 wineries could be developed with the co-op's help. Plans also included having a restaurant in the building, offering viticulture classes, hosting meetings and receptions, and even developing a cooking school.

Old North State tasting room

Old North State display

In 2003, the co-op began to release wine under the Carolina Harvest label. Then it developed the 38 Vines label to recognize the 38 vineyards of its original members. However, it quickly ran into a number of challenges, including financial and organizational difficulties. Start-up costs and operating expenses were much higher than anticipated, and the co-op couldn't generate enough income from sales to remain viable. By 2005, it became clear that the experiment was not working. In 2006, just as the winery was about to go into foreclosure, Tom Webb, his son Ben, and Michael Thomas—all original co-op members—took over the winery's operations by assuming loans on the building and equipment.

Tom has a banking background, which he believes will help him get the winery on good financial footing. Yet even though Old North State is no longer a cooperative, Tom insists that he and his partners "want to keep the idea alive" and that they plan to pursue many of the co-op's original aims. For example, they have been developing the winery's custom crush business, which will allow vineyards to have wine made under their own labels. Under this system, Tom says, growers "won't just dump the grapes at the back door. It will be a hands-on process. The grower will be assisted in applying for all of the federal and state permits, label approval, and compliance issues. They will contribute, work in the cellar, work in the tasting room, and learn the business." In this way, Tom believes Old North State can provide "a hands-on comprehensive program that's an extension of the one at Surry Community College." He also sees the winery as a resource for those who want to use only some of the facilities, such as the bottling line. For them, "the equipment can be used à la carte."

With the winery's custom crush program, Tom believes that he's providing not only a way for grape growers to enter the business but also a method "to develop some really good wines that would be labeled 'cult wines' in other places." He points to Ben as a model. Old North State's winemaker and general manager, Ben also has his own 10-acre vineyard where he grows grapes organically. In 2005, he produced 300 cases of a fine-quality wine in a custom crush operation. Tom points out, "When you sell grapes by the ton, you fill that bin up. When your name is on the bottle, you pick only the best fruit."

After taking over the winery, Tom and his co-owners quickly revived another co-op feature—the restaurant next to the tasting room. Scuppernongs is both a deli and a sit-down restaurant. Meals are designed around Old North State wines and often feature the wines in the recipes. For the most part, Scuppernongs is open at the same time as the tasting room. The space is also available for meetings, receptions, and group events.

Tom is realistic about the challenges ahead. He acknowledges, "It's definitely a hard go right now in the wine industry. We're not just competing with the wineries down the street, but with ones in Chile, Argentina, Australia—all over the world." But he believes that Old North State Winery has the potential to be a success. It has an excellent location in a historic town that attracts an estimated 300,000 visitors a year. It has access to quality grapes, both in its own 15 acres of vineyards and from other growers. It has facilities with a production capacity of 15,000 cases, and it appeals to a wide variety of consumers by offering both vinifera and muscadine wines. In short, the winery has many assets.

Although Tom may joke about the difficulties of being in the wine business, he believes in the importance of what he is doing. He says, "We have to do something to keep the farmers in business. Farms are being bulldozed, and houses are being planted. We have to figure out ways to keep green space." Wineries like Old North State may help.

Raffaldini Vineyards

450 Groce Road
Ronda, N.C. 28670
Phone: 336-835-9463
Fax: 336-835-9330
Website: www.raffaldini.com
E-mail: info@raffaldini.com
Hours: Wednesday–Saturday, 11 a.m.–5 p.m.; Sunday, 1–5 p.m.

RAFFALDINI®
Vermentino
2005
Yadkin Valley
Alc. 12% by Vol.

Owners: The Raffaldini family
Winemaker: Stephen Rigby
First year as bonded winery: 2005
Tasting fee: Yes
On-line ordering: Yes
Wine club: Yes

Wine List
Whites: Fiori (white blend), Pinot Grigio, Vermentino
Blush: Chiara (semisweet rosé)
Reds: Bella Misto (red blend), Montepulciano, Sangiovese

Directions: From Interstate 40, follow U.S. 421 North. Take Exit 267 (Windsor Road) off U.S. 421. Turn right on Windsor Road and follow the signs. Go left and follow Old U.S. 421 for approximately 1.5 miles. Go right on Swan Creek Road, drive 2.5 miles, turn left on Clingman Road, drive 1 mile, and turn left on Groce Road.

When Stephen Lyons was planning the estate for Raffaldini Vineyards, he knew there needed to be a well, but he wasn't sure where to dig one. Jeremy Childress, a person helping in the vineyards, told him, "My mother does well-witching—dowsing with two copper wires. Where they cross is where there's water." Jeremy claimed that she had a 100 percent success record. Although she was just about to have surgery for breast cancer, she was willing to come out to the site.

Stephen remembers the experience. "She walked over the 40 acres, and she found three places that had water, including one which was really good. She put a stake in the ground and said, 'Tell them to drill here.' She said, 'You've got to remember, it's drill here. Not five feet there. Not eight feet over there. It has to be here.' The well driller came out, and he said, 'Where you going to drill?' I said, 'Right where the stake is.' He said, 'We'll have to move it a little bit over.' I said, 'No, it's where the stake is.' He said, 'You had this witched, didn't you?' I said, 'You have to do this. There is a lot of emotion in this. Jeremy's mother is going into the hospital.' He started drilling, and the drill broke down. He broke his bit, and he had to get another one. This went on for two weeks. It

Raffaldini Vineyards
COURTESY OF RAFFALDINI VINEYARDS
PHOTOGRAPH BY MAIA DERY

should have been a two-day job, and two weeks later, he's just getting down. He hits granite. Big granite rock. At 100 feet, he had 10 gallons a minute, and he said, 'Is that enough?' I said no. So he kept on drilling and drilling, and then he had to go to a hydraulic hose. Probably three weeks after he started, he gets down to just under 200 feet—he's going through granite—and suddenly the whole rig lifted off, and the water just went straight up, just like an oil gusher. It was 100 gallons a minute. And Jeremy's mother was right. Another eight feet over there, because it's under rock, the bit could have gone off to the left or the right, and it would have been five gallons a minute instead of 100."

In many ways, this story epitomizes the values of Raffaldini Vineyards. You have to be open-minded, you have to be committed to seeing a project through, and you have to trust one another and work together. People at Raffaldini frequently use words like *team* and *teamwork*. Susan Lyons, the winery's marketing director, insists, "It takes a team to make good wine," and Stephen Rigby, the winemaker, points out, "The teamwork goes all the way back to the land."

The winery began in 2000, when businessman Jay Raffaldini contacted Stephen Lyons. The Raffaldini family, including Jay, his wife, Maureen, and his sister Barbara, wanted to establish vineyards in North Carolina. Jay had heard that few people knew the industry as well as Stephen. As a vineyard consultant, Stephen, who began his career in California, had helped develop dozens of North Carolina's vineyards and many of its major wineries. After talking with Jay and gauging his commitment, he agreed to look for property, to help establish the vineyards, and to become the estate's general manager. He and Susan Lyons also became partners in the enterprise with the Raffaldini family.

Stephen Lyons estimates that he considered over 100 sites and physically surveyed more than 50 before narrowing it down to five possibilities. He showed these to the Raffaldini family, and they chose the current location in the Blue Ridge foothills. With its elevation of 1,200 feet and its stony terrain, it is excellent for grapes. Stephen insists of the land, "It was the biggest blessing I could have, outside of my wife. . . . We are very, very lucky to have this site."

Stephen Rigby

The location resembles parts of the Italian Piedmont, which is important because the Raffaldinis honor their heritage by making Italian wines. In fact, Raffaldini Vineyards bills itself as "Chianti in the Carolinas," and its website may be the only one in the wine industry that features a biography of the poet Virgil. In the vineyards are Italian varietals such as Sangiovese, Pinot Grigio, Montepulciano, Vermentino, and Aleatico. Since some of these grapes had never been grown on the East Coast and are extremely rare in the United States, Stephen is constantly doing research and gathering data to determine how best to cultivate them.

Just as Stephen Lyons is educating himself in the vineyards, Stephen Rigby is educating himself in the winery. Although he has been a winemaker for over 20 years, he hadn't worked with some of the more uncommon Italian varietals before he joined Raffaldini. Consequently, he talks about "figuring out" a wine as he traces a grape's development over several vintages. However, regardless of the varietal, Stephen Rigby also says that his basic guidelines always remain the same: "Follow good-quality winemaking practices" and "let the grapes and the wine express themselves; do not manipulate them." These principles clearly work, since Raffaldini Vineyards frequently wins medals at international festivals, including a prestigious gold for the 2005 Vermentino at the 2006 San Diego International Festival.

Although Raffaldini Vineyards already has had notable successes, it is a young winery. Stephen Lyons insists, "Vines live as long as human beings. So we're still in the childhood of these vines. They're still in elementary school." There is much to learn about the vines as they age, and sometimes the education can be painful. Originally, Raffaldini Vineyards planted Nebbiolo, Dolcetto, and Barbera, but after several years, it decided to pull many of these vines out. Although Stephen says that "we knew from the start we would pick and choose" the best varietals, it was still a difficult decision, since so much work had been put into growing the vines. Taking out the Barbera was particularly difficult: "It broke our hearts. We loved it, but it wasn't working."

Stephen Rigby suggests that the decision to pull out the varietals "is one that is easy to criticize." However, "we have to be receptive to what our vineyards are giving us, not what we want the vines to be." In the case of the Barbera, Raffaldini was willing to sacrifice the short-term profits from already-planted vines to pursue a higher-quality wine in the future. This commitment to the long term can be seen in almost all of the decisions. The site was selected with care. Instead of immediately building a winery, Raffaldini has in the first years shared a facility with Buck Shoals Vineyard. Similarly, it waited for several years to build a permanent tasting room. Finally, in 2006, it began construction of a two-story tasting room and event space to be known as Villa Raffaldini, which will showcase the mountain views, the landscape, and the vineyards. For the Raffaldinis, a quality wine takes time, and a quality winery does as well.

Raffaldini Vineyards also believes that a successful winery is the result of many people's efforts. Stephen Lyons insists that it takes at least five people with vision to get a good bottle of wine to a customer: the person with the capital, the person in the vineyards, the winemaker, the tasting-room staff, and the marketer. No one person can do it alone, and each must be dedicated to his or her job. Raffaldini believes it has those people. As Susan Lyons puts it, "We have a wonderful team. We love what we're doing, and we strive to do it the best."

RagApple Lassie Vineyards

3724 RagApple Lassie Lane
Boonville, N.C. 27011
Phone: 866-RAG APPLE (866-724-2775)
Website: www.ragapplelassie.com
E-mail: info@RagAppleLassie.com
Hours: Open daily, noon–6 p.m.

Owners: Frank and Lenna Hobson
Winemaker: Linda King
First year as bonded winery: 2002
Tasting fee: Yes
On-line ordering: Yes
Wine club: Yes

Wine List
Whites: Boonville Blanc (Viognier), Chardonnay, Pinot Gris, Viognier
Blush: First Blush
Reds: Cabernet Sauvignon, Merlot, Rockford Red, Syrah, Zinfandel
Dessert: Evening Sunset

Directions: Boonville is located at the junction of U.S. 601 and N.C. 67 in northern Yadkin County. The winery is 3 miles east of Boonville off N.C. 67.

Lenna Hobson calls her husband, Frank, "the quintessential farmer." She says, "He has a farming heritage, but he also loves farming. He's a farmer to his toenails." Years ago, when Frank worked for a fertilizer company and was told that he had to quit farming and concentrate on running its stores, he quit the company instead. For most of his life,

Frank has grown tobacco, but in the 1990s, as the government steadily reduced his allotment, he began looking for a new crop. His choice was "a process of elimination," Frank says. "I don't like chickens. The neighbors don't like hogs. And I've run all the cows and pasture that I'm going to run." Lenna laughs, "He said he didn't want anything you had to feed that would get out when you wanted to go somewhere on a Saturday night." Intrigued by the development of Shelton Vineyards, the Hobsons visited it several times. One evening, Frank said, "Well, why don't we plant grapes, then?" It was, Lenna remembers, like a light bulb clicking on. Now, visitors to RagApple Lassie Vineyards can see rows of tobacco growing next to acres of grapes. It's a symbolic juxtaposition of what some consider the Yadkin Valley's past and future.

Frank says, "The vineyard business has been our salvation here," but the Hobsons did not jump into the industry rashly. They methodically educated themselves, planned, and moved ahead in stages. First, Frank, who also co-owns a farm supply store, began making calls and doing research. In the process, he discovered that "there are very few suppliers of everything you need in the vineyard business except on the West Coast." So he expanded his business to supply poles, equipment, and chemicals to the area's grape growers. He also planted his own vines. Lenna says, "At first, it's all so overwhelming because it's so totally brand-new. You're

Linda King

not sure what's required." But after going through a year's cycle, they realized that grape growing "dovetails nicely with the other farming operations." They decided to take the next step and build a winery.

When the University of North Carolina at Charlotte's School of Design heard about the Hobsons' intentions, it asked if the winery could be used as a design project for the senior class. Students came to the area several times, interviewed Frank and Lenna, walked the property, and came up with different concepts. During the process, the Hobsons learned that the professor, Greg Snyder, did private commissions. When they approached him to be the architect, he agreed. His design situated the winery where it could take advantage of views of Pilot Mountain and also be next to a natural amphitheater where musical events could be held. A silo with a circular stairway to the barrel room was to offer an architectural reference to the area's farming heritage. The event room, designed to seat approximately 270 people, was to open onto a covered terrace. The Hobsons loved the design. Before beginning construction, however, they went to Napa Valley to meet a winery consultant. They knew "textbook theory" but wanted to talk to someone about the practical aspects of the building. Lenna says the consultant "showed us nuances of what makes the workspace of a winery a nightmare and what makes it a dream. It's as simple as sloping the floor so that the water runs towards the drain, and that way, you don't have to squeegee it."

To counterbalance their inexperience, the Hobsons knew they wanted a veteran winemaker. Steve Shepard, the winemaker at RayLen Vineyards and Winery, suggested they contact Linda King, the winemaker at Chalet Debonnet, the largest estate winery in Ohio. Linda, who also is a professional wine judge, wasn't looking for a new job, but the Hobsons' enthusiasm, the quality of Frank's vineyards, and the opportunity to have more control over her wines convinced her to join RagApple Lassie.

Before Linda arrived, for its initial releases, RagApple Lassie offered wines that were custom-crushed by Steve Shepard. To Lenna, the experience with these first wines was a sign that she and Frank were

RagApple Lassie winery

in the right business. Once they had a harvest, the Hobsons needed French oak barrels, but no one believed they could get them in time. The barrels come from two different French forests (depending on whether they will be used for white or red wine), and they must be ordered and paid for a year in advance. Frank called a company in France and explained the situation. In less than a month, the barrels arrived. He says, "They shipped just exactly what we needed." The bill came later. Meanwhile, other wineries were still waiting for orders that they had paid for months earlier. Lenna says, "I viewed that as a sign that we're exactly where we're supposed to be, doing what we're supposed to be doing."

Besides acquiring the first barrels, the easiest part of establishing the vineyards was choosing the name. As a teenager, Frank had a Grand Champion Holstein named RagApple Lassie. Even now, decades later, he talks fondly about carrying alfalfa pellets in his pockets and having RagApple Lassie come running to him and stick her nose in his clothes. She was, Frank says, "a big pet." Consequently, the winery's website explains, "the opportunity to combine the farm heritage of Frank's life, with a name that was both unique and memorable made 'RagApple Lassie' the obvious choice." A photograph of RagApple Lassie (and a young Frank) can be seen in the winery. She also is prominently featured in the winery's marketing, from its logo to its website.

If Frank is "the quintessential farmer," then Lenna might be "the model marketer." Promotional ideas pour from her. Before its first wine release, Lenna decided the winery needed a product, so she arranged to have RagApple Lassie Bottled Water available at events. In October 2001, she organized "A Celebration of Firsts," which was, she explains, "the first annual vineyard party celebrating the first year's growth of the first year's planting of the first Boonville vineyard on the first Saturday of October at the first minute after four." It was also a charity event. Habitat for Humanity brought two-by-fours that were to be used in its next house, which guests could sign if they offered a donation. The party raised $6,000. Lenna subsequently instituted an "Adopt-A-Vine" program at the vineyards; people who make donations to Habitat for Humanity choose a vine that is "theirs," complete with a plaque. Lenna's efforts have paid off. RagApple Lassie has won awards in competition not only for its wines, but also for its labels, logo, and design.

In addition to fundraisers, RagApple Lassie hosts events such as regular outdoor concerts. The winery has picnic areas, and paths wind through nearby woods to the vineyards. For those who would like to stay longer in the area, guesthouses are available for rent.

The Hobsons have enjoyed establishing RagApple Lassie, which now produces around 6,500 cases a year. Although the process has involved "stomach-turning investment decisions," Lenna insists that "it's been exhilarating and great fun. There has never been a day that we haven't considered it fun and fascinating." They also have discovered an unexpected social phenomenon. When they travel, people respond very differently if they say they own vineyards instead of a tobacco farm. Lenna says the reaction is astounding; people's eyes open wide, they ask numerous questions, and they seem fascinated. No one, Lenna laughs, treats them like this when they present themselves as "farmers." Yet farmers are proudly what Frank and Lenna are. In addition to the vineyards, which now include 35 acres of grapes, they continue to grow corn, wheat, soybeans, and tobacco. They know, however, that their children and grandchildren will probably not farm multiple crops like they do; consequently, they believe that RagApple Lassie is their legacy to future generations. Lenna says, "They are the ones who are really going to benefit and who are really going to have the opportunity to do neat things with the winery."

RayLen Vineyards and Winery

3577 U.S. 158
Mocksville, N.C. 27028
Phone and fax: 336-998-3100
Website: www.RayLenvineyards.com
E-mail: info@RayLenvineyards.com
Hours: Monday–Saturday, 11 a.m.–6 p.m.

Owners: Joe and Joyce Neely
Winemaker: Steve Shepard
First year as bonded winery: 2000
Tasting fee: Yes
On-line ordering: Yes
Wine club: Yes

Wine List
Whites: Chardonnay, Pinot Grigio, Riesling, South Mountain Chardonnay, Viognier, Yadkin Gold
Reds: Cabernet Franc, Carolinius, Category Five (Bordeaux blend), Eagle's Select, Merlot, Pale Red, Shiraz

Directions: From Interstate 40 West, take the exit for N.C. 801 and drive south. Go right on U.S. 158 West. The winery is on the right after 4 miles. From Interstate 40 East, take the exit for Farmington Road. Turn left at the stop sign onto U.S. 158 East. The winery is on the left after 2 miles.

In the late 1990s, Joe Neely considered the prospects of the North Carolina wine industry and liked what he saw. In fact, he liked the prospects so much that, although he was supposedly retired, he couldn't

RayLen winery

RayLen winery

resist getting involved. Inspired by trips to Napa Valley with the Martins and Littles of Round Peak Vineyards and with Marilyn Thomer of Parducci Wine Cellars in California, Joe and his wife, Joyce, planted six acres of vineyards in Lewisville. Then, encouraged by their friends Ed and Charlie Shelton, the owners of Shelton Vineyards, they decided to establish their own winery. They bought a 115-acre dairy farm, began planting vines, and built a showcase winery that they named RayLen, a combination of their daughters' names, Rachel and Len.

Steve Shepard

Because Joe had been involved with a number of successful entrepreneurial start-ups, the Neelys had confidence in their business plan. They chose the land because of its location in the Yadkin Valley and its proximity to Interstate 40. Their smartest business decision, however, may have been hiring Steve Shepard as RayLen's winemaker and general manager. When the Neelys offered him the chance to be involved, Steve, known for his award-winning work at Westbend Vineyards, couldn't resist. He says, "I decided to jump on board and start all over again. I really like the challenge of starting with nothing and building it up."

For Steve, it was a chance to create an ideal winery. Working with architect Ray Troxell and others involved in the design of Shelton Vineyards, he helped plan RayLen's physical layout, including the crucial placement of tanks, water lines, and electrical lines. He ordered state-of-the-art equipment ranging from a computerized European press to a portable water heater that produces a high-volume spray of scalding water for cleaning. Steve says, "I've been making wine for 25 years, and I've done four or five different wineries. I took the best of everything from those other wineries and put in everything I could think of here." When RayLen began production, Steve found that the winery worked "like a dream." At 11,000 square feet, it was designed for growth, and it now produces 10,000 cases a year.

Steve also has had a free hand in developing the wines. Pointing out that "different winemakers have different styles," he says, "I like wines that are high in acid. They go better with foods. . . . I like something that's going to wake up your taste buds." He doesn't, however, try to please only himself; his goal is "to make wines that people enjoy drinking." Steve insists that winemaking is an art, and that a winemaker should therefore have an artistic sensibility and a sense of personal style. But he or she also needs to consider audience tastes. There must be a balance as a winemaker tries "to develop something that's really creative" and also a wine "that people are going to go head over heels over."

The vineyards at RayLen now include 35 acres of vines and supply 70 to 80 percent of the fruit for its wines. The winery also purchases grapes from local and state growers. In particular, Steve has a relationship with Larry Kehoe of South Mountain Vineyard, and RayLen offers a special South Mountain Chardonnay. Kehoe, a longtime wine enthusiast, praises the result because he feels "it's not a California style—that pineapple juice with oak logs floating in it. It's much more French."

From the very beginning, RayLen wines have been popular with both drinkers and wine judges and have earned a number of significant awards. In fact, Joe says of RayLen's early years, "If I had known that the wines were going to be as good as they were, I would have gone a lot faster." Steve, however, downplays such recognition. He insists, "Winning medals and awards is part of your job. You should win them. If you're not winning awards, then you've got a problem."

For Steve, the important thing is not a wine's award, label, or mystique, it's what's in the bottle. This is why he champions screw caps, which he believes preserve wine more reliably than corks, and why he prefers blends, even though it may be easier to market a specific varietal. Blending allows a winemaker to take what's best from each grape and create a whole that's greater than the sum of its parts. Over the years, Steve has developed a number of proprietary Bordeaux-style blends for RayLen, including Carolinius and Category Five. And as RayLen's vines age, Steve finds himself able to create wines of greater complexity and potential for cellaring. Consequently, RayLen has now begun to release reserve wines such as Eagle's Select.

RayLen's tasting room has windows that provide views of the vineyards' rolling hills. The building also features a wraparound porch with rocking chairs, and visitors are encouraged to bring picnics. RayLen often sponsors events, including concerts and release parties. Its large second floor can be reserved for private business meetings.

In addition to wines and clothing, RayLen's tasting room displays for purchase several pieces of handcrafted furniture, wooden boxes, and other pieces of woodwork. These are the products of another business with which Joe is involved—or, as he puts it, "another one of my dabblings." Although he insists that he's retired, you wouldn't know it by his schedule. Not only does he have RayLen and his "dabblings," he is the president of the Yadkin Valley Winegrower's Association and is involved in the promotion of the state's wine industry. Thanks to the success of RayLen and the increase in North Carolina's wineries, retirement for Joe is a lot of work.

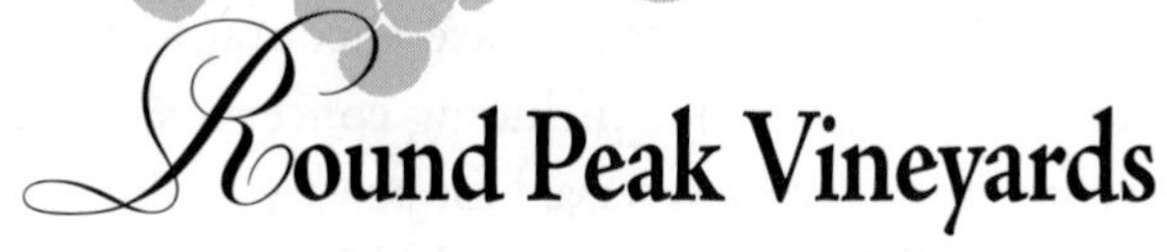

Round Peak Vineyards

765 Round Peak Church Road
Mount Airy, N.C. 27030
Phone: 336-352-5595
Fax: 336-352-5581
Website: www.roundpeak.com
Hours: Monday and Thursday–Saturday,
10 a.m.–5 p.m.; Sunday, noon–5 p.m.;
or by appointment

Owners: George and Susan Little and
Lee and Janet Martin
Winemaker: Sean McRitchie (consultant)
First year as bonded winery: 2005
Tasting fee: Yes
On-line ordering: No
Wine club: Yes

Wine List
Whites: Chardonnay, Sweet Niagara
Blush: Sweet Rosé
Reds: Cabernet Franc, Cabernet Sauvignon, Fiddler's Red (blend), Merlot, Nebbiolo, Sangiovese

Directions: From Interstate 77, take Exit 100. Turn left on N.C. 89 West toward Low Gap. Turn right on Round Peak Church Road and go approximately 1.5 miles. The winery is on the left. From U.S. 52 North, take Interstate 74 West to Exit 6. Turn onto N.C. 89 West. Turn right on Round Peak Church Road and go approximately 1.5 miles. The winery is on the left.

Round Peak vineyards

In 1998, the Martins and the Littles took a vacation together to San Francisco. In addition to eating at good restaurants, visiting one of their children, and going to a football game between the University of North Carolina and Stanford, they decided to do the obligatory wine tour. It ended up changing their lives.

The third night in Napa Valley, the men were relaxing by the pool. They had been, in the words of one of them, "hitting the wine trail hard," and they began talking about starting their own vineyards when they returned to North Carolina. When the husbands told the wives their plans, the women didn't take them seriously. Looking back on it, Susan Little admits she thought, "It's all just talk," and Janet Martin says, "We thought it was a passing phase . . . but it never passed." Upon returning to North Carolina, they began looking at properties. George Little remembers, "We had fun laughing and joking, and when we came back, it ceased to be a joke." In 1999, the two couples bought land together in Surry County and began establishing Round Peak Vineyards.

To find the right property, the Littles and Martins hired Stephen Lyons, one of the state's premier vineyard consultants (and now the

The Martins and the Littles

general manager of Raffaldini Vineyards). He found a 32-acre site in the rolling foothills of the Blue Ridge Mountains and helped them lay out the vineyards. The property came with a house and a back deck. Janet remembers, "Night after night, we would sit on the deck, and we would talk about how we wanted to prove that we could grow high-quality grapes in the Yadkin Valley."

Initially, the Martins and Littles planted eight acres of French and Italian varietals. At first, they intended to grow grapes and sell them. As they began learning about the industry, in part by taking courses at Surry Community College, they realized that it made more financial sense to make and sell the wine themselves. Consequently, they began to have other wineries provide custom crushes, which they sold in the Round Peak tasting room. In 2005, they established their own winery.

With an annual production of approximately 2,000 cases, Round Peak Vineyards is small, but there is plenty of work. The Martins and Littles trade off weekends in the tasting room, and although they acknowledge the work is tiring, they also find it rewarding. Lee Martin, who has devoted himself to the winery after retiring from a career at Wachovia, says, "This is harder work, but more fun." He particularly loves the harvest. "I love working the tasting room," he insists. Susan agrees. She finds it rewarding to be able to offer a product grown, made, and bottled on their own property. She admits, "It's especially thrilling to sell to people from California." She fondly remembers the day two motorcyclists wanted to do a tasting. They asked her about Pierce's disease, a problem that affects vineyards but one most customers don't know about. As they talked about the state's industry, one of the men explained that he was a viticulturalist from the University of California at Davis. He not only complimented the wines, he bought a bottle to pack in his saddlebag and take back west.

Although Round Peak had its origin in vacation talk, it has become a substantial accomplishment. George Little says with pride, "We've got as good a vineyard as there is. Period." He also emphasizes Round Peak's contributions to the community. For example, the winery takes part every year in the Tommy Jarrell Festival, which honors the notable old-time musician who developed a distinctive Round Peak style.

Round Peak Vineyards requires so much attention that the Littles and Martins have not taken many vacations together in recent years. This may be just as well. Considering what happened when they went to California, Janet Martin laughs, "it's dangerous when we travel."

Shelton Vineyards

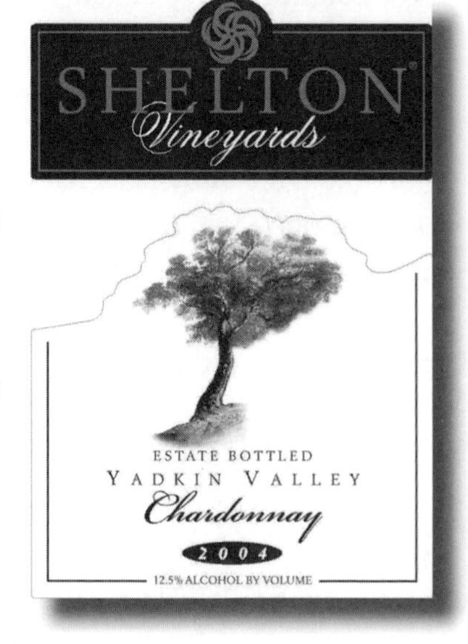

286 Cabernet Lane
Dobson, N.C. 27017
Phone: 336-366-4724
Website: www.sheltonvineyards.com
E-mail: sales@sheltonvineyards.com
Hours: Open daily, 10 a.m.–6 p.m.

Owners:
Charles M. and R. Edwin Shelton
Winemaker: Murphy Moore
First year as bonded winery: 2000
Tasting fee: Yes
On-line ordering: Yes
Wine club: Yes

Wine List
Whites: Chardonnay, Family Reserve Chardonnay, Madison Lee White, Riesling, Salem Fork Snow Hill White
Blush: Salem Fork Sweet Blush
Reds: Cabernet Franc, Cabernet Sauvignon, Family Reserve Claret, Madison Lee Red, Merlot, Pinot Noir, Salem Fork Zephyr Red, Syrah
Specialty: Yadkin Valley Port

Directions: From Interstate 77, take Exit 93 (the Dobson exit). Turn right, then take the first right onto Twin Oaks Road. The winery's entrance is on the right after 2.5 miles. From Interstate 74, take U.S. 601 to Dobson and follow the signs.

According to Charlie Shelton, the origins of Shelton Vineyards were an impulse buy and a late-night television commercial. In 1994, Charlie bought an old dairy farm at an auction. He had no plans for it.

Pond at Shelton Vineyards
COURTESY OF SHELTON VINEYARDS

"I just thought," he says, "that we ought to own a farm." After a few years, he and his brother and business partner, Ed, began to seriously ask, "What can we do with this land? What can we do to help some of the people's thinking in this county, that there's other things that you can do besides tobacco?" Then, one night as he watched the NIT basketball finals, Charlie saw a promotion for the viticulture program at the University of California at Davis. He called the school to get information about growing grapes. Someone at the school referred him to someone at Virginia Tech, who referred him to someone else, who referred him to someone else. Charlie persisted. Eventually, he made contact with a consultant in Tryon, North Carolina, who visited the farm, tested the soil, reviewed the climate, and pronounced it a good place to grow grapes.

After the Sheltons decided to establish vineyards, they went, as one friend puts it, "about 90 miles an hour." In 1999, they planted European varietals on 60 acres. Each year, they expanded, and now the 400-acre estate contains 200 acres of vineyards with a dozen varietals.

To design the 33,000-square-foot winery, Charlie and Ed convinced North Carolina architect Ray Troxell, an old friend and business associate, to come out of retirement. Troxell has enjoyed working with the brothers and their construction company, Shelco, Inc. He says, "Charlie and Ed are most unusual people. They are the salt of the earth, in my book." He appreciates that the brothers "were not interested in budget work. They wanted first-class. They always do, and they always get it. I think that job probably went as smoothly as any job they ever built."

Believing that if, as Charlie puts it, "you've got the right people and the right equipment, it will make the right wine," the Sheltons hired industry experts, including Sean McRitchie from Oregon's Willamette Valley. And they outfitted the winery with top-of-the-line equipment. McRitchie says that the Sheltons told him, "'We want to do it right. If it improves the wine even a little bit, let's do it.'" For example, they decided to incorporate a gravity-flow system that requires minimal pumping of wine. The effort paid off. With its first releases, Shelton Vineyards began winning awards. By 2006, it had won almost 300 in regional, national, and international competitions.

The brothers insist that they didn't create the state-of-the-art winery simply as a business venture. They also intended to make a statement. They wanted to demonstrate the land's possibilities. In an area that has increasingly lost jobs due to changes in the tobacco, textile, and furniture industries, finding new sources of revenue is crucial. The Sheltons believe that one of these sources may be grapes. According to Charlie, a survey done by researchers at Virginia Tech found that almost 95 percent of Surry County is ideal for growing vinifera. Part of the Yadkin Valley, it has a good climate—warm summers and mild winters—fertile soil, and rolling hills, which provide drainage. Shelton Vineyards, then, serves as a model to area farmers of what can be done. And in fact, many Yadkin Valley winery and vineyard owners mention Shelton as an inspiration for them.

Having been born and raised in the North Carolina Piedmont, the Sheltons emphasize their desire to give something back to the community. Charlie says of the winery, "The most rewarding thing is to see what it has done for Surry County—in particular, this area, Mount Airy. It's sort of put a new breath of life in these folks." At one time, the Mount Airy region had a significant tourism industry, and the Sheltons believe that this can be rebuilt. Ed remarks, "I'd love to see 100 wineries up here in this area. I'd like to see people doing things that use the land. I think that rural North Carolina has got to develop its rural character." To that end, the brothers intend Shelton Vineyards to be a "destination area." Larry Kehoe, the owner of South Mountains Vineyard, believes they have succeeded. He says of the Sheltons, "What they've done is so magnificent. You drive down that lane and suddenly say, 'My God, I'm in Napa Valley.' It's amazing."

The winery has a 50,000-case production capacity. Tours for visitors were planned as part of the building's layout. Consequently, as Troxell points out, "the public can walk through this facility and see the different operations and not interfere with them and yet have a very comfortable path." Organized tours run every half-hour, and windows offer views of the various work areas, such as the bottling and fermentation rooms. The tasting room is a large, beautiful space with a three-story atrium lit by an enormous chandelier.

Outside, the wraparound porch has rocking chairs situated to overlook some of the vineyards. Troxell says, "The vistas and views of that land are magnificent. That was an integral part of the design." The grounds include picnic areas and a small pond. Shelton often hosts concerts and festival events.

In 2001, to complement the winery, the brothers opened Shelton Cheeses, a facility that makes handcrafted cheeses from goat and Jersey cow milk processed by a local dairy. In May 2005, the Harvest Grill opened at the winery. It offers lunch daily and dinner Thursday through Saturday.

The brothers set out to make a statement, and they have. Their impact on the state's wine industry has been enormous. Their example has convinced other farmers to grow grapes and has inspired the development of several other wineries, including RayLen and RagApple Lassie. They sponsored the application for the official designation that would make the Yadkin Valley an "appellation," a distinct winegrowing region. In 1998, they started a viticulture and oenology program at Surry Community College, and they funded the program for its first two years. According to one small winery owner, the brothers' political and business clout has allowed them "to open doors a lot of us have been hammering on for years."

The Sheltons are leaving a legacy not only for their community but also, they hope, for their families. In a variety of ways, Shelton Vineyards pays tribute to both their ancestors and their descendants. The red-wine blend Madison Lee is named after their grandfathers. A trophy case visible on the tour displays photographs of the brothers' lives, families, and careers. The winery's design of five *S*'s represents the five children who someday will inherit Shelton Vineyards. In fact, when the winery opened, Ed stated that "at Shelton Vineyards, we are creating a place that will soon produce the best wine on the East Coast. After that, it will be our children's responsibility to make it the best wine in the United States. And after that, it will be up to our grandchildren to make it the best in the world." The sentiment suggests how much rural North Carolina and its families have changed. After all, Ed and Charlie grew up in a family of teetotalers and were hesitant to explain to their 93-year-old father that they were going into the wine business. Once they finally did, their father thought for a moment and then said, according to Charlie, "'Well, the old folks used to eat a little vinegar with their food to help digestion, and I think wine is vinegar, so you'll be all right.'"

Stony Knoll Vineyards

1143 Stony Knoll Road
Dobson, N.C. 27017
Phone: 336-374-5752
Fax: 336-386-8170
Website:
www.stonyknollvineyards.com
E-mail: vancoe@surry.net
Hours: Saturday, noon–6 p.m.;
Sunday, 2–6 p.m.

Owners: Van and Kathy Coe
Winemaker: Lynn Crouse
First year as bonded winery: 2004
Tasting fee: Yes
On-line ordering: Printable order form
Wine club: Yes

Wine List
Whites: Ardella Blanc (Niagara), Chardonnay
Reds: Cabernet Franc, Cabernet Sauvignon, Syrah

Directions: From Interstate 77, take Exit 82 (Elkin/Jonesville). Drive east on N.C. 67 for 10 miles. Turn left on Rockford Road, go 7 miles, and turn left on Stony Knoll Road. The winery is on the left after 0.5 mile.

In the late 1990s, inspired by the state's growing viticulture industry, Van and Kathy Coe began to consider devoting part of their 48-acre farm to growing grapes. The land had been in the family since 1896,

Stony Knoll Vineyards

and for much of the 20th century, it had been planted in tobacco. However, following the reduction in government quotas in the 1980s, the land had been allowed to lie fallow. The Coes felt grapes might be a viable new crop.

Since many members of the family are teetotalers, the decision to plant a vineyard was not an easy one. Van himself was raised to believe alcohol should be avoided. Consequently, before moving ahead with the project, he says that he "spoke with older members of the family. They knew me, and I knew them." Although there was no official family meeting, Van remembers talking about the idea over a period of time: "Each Sunday after we go to church, the whole family gets in an automobile and goes for Sunday dinner. Many, many discussions were held informally then. That's where we talked about it."

The family trusted Van, eventually deciding that "maybe there was a right way to do this." They became convinced that they could offer a positive, healthy product that could improve a person's quality of life and be sold in a responsible manner. Consequently, Van enrolled in the viticulture program at Surry Community College, and his brother-in-law, Lynn Crouse, enrolled in the oenology program. They laid out the vineyards in 1999 and 2000 and planted the first vines in 2001. In 2004, Stony Knoll Vineyards officially opened.

Establishing the winery has been an education with, as Van puts it, "a steep learning curve." He says, "We're learning how to grow grapes

Van Coe at Salute!

every year." Some seasons, one varietal will do well, and the next year, everything will change. Although the area's rocky soil is good for vines, the weather in North Carolina can be unpredictable. As a result, according to Van, the climate makes goals "a moving target." There are other challenges as well, including birds, deer, and other animals that eat the crops. Despite all the difficulties, Van appreciates the opportunity to work outside after having spent over 20 years in the banking industry: "I really enjoy watching the vines come out. It's amazing what humanity knows about plants. It's amazing we can direct a plant to do what we want."

Stony Knoll is located along beautiful country roads near the historic remains of Rockford, a 19th-century village. The winery was designed by Van after the model at Surry Community College. Its main feature is an exceptionally large, uncluttered tasting room suitable for receptions and other gatherings. A small kitchen allows for catered events; in the future, Stony Knoll might offer prepared deli foods for people to eat at its outdoor picnic tables. Although Stony Knoll might expand its wine list, Van doesn't envision the winery growing very quickly. He insists, "We're taking baby steps. We're not interested in being a large corporation. We want to figure out what we're doing, what we can do well, and provide a valuable beverage for the future."

Van hopes that Stony Knoll can eventually help diversify the local economy and create job opportunities. He believes the area can become a tourist destination. For now, he's pleased that he can offer work to family members who want it. He remembers as a boy helping his grandfather grow and sell strawberries, and now he finds it gratifying to work with his own children, nieces, and nephews. He laughs that whenever someone asks, "Uncle Van, is there anything I can do?" the answer is always yes. Sometimes, this means helping to bottle the approximately 1,000 cases of wine Stony Knoll produces each year. Sometimes, it means staffing the tasting room or working in the fields. When you run a winery, Van points out, "there is never any idle time. We're a very busy family."

484 Hartman Road
Winston-Salem, N.C. 27127
Phone: 336-775-9717
Fax: 336-248-2800
Website: www.weathervanewinery.com
E-mail: sproctor3@triad.rr.com
Hours: By appointment only

Owners: Sid and Miranda Proctor
Winemakers: Sid and Miranda Proctor
First year as bonded winery: 2005
Tasting fee: No
On-line ordering: Via e-mail
Wine club: No

Wine List
Whites: Pinot Grigio, Sauvignon Blanc, Tropical Wave (kiwi-flavored Gewürztraminer), Viognier
Reds: Grand Vieux Chateau du Roi, Merlot, Rooster Black (Merlot with blackberries), Rooster Red (Chianti-style with cranberries), Stratosphere (Zinfandel), Strawberry Breeze (Riesling), Sweet Mountain Bliss (Zinfandel with raspberry), Temperature Rising (Chianti)

Directions: From Winston-Salem and points north, take U.S. 52 South to Exit 100 (Hickory Tree Road). Turn right on Hickory Tree Road and then take the second left onto Hartman Road. The winery is located at the second house on the right. From Lexington and points south, take U.S. 52 North to Exit 100 (Hickory Tree Road). Turn left on Hickory Tree Road and then take the second left onto Hartman Road. The winery is located at the second house on the right.

Weathervane wine

After Bob Bowers built a cabin in the Blue Ridge Mountains in 2001, he decided to throw a party to thank everyone who helped him. He rented the Burgiss Barn in Laurel Springs and asked his son-in-law, Sid Proctor, to check the sound system. When Sid did so, he met the proprietor, Tom Burgiss, who assured him the equipment was fine and then asked if he could show him something. Sid recalls thinking, "Uh-oh," but when Tom gave him a tour of Thistle Meadow Winery and Grapestompers, his do-it-yourself winemaking store, Sid's hesitation turned to interest. He thought the hobby looked like fun. He says, "One thing led to another, and I bought some equipment."

Sid made his first batch of wine at home, and when it was finished, he returned to Thistle Meadow and offered some to Tom. After sampling it, Tom said, "This is the worst stuff I've ever tasted. You rushed it." Chastened, Sid tried again. And again. He developed patience, kept getting advice from Tom—whom he calls "a terrific mentor"—and began to make better wines.

As Sid became more involved in winemaking, he began to wonder about the commercial possibilities. He talked it over with his wife, Miranda, and they decided to research the licensing process. Again, one step led to another, and as Sid puts it, "a hobby ended up as a little business" when the Proctors established Weathervane Winery in the basement of their house.

Initially, the Proctors intended to sell their wine only at festivals. They went to their first one at Tanglewood in June 2005. "We knew it was going to be busy," Sid recalls, "but we were slammed. Everyone had a great time, but by the end of the day, we were worn out. And we knew we had something special." Sid and Miranda thought they would have until October to prepare for the next event, but the day after Tanglewood, "phones started ringing, and people wanted more." Consequently, the Proctors decided to distribute their wines in local outlets, and Sid began "running up and down the road to keep shelves stocked."

In the first year, Sid and Miranda estimated they might sell 100 cases. Instead, they sold 300. Sid says, "We've been behind in production ever since." The following year, Weathervane increased production to almost 1,000 cases and still sold out many of its offerings.

Sid attributes the immediate success of Weathervane in part to his 25 years of experience in marketing. The first questions he asks are "What are the needs?" and "What's the demand?" To find answers, he test-markets each offering. For example, he might make three cases of Malbec, take it to a tasting, and ask, "Is this something you're interested in?" For the wine Stratosphere, he took 20 cases to an event in Blowing Rock, and when they sold out, he knew he had a popular selection.

The Proctors can do such test marketing because Weathervane works mainly with concentrates and grapes from local growers. This means it can develop a recipe, keep improving it, and then follow it for future batches. Small batches also mean that if a wine doesn't sell, it can be taken off the market, and the Proctors aren't stuck with a large inventory. Sid compares this to the "just-in-time" processes of modern manufacturing, in which product is made according to demand. He says, "We're not the volume guys, but we're right where the market is. We can move quickly and make what the market wants."

Sid acknowledges that Weathervane has followed the reverse of most business plans: "We did it backwards. Instead of building a plant and seeing if the wine was good, we said, 'Let's see if the wine's good and if there's a demand, and then we'll build a plant.'" Since there clearly is a market for their wines, the Proctors have begun looking for property to build a tasting room. In 2007, they plan to build a separate winery.

Sid thinks they would eventually like Weathervane to produce about 1,500 to 2,000 cases. "That's all we'll be interested in doing. We want something manageable, that doesn't kill us, and that's still fun." Sid also believes that winemaking on a small scale is better. For one, it's more intimate. Working with carboys and buckets instead of tanks "allows people to see what's going on." You can watch the fermentation up close. And Sid insists that there's an additional benefit: "When you're picking up and putting down those containers each day, you don't have to worry about losing muscle or bone-mass density. All that lifting is good exercise."

Westbend Vineyards

5394 Williams Road
Lewisville, N.C. 27023
Phone: 866-901-5032 or 336-945-5032
Fax: 336-945-5294
Website: www.westbendvineyards.com
E-mail: westbendvineyards@alltel.net
Hours: Monday–Saturday, 11 a.m.–5 p.m.;
Sunday, noon–5 p.m.
Winter hours may vary.

Owner: Lillian Kroustalis
Winemaker: Mark Terry
First year as bonded winery: 1988
Tasting fee: Yes
On-line ordering: Yes
Wine club: Yes

Wine List
Whites: Chardonnay, Pioneer White, Riesling, Viognier, Yadkin Fumé
Blush: Carolina Blush
Reds: Cabernet Sauvignon, Carolina Cuvée, Chambourcin, Lucky Lucci, Merlot, Pinot Noir, Pioneer Red, Vintner's Signature
Dessert: Lilly B

Directions: Heading west from Winston-Salem, exit Interstate 40 onto U.S. 421 North. After 15 miles on U.S. 421, take Exit 246 (Shallowford Road) and turn left. Go 2 miles and turn left on Williams Road. The winery is the fourth drive on the left. From Statesville, take Interstate 40 East to the Farmington Road exit. Turn left and go 10 miles. Turn right at the second stop sign onto Courtney-Huntsville Road. Drive 2 miles, then make a hairpin right onto Williams Road. The winery is the fourth drive on the left.

For Jack and Lillian Kroustalis, a passion for wine meant committing themselves to a lifelong education. Lillian says of wine, "You live it and learn. You're always learning. Wine is not static. There's always something different about it."

The Kroustalises lived it together for over 30 years, but they wouldn't have if they had listened to other people. In the early 1970s, as they considered planting vineyards specializing in European varietals, almost everyone counseled them against it. No one had ever grown French vinifera grapes in the Piedmont. They tried to get advice from state officials, farming experts, and professors at North Carolina State University and the University of North Carolina, but no one could help them. Lillian says, "They just didn't know. They had no experience except with muscadines. The agricultural people said, 'Would you be interested in growing some blueberries?' They wanted us to grow what they knew." The Kroustalises decided to experiment with the grapes anyway, on farmland they had bought near the Yadkin River.

Although Jack and Lillian didn't know it at the time, the land's fertile soil, sloping drainage, and elevation of 950 feet above sea level turned out to be excellent for vineyards. They started on a small scale, planting various varietals including Chardonnay, Cabernet, and Gamay

Westbend Vineyards winery

Westbend Vineyards patio

on a few acres at a time. As they traveled the Eastern states to attend viticulture conferences and visit other wineries, they discovered vineyards growing the French-American hybrids Chambourcin and Seyval. Since people continued to insist that their experiment with Chardonnay would fail, Jack and Lillian decided to plant the hybrids as well, as a form of security.

Although the Kroustalises always envisioned a winery as a long-term goal, they developed the vineyards slowly, as they educated themselves. Westbend's basement, which Lillian laughingly refers to as "the dungeon," still contains wine in unlabeled bottles, leftovers from those early years. For those "vintages," they destemmed the grapes at the kitchen table, crushed them in a pot, and used a manual bottling machine. "We had a lot of fun," Lillian recalls. "We were playing. It was a hobby." They would put a C on the cork to indicate the wine was a Chardonnay or an *R* to show it was a Riesling. At one point, however, the hobby caused problems. While they were traveling in Europe, an airport x-ray machine outlined some bottles in their baggage. The security guards insisted they unpack and explain the objects. Lillian says, "They wanted to know what it was, and we had to show them. And of course, none of it was labeled. It could have been anything."

By the mid-1980s, the Kroustalises had 30 acres of vines and a 70-ton grape harvest, which they sold to regional wineries. Château Morrisette in Virginia bought much of their crop. When Morrisette's winemaker visited the vineyards and pronounced the grapes excellent, Jack and Lillian knew they were on the right track.

Having successfully grown high-quality grapes, they decided to become more serious about the winemaking itself. They began to convert the farmhouse into a winery, starting with the stable, which was available because, Lillian explains, "my daughter found boys and lost horses." They renovated the space and placed vats where the stalls used to be, but the original double doors can still be seen on tours. They bought professional equipment and became a bonded winery. As part of the process, they had to decide on a permanent name. It was a difficult choice. They considered and rejected several names, including Yadkin Valley. Lillian recalls, "We didn't want to call it Château something or something French-sounding. And our name, Kroustalis, doesn't flow well on a label." Eventually, they decided to recognize and honor their geographical location. "We are who we are because of where we are," Lillian says. The area around the winery is known as the West Bend region

Grape stomping at Westbend Vineyards
COURTESY OF WESTBEND VINEYARDS

because of a bend to the west in the Yadkin River, and the Kroustalises took that name with only a slight modification—the two words became one.

Westbend had an important early success. Its first vintages, the 1990 Chardonnay and Chambourcin, were awarded several gold medals at the Eastern International Wine Competition. In fact, Westbend was the only winery east of the Mississippi so honored. The medals were particularly impressive because the major California wineries participated in the event, and Westbend's barrel-fermented Chardonnay won in a head-to-head competition against Kendall-Jackson. At the time, wine news didn't garner the media attention it now gets, and the only announcement was a blurb in the local newspaper. However, it did mean immediate credibility for the new winery. Though people at Westbend had considered the wine good, Lillian wryly notes that, "as a mother, you look at your child and you think it's beautiful even when it's homely." The gold medals were crucial outside corroboration.

Westbend quickly gained additional recognition. Some of its 1994 wines were listed as "Best Values" in *Wine Spectator*, and Robert Parker of the *Wine Advocate* called Westbend "one of the South's best kept wine secrets." Praising its Chardonnay, Seyval, Sauvignon, and Cabernet Sauvignon, Parker remarked, "As fine as these wines are, I am surprised they are not better known outside of North Carolina." His view of the wines' quality was shared by others through the 1990s, as Westbend continued to win medals at national and international competitions.

Because of their stubbornness, hard work, and dedication, the Kroustalises proved that excellent European varietals can be grown in the Piedmont. Larry Ehlers of Chateau Laurinda says, "I think all the wineries in North Carolina have to look back at Westbend with a little bit of gratitude. They did experiments and research on plantings at their own expense, without any outside help, that we all benefit from today. Anybody that makes wine in this state has to recognize that."

Lillian admits, "We had no master plan. . . . We were not in a hurry. We just evolved." Although Westbend is seen as pioneering the vinifera wine industry in the state, Lillian says that wasn't the attitude at the time: "You have to be here for a while and look back. When you're in the infancy, who's a pioneer?"

Westbend's vines now cover over 60 acres and include more than a dozen varietals. The winery produces between 5,000 and 7,000 cases a year under the guidance of winemaker Mark Terry, who joined Westbend in 2004 after a 20-year career at Hargrave Vineyard on Long Island.

In 2007, Westbend will celebrate the 35th anniversary of the establishment of its vineyards, and the winery plans to hold a number of special events. Unfortunately, Jack will not be there to take part. He passed away in March 2006. After his death, people throughout the industry paid tribute to his example.

Westbend's importance in the history of North Carolina wine is clear, but Lillian wants the winery to have a part in its future as well. Working with her son Alex, Mark Terry, and Jane Murray, the winery's sales representative, Lillian has begun to plan a number of projects, including the renovation of old structures and the building of new ones. After a lifetime dedicated to wine, she remains as enthused as when she began: "Wine is seductive. It gets you. It grabs you. It won't go away."

Windy Gap Vineyards

837 Pardue Farm Road
Ronda, N.C. 28670
Phone: 336-984-3926
Website: www.windygapwines.com
E-mail: wineman@wilkes.net
Hours: Tuesday–Saturday,
11 a.m.–5 p.m.; Sunday, noon–5 p.m.

Owners: Allen and Sandra Hincher
Winemaker: Allen Hincher
First year as bonded winery: 2000
Tasting fee: Yes
On-line ordering: No
Wine club: No

Wine List
Whites: Chardonel, Three Dawg Nite, Viognier
Blush: Froglevel Swing
Reds: Cabernet Franc, Cabernet Sauvignon, Chambourcin, Fat Basset Red, Tory Oak Red (Bordeaux blend)
Fruits: Blackberry, Blueberry

Directions: From U.S. 421, take Exit 272 (Clingman Road) and follow the signs. Drive approximately 0.5 mile on Clingman Road to Pardue Farm Road and turn left. Go 0.25 mile and turn left (again) on Pardue Farm Road. The winery is at the end of the road.

Vacations seem simple. You travel to interesting places and meet new people. Often, you take stock of your life, and as you relax in a romantic locale, you fantasize about making huge changes. These daydreams appear harmless, but they can have unexpected consequences. For Allen

Sandra and Allen Hincher

and Sandra Hincher, a vacation in Virginia dramatically altered their lives.

Enticed by Virginia's tourism promotions, the Hinchers drove through the Shenandoah Valley touring the area's wineries in the fall of 1995. They spent several days traveling country roads, tasting wine, and talking to owners and winemakers. The more they realized that the area resembled North Carolina's Wilkes County, where they were raised, the more an idea began to grow. For years, they had been working corporate jobs in Charlotte, and they were tired of the commutes, the days spent looking at computer screens, and the *Fortune* 500 mentality. They wanted to move back to the northern part of the state and wondered if a winery could provide a way to do that.

After their vacation, Allen and Sandra talked to family members who owned farmland near U.S. 421. At 1,100 feet in the foothills of the Brushy Mountains, it seemed a good place for grapes. Allen says, "When we originally concocted the idea of planting vineyards on it, . . . [the family] all thought it was a fool's folly, but they said, 'If you want to plant it, go ahead and plant it.'" The Hinchers decided to start slowly. They put vines on one acre, thinking that if they didn't grow, they'd lose the price of a medium-sized new car. It was a calculated investment. A failure would be disappointing but not financially devastating. Thus, they sensibly began an endeavor that would end up putting an enormous strain on their energy, finances, and emotional resources.

Windy Gap Vineyards

Although they come from farming families, Allen and Sandra had never worked in the fields. They taught themselves as they went along. "We've learned it the hard way," Allen says. After renting a tractor, they had to figure out how to drive it. To find out how to care for vines, they pored over books, questioned people in the business, and went to seminars. The advice they received wasn't always the best. Following a friend's suggestion, they first planted the varietal Melody. "As it turned out, that was probably the worst varietal to plant in North Carolina because it's a French hybrid that's very, very vigorous," Allen admits. Melody requires twice as much time for pruning and being cared for as other varietals. Allen remembers, "It about killed us that first summer, trying to take care of that one acre." On Saturdays, they would drive 65 miles from their house on Lake Norman to the vineyards, work all day in the fields, and then drive home. On Sundays, they would make the 130-mile round-trip drive again, returning to the vineyards to put in another eight to 12 hours.

Allen notes, "We thought the first year was bad, but in the second year, '97, it was even worse because we had the trellis up. It was hell." The Hinchers refused to quit. Instead, they decided to expand. They planted four acres of Viognier, Cabernet Franc, Chardonel, and Chambourcin. Nothing, however, seemed to go smoothly. They bored 800 holes for new rootstock. The night before they intended to plant, it rained 10 inches in 18 hours. Working in rain gear, the Hinchers and some loyal friends had to bail out the holes with milk jugs. Unfortunately, this proved one of the last rains in a summer of drought. Later, they had to bring in water trucks to ensure the young vines' survival. Each season brought new problems. Although a contractor had guaranteed a completion date of the building that would serve as both the winery and the Hinchers' new residence, it wasn't finished in time for the harvest. As a result, between five and six tons of grapes rotted on the vines because there was no place to put them. Allen says of those years, "My wife and I have a very strong relationship, to have made it through."

Luckily, the process of making wine has not been as difficult as growing grapes. For years, Allen was a serious hobbyist. He insists that there is no fundamental difference between making five gallons of wine and making 500. The key, he says, is to stay out of the way. According to Allen, if you grow good grapes and pick them at the right time, "the best thing the winemaker can do, other than dealing with problems that come up, is to intervene as little as possible." He concentrates on making small batches of no more than 500 gallons, so Windy Gap's wine list is subject to change.

After the winery was bonded in 2000, the Hinchers ran into additional difficulties. Following the terrorist attacks on September 11, 2001, the approval of wine labels became a low priority for the Bureau of Alcohol, Tobacco and Firearms. Consequently, Allen and Sandra had to delay releasing their first vintage and opening their tasting room. Finally, after years of struggle, Windy Gap Vineyards celebrated its grand opening in April 2002. At last, the Hinchers had the satisfaction of seeing people gather in a building they had designed to drink wine they had made from grapes they had grown. Through persistence and determination, they had succeeded in fulfilling their vacation vision.

By 2006, the Hinchers' vineyards had grown to seven acres, and the winery was well established. However, despite Windy Gap's location in the Yadkin Valley appellation and its status as part of the Vineyards of Swan Creek Wine Trail, Allen and Sandra have discovered that selling wine can be as challenging as making it. Originally, they planned to grow the winery to an output of 2,000 cases a year, but instead they have limited their production to 1,200 cases, and they sell the excess grapes to other wineries. Nevertheless, Allen insists that the worst day in the vineyards is better than the best day behind a computer terminal. Several years ago, he quit his corporate job, and while he misses the paycheck he used to have, he also traded in an hour commute for a 30-second one. "The real payback," Allen says as he gestures around the tasting room, "is the joy of working here."

Wineries of Piedmont North Carolina

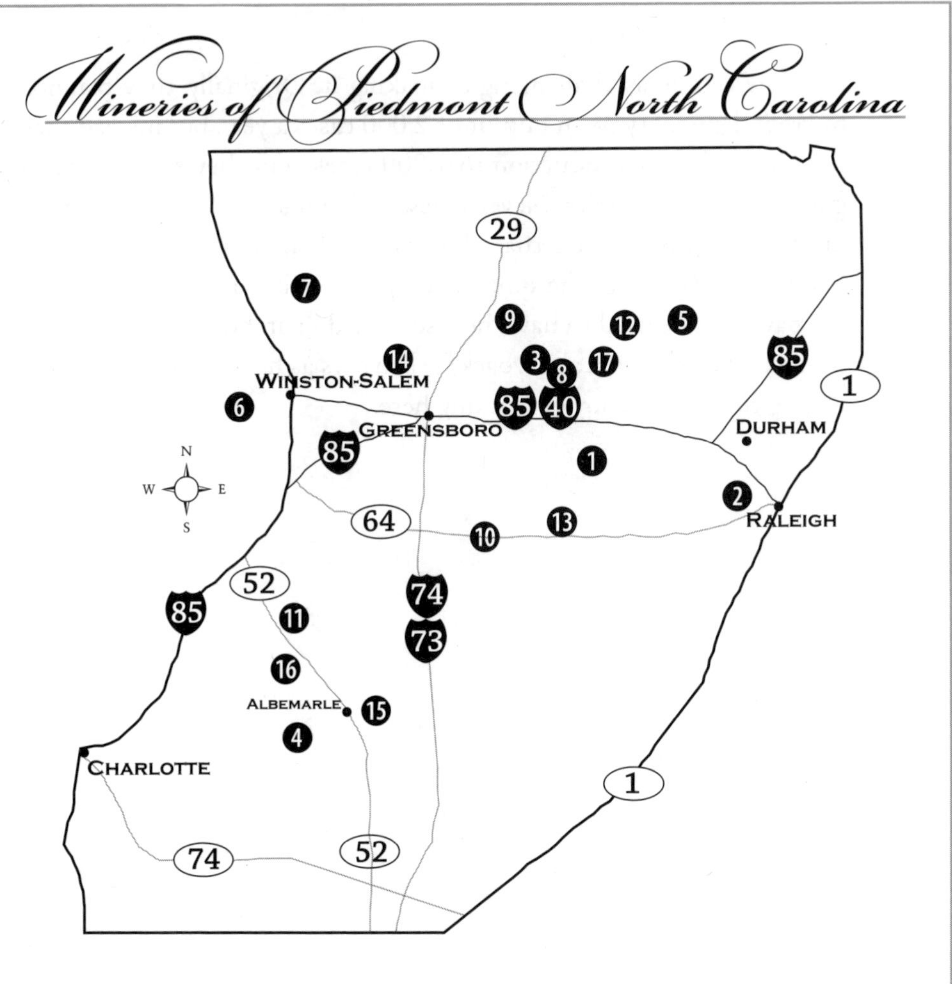

1. Benjamin Vineyards and Winery
2. Chatham Hill Winery
3. Creek Side Winery
4. Dennis Vineyards
5. Desi's Dew Meadery
6. Garden Gate Vineyards
7. Germanton Art Gallery and Winery
8. GlenMarie Vineyards and Winery
9. Grove Winery
10. Horizon Cellars
11. Old Stone Vineyard and Winery
12. Rock of Ages Winery and Vineyard
13. SilkHope Winery
14. Stonefield Cellars
15. Stony Mountain Vineyards
16. Uwharrie Vineyards
17. The Winery at Iron Gate Farm

Wineries of Piedmont North Carolina

Andy Zeman

Benjamin Vineyards and Winery

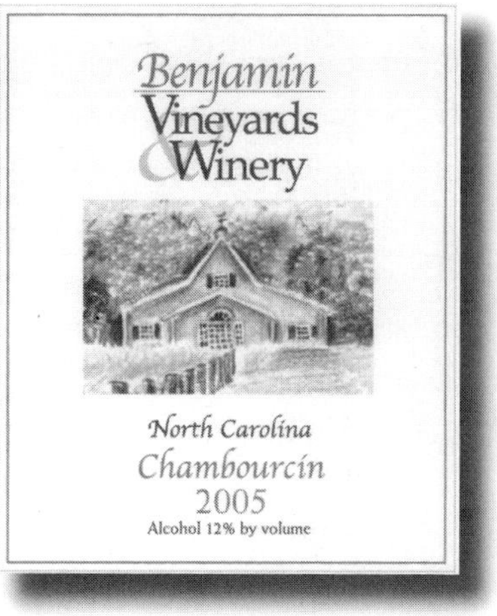

6516 Whitney Road
Graham, N.C. 27253
Phone: 336-376-1080
Fax: 336-376-1080
Website: www.benjaminvineyards.com
E-mail: benjaminwines@cs.com
Hours: Thursday–Sunday, noon–5 p.m.

Owners: Andy and Nancy Zeman
Winemaker: Andy Zeman
First year as bonded winery: 2004
Tasting fee: No
On-line ordering: No
Wine club: No

Wine List
Whites: Carlos, Chardonel, Chardonnay, Magnolia, May Wine (Chardonnay, strawberries, and woodruff), Sauvignon Blanc, Scuppernong
Reds: Cabernet Sauvignon, Chambourcin, Hunt (muscadine), Merlot
Fruit: Blackberry Bramble

Directions: From Interstate 40/85, take Exit 154 (Mebane Oaks Road) and drive south for 8.5 miles. Continue across N.C. 54, where the road becomes Saxapahaw-Oaks Road. Go 4 miles. Just over the Haw River bridge, turn left on Whitney Road. The vineyard is on the left after 1.2 miles.

Over 20 years ago, Nancy Zeman bought her husband, Andy, a beginner's winemaking kit. It was a small gift that ended up having a major impact on their lives. Andy found he enjoyed winemaking, and over the years, he progressed from the small plastic kit to working with concentrates to using fresh grapes. He also made wine in increasing amounts. Andy laughs, "It starts with one gallon, then five, then 10, then you have to buy a barrel, then the garage is full." He says that his hobby reached the point where "we were kind of like the neighborhood bootleggers, giving wine to everyone."

Although Nancy suggested several times that Andy should consider becoming a commercial winemaker, he resisted. He was afraid that doing it as a job might kill the pleasure. He insists, "You have to do it because you love it." Finally, however, as he started to plan his retirement from his job as a chemical engineer for Liggett & Myers Tobacco, he decided to try to make the transition.

In 2000, the Zemans began to look for suitable land on which to establish Benjamin Vineyards. Andy remembers that the real-estate agent regarded them strangely, since they carried a shovel everywhere. At each prospective site, they would scoop up dirt and send it to a laboratory to have it analyzed. Eventually, they found 10 acres with a soil composition that they liked. After buying it, they began planting vines.

The first year, the Zemans put in an acre of muscadine, which they chose in part because it's easy to tend and resistant to disease. Andy says, "We're big advocates of sustainable agriculture." As much as possible, they try to stay true to the principles of organic farming. In their third year, they planted French-American hybrids, and then, as their confidence in their farming abilities grew, they added Merlot and Cabernet. Andy points out, "In the Piedmont, we're unique because we can grow most of the vinifera and the muscadine."

In 2004, Andy and Nancy opened their tasting room. The Zemans had lived in North Carolina for 14 years, but they were still apprehensive about the reception of a winery in "the Bible Belt South." However,

Andy says, "our neighbors are our best customers. It's rewarding to come into this community and be so accepted." In fact, people in the area appreciate that the land is being cultivated, rather than developed. When the Zemans initially staked out the vineyards, a worried neighbor came by and asked about all the red flags. When he learned their plans, he said with relief, "Oh, thank goodness, we thought you were laying out a trailer court."

People also appreciate the Zemans' commitment to showcasing local artists. Every two months, a different artist exhibits work on the tasting-room walls, and each Fourth of July weekend, the winery hosts a pottery festival. Because of the small size of Benjamin Vineyards and Winery, however, events quickly can become crowded, so eventually the Zemans would like to expand their event and hospitality areas.

Andy enjoys meeting people, particularly those who, like himself, have made wine in their basements. He remembers that when the 2,000-square-foot winery opened, "one of our earliest customers was someone who lived on the other side of town. A former bootlegger, he walked around, looked at the barrels, and said, 'Are you sure this is legal?'" By the end of his visit, he was even offering some of his old recipes.

Andy notes with regret that he usually can't make country recipes like those of the ex-bootlegger. A hobbyist can "throw anything in," but a commercial winemaker needs to be more rigorous. Not only does the

Andy Zeman

government have to approve the ingredients and recipes, but according to Andy, to be cost effective, he needs to make at least 100 cases of a particular wine. Consequently, he can no longer make something like an apple-raisin wine on impulse, and he admits that he misses this flexibility. Still, he might do some "country custom wines" at some point, and he does play around with some recipes, such as his May Wine, which contains strawberries and woodruff.

Overall, Andy tries to offer a range of wines from dry to sweet. Each year, Benjamin Vineyards and Winery produces approximately 1,000 cases, and the winery has the capacity to triple that production. The Zemans would also consider expansion, depending on customer demand, which, according to Andy, keeps increasing. He points out, "People keep coming back, so that's good," and he believes that "we reached a milestone when stores started calling us and asking for our wine."

For all of Andy's anxieties about killing the fun of his hobby, that hasn't happened. He says, "Every year, the grapes get a little more mature and the wines get a little better, so I'm looking forward to the future."

Chatham Hill Winery

3500 Gateway Centre Boulevard, #200
Morrisville, N.C. 27560
Phone: 800-808-6768 or 919-380-7135
Fax: 919-380-1310
Website: www.chathamhillwine.com
E-mail: info@chathamhillwine.com
Hours: Monday–Wednesday and Friday,
11 a.m.–5 p.m.; Thursday, 11 a.m.–7 p.m.; Saturday, 11 a.m.–6 p.m.; Sunday, 1–5 p.m.

Owners: Marek Wojciechowski and Jill Winkler
Winemaker: Marek Wojciechowski
First year as bonded winery: 1999
Tasting fee: Yes
On-line ordering: Yes
Wine club: Yes

Wine List
Whites: Chardonnay, Pinot Grigio, Riesling, Sweet Carolina White, Viognier
Reds: Cabernet Franc, Cabernet Sauvignon, Merlot, Sweet Carolina Red, Syrah, Zinfandel

FRUITS: BLACKBERRY, BLUEBERRY, PEACH, POMEGRANATE, RASPBERRY, STRAWBERRY
SPECIALTIES: CHRISTMAS RED, CHRISTMAS WHITE

DIRECTIONS: FROM INTERSTATE 40, TAKE EXIT 285 AND PROCEED TOWARD MORRISVILLE ON AVIATION PARKWAY. TAKE THE FIRST RIGHT, GATEWAY CENTRE BOULEVARD. GO APPROXIMATELY 0.3 MILE, THEN TURN RIGHT ON NORTHGATE COURT AT THE SIGN FOR NUMBER 3500. THE WINERY ENTRANCE IS IN THE CENTER OF THE BUILDING.

The conversation of Marek Wojciechowski, the winemaker at Chatham Hill Winery, contains two key words.

The first is *experiment*. Marek continually talks about experimenting with techniques, machinery, and processes. He believes in exploring possibilities. For example, the winery offers three types of Chardonnay: one that is unoaked and aged in stainless steel, one that is lightly oaked (either by being blended or spending less than six months in wooden barrels), and one that is fully oaked. This penchant for experimenting isn't surprising, considering Marek's background. A scientist with a Ph.D. in chemistry, he moved to North Carolina to become the research director at a biotechnology company. Consequently, he is one of only a few winemakers who feel equally comfortable talking about

Marek Wojciechowski and Jill Winkler
COURTESY OF CHATHAM HILL WINERY

Chatham Hill wine
COURTESY OF CHATHAM HILL WINERY

a grape's taste and its molecular structure. He approaches winemaking with a scientist's disciplined concentration, attention to detail, rigorous sanitation standards, and passion for discovery. However, although his scientific background is invaluable, he points out that "making wine is not pharmaceutical. You're not making drugs. You're making something to be enjoyed." For him, wine is about the creation of pleasure.

The second word Marek uses frequently is *classy*. In his experiments, he searches to create a wine with style, elegance, and class. Accomplishing this requires a mind that is not just scientific but artistic, too—particularly, Marek insists, when it comes to blending the wines. It also requires a commitment to high-quality materials. On tours, Marek points out with pride the stainless-steel equipment, the heavy bottles, the embossed Portuguese corks, and the distinctive labels—in short, all the elements needed to accomplish Chatham Hill's mission of producing premium fine wines.

The stylishness of the wines contrasts markedly with the winery's location. Visitors who expect the usual rural surroundings will be surprised. Chatham Hill Winery is in a business park only two miles from Raleigh-Durham International Airport. The site is the result of a key decision made by Marek and his original partners, Robert Henkens and Steven Wegner, during the winery's planning stages. At first, they intended to buy land in Chatham County, but they soon realized that trying to simultaneously establish vineyards and a winery might overextend their resources. So they decided to concentrate on making wine rather than growing grapes.

As a winemaker, Marek likes "the heavy, full-bodied, more distinctive wines." He says, "In every wine, I try to emphasize fruitiness." His wines compare favorably with those of Europe and California. In fact, one winery employee, annoyed by a friend who kept insisting on the superiority of Italian wines, poured a Chatham Hill wine into an Italian bottle and gave it to him. Tasting it, the friend was ecstatic. "You see," he said, "if you want a good wine, you have to buy Italian." Although Marek likes this story, he points out that varietals grown here represent distinctive North Carolina versions. Even when wine is made in a particular style, the influence of geography—the terroir—leads Marek to tell people, "Don't expect it to taste like California because it will be different."

At first, Marek planned to focus on only a few wines, but he has since realized that a winery needs diverse offerings to appeal to different tastes. Making a narrow range of wines essentially tells people that the winemaker doesn't care what they want to drink, he feels. Although he was reluctant to make non-French wines, Marek began experimenting with French-American hybrids. He admits, "I'm glad that I did. These wines turned out very good. I can tailor more for the customer, and people appreciate it." Chatham Hill now also has a line of semisweet fruit wines called "Sweet Carolina."

In recent years, Chatham Hill has gone through a number of significant changes. The winery has nearly doubled its size by adding a large tasting room. This space gives the winery the capability to do events such as receptions, corporate meetings, and wine dinners. The most significant change, however, occurred when Marek and his wife, Jill Winkler, bought out the other partners and decided to alter the business model. They significantly increased production and distribution. The winery now produces 6,500 cases a year, and its products are available at over 300 retail outlets.

Both Marek and Jill see themselves as educators committed to increasing people's appreciation of wine. They have designed classes and events ranging from "Wine 101" to dinners with local chefs and blind tastings. Marek also helps other winemakers. He works on the North Carolina Grape Council, gives numerous presentations at conferences and meetings, and is almost always available for consultations. He says, "It gives me, personally, a lot of satisfaction when I can pass information along to somebody."

Like all true educators, Marek and Jill not only seek to share their knowledge but are constantly learning. They listen carefully to one another, their customers, and other people in the industry. As a result, the winery and its wines are continually changing as they strive to apply what they've learned. In the future, they plan to move the winery from its current location but remain in the area. They would like to find a space, Jill explains, "that will allow us to increase production as well as continue our efforts in education in the wine, art, and culinary experience."

Marek has spent almost 10 years establishing Chatham Hill Winery, and he has never been as excited about its possibilities as he is now. Jill shares his enthusiasm. She says, "We're doing what so many people would like to do. We're living the dream."

Creek Side Winery

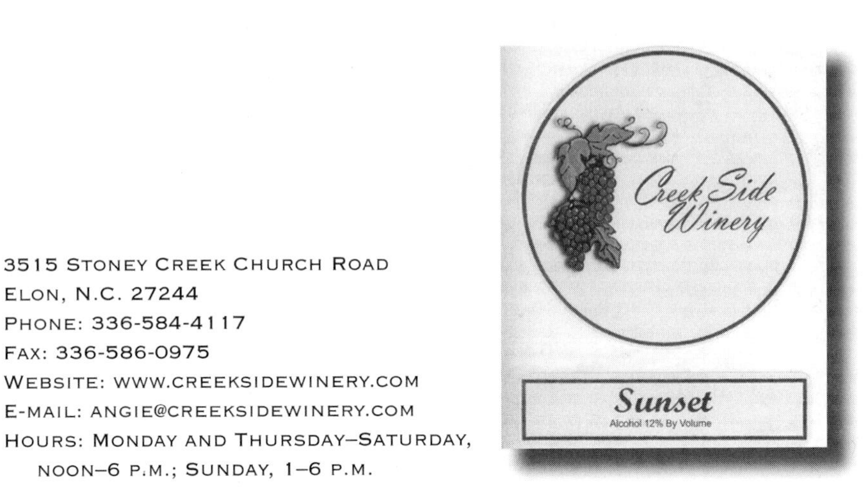

3515 Stoney Creek Church Road
Elon, N.C. 27244
Phone: 336-584-4117
Fax: 336-586-0975
Website: www.creeksidewinery.com
E-mail: angie@creeksidewinery.com
Hours: Monday and Thursday–Saturday, noon–6 p.m.; Sunday, 1–6 p.m.

Owners: Fred and Angie Wallace
Winemaker: Robert Wurz (consultant)
First year as bonded winery: 2005
Tasting fee: Yes
On-line ordering: No
Wine club: No

Wine List
Whites: Chardonnay, Creek Side Sunset (white blend), Creek Side White (dry white)
Blush: Creek Side Blush
Reds: Cabernet Sauvignon, Deep Creek Red (Cabernet Franc), Merlot, Stoney Creek Red (red blend)
Fruits: Chillin' Berry (raspberry), Misty Peach
Specialty: The Reverend's Creek Side Port

Directions: East of Greensboro, take Exit 141 off Interstate 40/85. Go through the town of Elon on Williamson Avenue (the name changes to Shallowford Road) to N.C. 87. Turn left onto N.C. 87 North and go approximately 7 miles. Turn right on Stoney Creek Church Road. The winery is on the left after 1.3 miles.

In 2002, Fred and Angie Wallace had to make a decision about 20 acres of their 52-acre family farm. They had planted vines a couple of years before, and they were considering expanding the vineyards, but as Fred puts it, he and his dad had been "weekend farmers messing with cows" for 20 years. Since they had full-time jobs, the Wallaces didn't think they could tend to both the grapes and the livestock. They decided that "the cows had to go."

Their first years of grape growing were educational. Fred says ruefully, "We've learned all that you can learn from bird control." One summer, they thought they could take a vacation because the grapes weren't yet ripe. It ended up being a costly trip because "we went to the beach and came back and had only one-third of the crop left."

As the Wallaces developed their acreage, local farmers offered helpful advice. Fred took the suggestion of some who said he should "ridge it up, like tobacco rows." This "ridged-row" method makes for better drainage, which is crucial for the vines' roots. Although it makes the rows difficult to work because there is no flat space, Fred says that "since we've done that, the vines have taken off. It's been tremendous." He believes that one key to farming is to remember "you're not going to beat Mother Nature, but you can work with her."

Angie and Fred Wallace

Initially, the Wallaces were part of the Old North State co-op in Mount Airy. However, because they are located much farther east than the other members, their grapes would ripen sooner, and it made scheduling difficult. Since they always intended to establish their own winery, they decided to accelerate their long-term plans and open Creek Side Winery in 2005.

The Wallaces had definite ideas about what they wanted for Creek Side, as they had been visiting wineries all around the country for several years. This hobby began in 1998, when they stopped by Château Morrisette on the Blue Ridge Parkway. Since then, Angie estimates they have visited more than 200 wineries, including ones all up and down the East Coast, across Texas, and even in Hawaii. At each one, they've made notes. Fred explains, "We learn a little of this and a little of that every time. If you can learn one thing, it's worth it."

The Wallaces say that what they value most in a winery are cleanliness and friendliness. They like the social interactions, which is why they prefer small wineries, where "you get that personal touch." They emphasize of Creek Side, "When you come here, you meet the owners." You also meet the builder. A database administrator at Duke University, Fred takes pride in working with his hands, and he built most of the winery himself. He says, "I was brought up to believe if you can do it, why pay somebody? You pay if you don't have the time." He constructed all of the winery's interior walls, the floors, and the ceilings with the help of his uncle and son. For the vineyards, he built a sprayer and the netting system. He even put together the 19 barrel racks. He laughs, "I didn't do the tasting-room counter. I know my limitations."

Creek Side now cultivates five and half acres of grapes. In 2005, the winery produced 1,200 cases. Fred and Angie would like to eventually grow to 3,000 or 3,500 cases. In its wine list, Creek Side tries to provide "a little bit of everything," but it also tries to find "small niches" between the extremely dry and really sweet offerings of other wineries. In the winery's first years, Robert Wurz of Stonefield Cellars has made Creek Side's wines. Eventually, Angie, who has a cooking degree and a background in food service, will become the winemaker.

Creek Side is truly a family affair. Fred's mother sells painted bottles and wine baskets in the tasting room. The Wallaces' son and daughter work in the fields and the winery. In fact, having the family together has been one of the most rewarding aspects of the project. The Wallaces named one wine Creek Side Sunset because of the times that the four of them have watched the sun go down in the vineyards. Fred says, shaking his head, "A lot of people don't see that because they're stuck in the house with videos or TV."

The Wallaces hope to expand their operations in the future. For now, "we're definitely a mom-and-pop shop," Fred states. "We're proud of where we've come from and what we've learned. We're not growing fast, but we've built it from scratch."

Dennis Vineyards

DENNIS
Vineyards
2001 NOBLE
NORTH CAROLINA
SEMI-DRY
ALCOHOL 12% BY VOLUME

24043 Endy Road
Albemarle, N.C. 28001
Phone: 800-230-1743 or 704-982-6090
Fax: 704-986-6128
Website: www.dennisvineyards.com
E-mail: mail@dennisvineyards.com
Hours: Monday–Saturday, 10 a.m.–6 p.m.

Owners: Pritchard and Sandon Dennis
Winemaker: Sandon Dennis
First year as bonded winery: 1997
Tasting fee: No
On-line ordering: No
Wine club: Yes

Wine List
Whites: Bear Creek White, Carlos (dry, semisweet, and sweet), Carlos in the Buff
Blushes: Ison (dry, semisweet, and sweet), Naked Noble
Reds: Bear Creek Red, Carnola (Carlos and Noble), Noble (dry, semisweet, and sweet), Spring
Fruits: Blackberry, Blueberry, Peach, Strawberry
Specialties: Christmas, Harvest Gold (ice-wine style), Sweetheart, White Christmas

Directions: From U.S. 52, turn west on N.C. 24/27 toward Charlotte. Go 5 miles to the Endy community and turn right on Endy Road. The winery is on the left after 0.5 mile.

In 2001, Sandon Dennis and his father, Pritchard, had a difficult decision to make. The family winery, Dennis Vineyards, had been expanding rapidly and badly needed additional space. The logical solution seemed to be to move into a nearby house built in the 1940s by Sandon's grandfather. It was a place, Sandon says, where "a lot of families were started" and where several generations of Dennises had lived. They discovered, however, that making the building compliant with commercial codes would be tremendously expensive, and it still wouldn't provide enough space. Eventually, they had to accept the fact that they should tear the house down and construct a new building. It was a wrenching realization. Sandon's wife, Amy, left town the weekend of the demolition because she couldn't bear to watch.

Most major decisions at Dennis Vineyards involve both personal and business considerations because the winery is fundamentally a family venture. The land has been owned by Dennises for generations. The first wine was made in Pritchard's basement, and the original "tasting room" was his sunroom and back porch. Father and son work together in the vineyards and the winery. Amy keeps the books and manages the tasting room. Sandon and Amy's children occasionally run the label and bottling machines, and nieces and nephews help out as well. Even the winemaking recipe has a long family tradition. Pritchard's grandfather, the area's original mail carrier, was known for his homemade muscadine wine. Sandon laughs, "If anybody had the bellyache or they just wanted

Dennis Vineyards patio
COURTESY OF DENNIS VINEYARDS

to get lit, they went to his house."

Pritchard inherited his grandfather's recipe and made wine as a hobbyist for years. He and his friends would pick grapes in the woods, and neighbors would bring him bucketfuls from vines on their property. He kept modifying and improving the recipe until the mid-1990s, when the wine was so good that Sandon became interested in making some himself. For a while, father and son engaged in a "battle of the batches." Then they started working together. Sandon remembers, "We were just going to have a glorified hobby. We were using the wine in church, in communion, and everybody fell in love with it and wanted to buy it." They began planting vines, but that "got out of hand, and it just kept snowballing." Eventually, they decided to go into commercial production. Now, Dennis Vineyards has over eight acres of muscadine vines and two acres under contract.

The Dennises regard muscadine grapes as part of the region's heritage, and the decision by many people to grow vinifera puzzles them. Because muscadines are native plants, they grow well with little trouble, and they are less prone than vinifera to disease. Sandon explains, "They're really smart vines. They'll only hold the grapes that they can basically carry to maturity. If the load gets too heavy and they get stressed—for example, by a lack of water—they'll start dropping what they can't carry and ripen the rest up. They won't overload themselves. European grapes, you have to thin out." Muscadines make flavorful wines, and Sandon insists they improve with age. A five-year-old wine made from Carlos grapes will be "just as smooth as silk."

In its first years, Dennis Vineyards quickly went from making 500 gallons to 15,000, and the increased production could never keep up with demand. Now, the winery produces approximately 25,000 gallons a year, and certain vintages still sell out. Sandon attributes this to the health benefits of resveratrol, an antioxidant found in some red wines, particularly muscadine wines. According to Sandon, resveratrol has been proven to reduce cholesterol. It also may help with Parkinson's disease, Alzheimer's, certain types of cancer, and problems with blood pressure and the circulatory system. In 1998, researchers at Cornell

University found that Dennis Vineyards' Noble wine contained the second-highest amount of resveratrol of all the wines it tested. This, Sandon notes, "put us on the map."

Many of Dennis Vineyards' customers swear by the wine's medicinal properties. One elderly lady claims that after she started drinking Dennis's Noble wine, her cholesterol dropped 60 points in six months, and that her doctor told her, "Go back and get some more of that!" Another customer buys several cases at a time. His mother has Parkinson's disease, and he believes the wine helps her. She's not healing, but her mind stays sharp, and she doesn't have "the real bad days." He told Sandon, "If you start running low, let me know, and I'll come by and buy the year's supply." The Dennises themselves testify to the wine's benefits. Pritchard had a cholesterol count of over 300, and according to Sandon, "he brought it down to 200 just by drinking the Noble wine alone. He didn't even change his diet." Even so, "sometimes he doesn't drink his wine like he ought to," Sandon says with mock concern. Sandon has brought his own high cholesterol down as well. Although doctors recommend three to four ounces of red wine a day, he admits with a laugh, "I push mine up to six or eight."

The Dennises are convinced that just being in the wine business provides health benefits. Sandon believes that the vineyards have prolonged his father's life. In 1985, Pritchard fell and tore an artery in his neck. At first, the doctors gave him three days to live, but after performing an operation that grafted a facial artery into his neck, they believed that he might live as long as 10 years. After a long and difficult recuperation, he followed medical advice and retired to the coast, where he fished and started studying wine in a serious way. Eight years later, his health had improved to the point that he moved back to Albemarle. A year after the doctors said he would be dead, Pritchard began the vineyards. Sandon says, "It's been unreal. I think if he hadn't come back and started this, I don't think he'd be here." Not only has Pritchard's health stayed strong, but his vision has improved. For years after the accident, he had problems with his sight and wore a patch over one eye. According to Sandon, Pritchard's "vision straightened out" when he

Dennis Vineyards tasting room
COURTESY OF DENNIS VINEYARDS

began working with the vines. Sandon says it can't be explained except by recognizing that "there are greater powers that be." Pritchard suggests that the Lord restored his sight to enable him to tend grapes. So almost every morning, that's what he does. He sets posts, irrigates the vines, and runs the tractor. Watching his father in the fields, Sandon says, "He loves it out there."

Sandon loves the work as well. When researchers discovered the resveratrol amounts in Dennis Vineyards' grapes, they suggested, "You can make medicine, or you can make wine." He responded, "I'm here to make wine." Winemaking is his passion. Sometimes, he becomes so involved in the process that he works past midnight without realizing it. He puts in long hours willingly, an attitude he didn't have in his previous career. Before working full time at the winery, he had a job in the computer industry, which "just burnt me totally out." Amy states bluntly, "He hated it." In contrast, Sandon says that winemaking "is probably one of the funnest things and the most rewarding things I've ever done." He insists that "no matter how bad the day was, I go home smiling. Not everyone can say that they've got a job they love. I love this. I can work day and night doing it."

Although he didn't like working in the industry, Sandon's computer background has been useful. For one, it enabled him to design the winery's labels, each of which displays a varietal or fruit. "What you see on the bottle is what's in the bottle," he says. The winery also offers special labels for Christmas and commemorative labels for events such as weddings and anniversaries. When the Cycle North Carolina tour went from Boone to Wilmington, it stopped at Dennis Vineyards. That afternoon, Sandon remembers, "there must have been $50,000 to $100,000 worth of bicycles scattered on the lawn." He designed a special label for the participants, then delivered their wine orders to them in Wilmington at the end of the tour. That kind of personal attention makes the winery a popular destination. Groups ranging from car clubs to elementary-school teachers hold meetings at Dennis Vineyards.

It was to better accommodate such groups that the family built the new tasting room. Although tearing down the old house was bittersweet, the construction of the new building enabled the winery to grow, and Sandon made sure it included ties to the past. Not only does the building have a shape similar to the former one, but the house's old kitchen was saved and installed next to the tasting room to allow catered events. It is a fitting symbol of the Dennises' effort to both pay tribute to their family history and address their present-day needs.

In 2006, Dennis Vineyards expanded again, opening a new events facility to host weddings, receptions, and meetings. Sandon also has other long-term projects in mind, which isn't surprising, since he says, "I feel like I can be doing this until 60-plus and probably won't quit until I die. My dad won't, and his dad didn't." Sandon tells the story of his grandfather, who lived to be 91. At 78, he had open-heart surgery. "When he got out of surgery," Sandon recalls, "he came to and said, 'I need to use the phone.' They said, 'Why?' He said, 'I've got to call my mother and tell her I'm okay.' They were like, 'You have a hot line to heaven?' He said, 'No, my mother's still alive.' She was 99 years old, and he had to call and reassure her." Sandon laughs, "I've got some long-lived people. My great-grandmother lived to 104, so I may be making wine for a long time."

Desi's Dew Meadery

8902 Charlotte's Mountain Road
Rougemont, N.C. 27572
Phone: 919-632-4770
Website: www.desidew.com
E-mail: bill.bailey@desidew.com
Hours: By appointment only

Owner: William Bailey
Mead maker: William Bailey
First year as bonded winery: 2000
Tasting fee: No
On-line ordering: No
Wine club: No

Wine List
Meads: Desi and Jack's Blackberry Mead, Desi's Tupelo Jubilee Mead, Raspberry Sparkling Mead, The Royal Table's Own Dry Mead, The Royal Table's Own Sweet Mead, Wildflower Sparkling Mead

Directions: From Interstate 85 in Durham County, take Exit 175 (Guess Road) and head north for approximately 10 miles. Go right on New Sharon Church Road, drive approximately 1.5 miles, and turn right on Charlotte's Mountain Road. The winery is on the left after approximately 0.25 mile.

Desi's Dew Meadery is not your typical winery. You won't find oak barrels, presses, or nearby vineyards. Its owner, Bill Bailey, makes only mead, or "honey wine," and it can take people awhile to realize what this means. Bill says, "There are some who constantly ask where the grapes

Bill Bailey

are, and after five or six times, they finally get it."

Bill was introduced to the drink in the mid-1990s by a friend who made mead and beer. He remembers thinking, "This is pretty good. I think I could do a good job doing it." He began making mead as a hobby. A few years later, as he was looking for an alternative to his work as a software engineer, he decided to open Desi's Dew.

Bill enjoys working with mead because "you can do all kinds of things with it. You can make it very sweet or dry. You can use all kinds of spices." Not only is Desi's Dew the only meadery in the state, it is one of only two in the country that offer "sparkling" meads, which are riddled and disgorged by hand in a champagne-type method. Since this is a rare variation on an unfamiliar product, Bill laughs that for a while many of his neighbors thought he was making "sparkling meat."

Bill named the meadery after a favorite cat, Desyrl, who died of kidney failure. "She was a beautiful cat," he explains. He honors her memory by putting her photo somewhere on every label. He also notes, however, that "it'd be ridiculous to name it after Bill Bailey. People would say, 'What's that guy smoking?'"

Since Bill had never run a business before, there have been "costly learning experiences." He remembers that when he opened, he told his

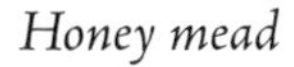
Honey mead

wife "I'd be in the black in a year or two. . . . She won't believe that again." He also admits, "If I knew some of the things I know now, I would be a bit more reluctant or a bit more cautious." Despite the financial struggles, Bill laughs that the business "does keep getting me into interesting and bizarre adventures." He also believes his products have been getting better each year. He is particularly proud of his Tupelo mead, which he says people like so much that he finds it difficult to make enough to meet demand.

As a meadery, Desi's Dew occupies a unique position in the state's industry. Bill says, "Other wineries treat me like a kid brother. They're not threatened by me. I'm an aberrant. They're probably thinking, 'He's nutty as a fruitcake.'" He does acknowledge, however, that local wineries like Chatham Hill have been helpful in sharing information and selling him equipment and supplies. Regarding the future, Bill sometimes thinks he might like to scale up production and move from the glass carboys he currently uses to stainless-steel tanks, but he acknowledges that his interests shift from day to day.

As for visitors to the meadery, which is a small storage building next to his house, Bill says, "I'm more than happy to entertain." However, people should be aware that there are no typical winery amenities such as picnic tables, and they should call and make an appointment first.

Garden Gate Vineyards

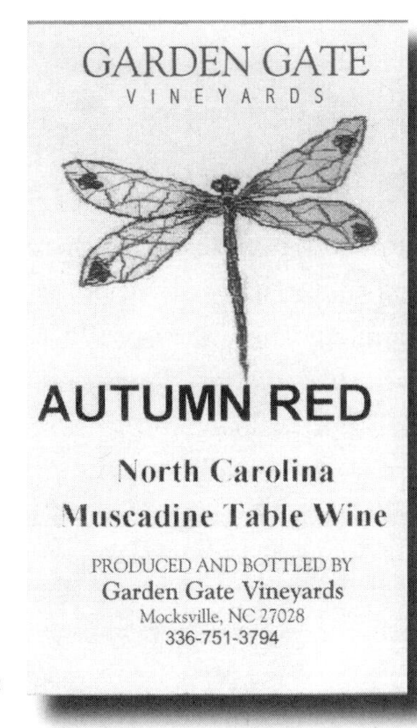

261 Scenic Drive
Mocksville, N.C. 27028
Phone: 336-751-3794 or
336-941-7721
Fax: 336-751-3794
Website:
www.gardengatevineyards.com
E-mail: gardengate@yadtel.net
Hours: Wednesday–Saturday,
noon–5 p.m.

Owners: Bob and Sonya Whitaker
Winemakers: Bob and Sonya Whitaker
First year as bonded winery: 2002
Tasting fee: No
On-line ordering: No
Wine club: No

Wine List
Whites: Jitterbug, Scuppernong
Blush: Scarlet Blush
Reds: Autumn Red, Muscadine
Fruits: Blackberry, Blueberry, Raspberry, Strawberry

Directions: From Interstate 40 west of Winston-Salem, take Exit 168. Turn east on U.S. 64 toward Mocksville. Go 0.25 mile, take a right on Green Hill Road, go 1.5 miles, take a left on County Home Road, go approximately 0.5 mile, and turn right on Scenic Drive. The winery is on the right.

Bob and Sonya Whitaker are doing what they've been told can't be done. They have built a winery, and they are running it without going into debt. What's more, they're enjoying themselves. They've managed to accomplish this rare feat by staying small, doing the work themselves, and keeping their goals modest.

When the Whitakers opened Garden Gate Vineyards at their house in 2002, they decided to try to make $50 a week. Sonya explains, "We didn't want any stress on us." They weren't out to create a large showcase winery. Instead, they wanted to make small batches of wine and sell it in a low-key, friendly atmosphere. In their first year, they made 600 gallons and sold it all, easily reaching their weekly goals. Each year, they made more, and now they produce about 2,000 gallons annually. However, even this amount, Sonya says, "doesn't go far enough."

Garden Gate specializes in fruit wines. Bob remembers that the first time he and Sonya went to a festival, other wineries called them rednecks. Although he says people were kidding, he points out that

Bob Whitaker

Sonya Whitaker

Garden Gate had the last laugh because "our wines sold out, and the next year, they all had fruit wines."

The Whitakers also make muscadine and scuppernong wines, and part of their vineyards are set aside for a you-pick operation each fall. The couple prefers American grapes to European ones for a number of reasons. Muscadine grapes have demonstrated health benefits. Since they are native to the area, they are more disease resistant, and growing them doesn't require irrigation or pesticides. Finally, they offer the unique taste of the area. Bob finds it puzzling that people constantly want North Carolina's wine industry to mimic California's or Europe's: "Why copy someone else's wine when you can make your own wine?"

The Whitakers emphasize the organic qualities of their wines. Bob notes, "We're proud to say our wine is as close to homemade as you can get." They do everything by hand, which has allowed them to remain out of debt. Sonya points out, "People think you have to have a million dollars. A winery's costly, but you don't need that. You can do it." It does require, however, a do-it-yourself work ethic. Bob explains, "Everything from the building to the cement porch—we haven't paid anyone to do anything. We probably saved $30,000 to $40,000 in labor doing it ourselves."

Bob sees an irony in the work he has put into Garden Gate. People tell him, "Your daddy was a good carpenter and farmer. You never liked to do it, and now you do more than he did." However, Bob knew when he retired from his job at a power company that he needed to find something that would keep him outside, active, and involved with other people. He joked at his retirement party that he was going to go home and "either make wine or make liquor." They're natural interests, since, as Bob explains, there is "a long line of bootleggers" in his family. Even before opening Garden Gate, he had made wine for years as a hobbyist.

The winery is a logical extension of Sonya's interests as well. An artist, she has thrown pottery since 1984, and Garden Gate provides her with a permanent exhibition space. In fact, the winery itself serves as an example of her work. She decorated the tasting room's interior, designed the patio arbor, and created the wine labels, which feature a dragonfly because, according to Sonya, "a dragonfly landing on you is a sign of good luck."

In designing Garden Gate, the Whitakers tried to create a place that would offer people a leisurely, personal experience. They have stools inside their tasting room, a separate room available for meetings and banquets, and picnic tables outside. Sonya insists, "No one aggravates you or wants you to go on." People will sometimes stay two or three hours, and that's fine with the Whitakers, who are happy to talk to them, listen, or leave them alone. As a result, "our customers bring people back, and they say it's because of the way they've been treated," Bob says. Yet Sonya points out that the appreciation goes both ways: "We meet the nicest people." They have developed several long-term friendships with customers and even have had people from out-of-state invite them to visit and stay in their homes.

The Whitakers have been told that they should charge for tastings, but they refuse because, as Bob explains, "if my neighbor comes across to taste my wine, it's an honor." Children are encouraged to explore the vineyards and even eat the ripe berries. Bob laughs at anyone who would be surprised by such generosity: "If I ever get that tight, just cut the vines down." The Whitakers know that people can be generous in return. One year, someone stole a crop of grapes at a vineyard they lease. When friends and customers heard the news, they offered grapes from their own land. People with only four or five vines picked bucketfuls and brought them in, and no one wanted money.

By staying small, the Whitakers have made Garden Gate successful, and they believe their winery might even serve as a model for others. Bob points out that in the 1960s, Davie County had 135 farms. Now, there are only five. He remembers his father telling him that if he wanted to go into agriculture, he needed to head west because "farming is over here." However, Bob believes that viticulture may offer people a way to go back to farming. Grapes are a viable crop, they don't hurt the land, and they offer a way to retain some open spaces. They offer another benefit as well. A vineyard is, Bob says, "one of the most beautiful things I've ever seen."

Germanton Art Gallery and Winery

3530 N.C. 8 and N.C. 65
Germanton, N.C. 27019
Phone: 800-322-2894 or 336-969-6121
Fax: 336-969-6559
Website: www.germantongallery.com
E-mail: sales@germantongallery.com
Hours: Tuesday–Friday, 10 a.m.–6 p.m.;
Saturday, 9 a.m.–5 p.m.

Owners: David and Judy Simpson
Winemaker: Jerry Pegram
First year as bonded winery: 1981
Tasting fee: Yes
On-line ordering: No
Wine club: No

Wine List
Whites: Chardonnay, Niagara, Seyval Blanc
Blush: Autumn Blush
Reds: Chambourcin, Merlot, Sweet Red Wine, Vermillion

Directions: From U.S. 52 north of Winston-Salem, take the N.C. 8 (Germanton Road) exit and go 7 miles north to Germanton. The winery and Germanton Art Gallery are on the corner of N.C. 8 and Friendship Road.

One year, artist Jim Wilson was in Alaska's Denali National Park taking a workshop with Robert Bateman, a world-famous artist and environmentalist. After dinner one night, the discussion turned to exhi-

Germanton Winery

bitions. Someone asked Bateman what his most memorable show was. He thought for a minute, then said, "There's this little gallery and winery in North Carolina that everybody ought to go to."

Not surprisingly, Wilson's friends David and Judy Simpson were pleased when they heard this story. They own the Germanton Art Gallery and Winery, two businesses combined in one building. It's an arrangement the Simpsons feel "works great" because "people that enjoy good wine enjoy nice art, too." They have exhibited work by Bateman and other internationally known artists in their unpretentious space, a renovated gas station. David says, "When you walk through the front door of this little building, I think it's just a warm little place that kind of grabs you."

The winery began as a type of cooperative in the 1970s. Several people who wanted to grow grapes started the venture on the farm of William "Big Bill" McGee. They also set up an experimental vineyard on his land in which they grew 18 different varietals. David remembers the day in 1981 when the winery opened for business: "We got up that morning, and there were people everywhere on the farm. People sleeping in sheds and in barns. They'd been there all night. There were people here from Kentucky, all over the country, to buy those first bottles of wine. . . . By midday, we realized that we were going to have to start limiting wine—so many bottles per person—so it would last. We sold out completely the first day."

David and Judy Simpson

Although many people were involved, Bill McGee was the winery's driving force. He served as president, accountant, salesman, and public-relations person. In short, according to David, "he took care of everything." Tragically, Bill was killed in 1986. "The farm was such a sad, sad place when he was gone," Judy remembers. "We just really had to start over then, and we, in most instances, have learned the hard way." Because they lived on the property, David and Judy were asked to take care of the winery. Finally, they decided to become partners in it as well. Eventually, they bought the others out.

As the Simpsons educated themselves about the wine business, they often went against conventional wisdom. For example, David notes that "in the beginning, a lot of people told us, 'Don't do blends' and 'Don't do sweet wines' because people won't buy them. Well, every wine magazine that you pick up now, all they're talking about is blends." They encountered numerous problems, particularly with distributors. Judy says, "We've had everything go wrong and made every kind of mistake that you can think of." Nevertheless, they persisted, in part because they felt a responsibility to Bill McGee, whose photograph they keep above the tasting-room bar. Judy says, "He's why we keep doing it." David adds, "I hate that Bill can't be here to see all this [excitement about the Yadkin Valley] because his vision was wineries all over this area. Just like Napa

Valley. He was so far ahead of his time in his dreams and beliefs."

The other half of the business, the Germanton Art Gallery, started with two dollars. One day while working at the R. J. Reynolds Tobacco Company, David was "sitting behind a cigarette machine and pretty much [thinking] that was where I was going to be the rest of my life." He brought a raffle ticket for two dollars and won. The prize was a Harley-Davidson motorcycle. Because he was interested in photography, he sold the Harley and used the money to buy framing equipment. That was the beginning of a gallery he ran out of his basement, where, as a matter of convenience, he began selling Germanton wine as well.

In the early years, the gallery concentrated on framing prints. Eventually, the focus changed to original works. Several times, its annual miniature show, which focuses on small-scale works and takes place the first weekend in December, has been voted one of the best art shows in the country by *U.S. Art* magazine. The gallery attracts visitors from all over the world, a fact David attributes in part to its website, which gets more than 60,000 hits a month.

So many artists want to exhibit their work at the Germanton Art Gallery that the Simpsons must turn away hundreds of submissions each year. Judy believes the gallery appeals to artists for a simple reason: honesty. She says, "Artists are battered all over the world. Their art is taken for granted. They're mistreated." By contrast, the Simpsons treat them with respect. "We don't cheat them," David says. "So many gallery owners have the mind-set that if it wasn't for them, the artists wouldn't be there. We have the opposite mind-set. If it wasn't for the artists, we wouldn't be here."

After years of running the gallery out of a basement, the Simpsons saw an opportunity to expand when a nearby gas station went up for sale. Built in 1929, it had been abandoned for a long time. David remembers, "It looked so bad that I was the only one who showed up at the auction." After buying it, they renovated the space and filled it with art and other materials. David laughs, "We collect junk. Most everything in this building is stuff that we had stored in our sheds at the farm." In one corner, they put an oak bar top to serve as the winery's tasting "room"—

or, as Judy calls it, "our liquid art department." Getting approval for the new facility, however, was not easy. Although the combination of gallery and winery seemed natural to them, it caused problems for the state's regulatory system. The various agencies didn't know how to classify the business. It took months to sort out the paperwork.

A display of Germanton wines fits nicely into a gallery environment because, as might be expected, the labels reflect the Simpsons' interest in art. The Germanton Winery does 10-color labels, which David believes is unique in the industry. Each wine features a different watercolor scene. The winery also does a variety of special labels and promotions. For example, one featured NASCAR legend Junior Johnson, who came to the gallery for a signing event. Others showcase artists. David points out, "An artist's dream is to get their work into a museum, but it's also now to get it on a wine label. It's really neat, if you're doing a show or a charity or whatever, to hand someone a bottle with your artwork on the label." The winery also does special labels to raise money for environmental groups, including the American Farmland Trust (the only nonprofit organization dedicated exclusively to preserving farmland) and the Florida Wildlife and Western Art Exposition.

The Simpsons feel a sense of responsibility and stewardship. They have worked hard to protect the legacy of Bill McGee. They believe strongly in preserving farmland and engaging in responsible practices that will protect it for the future. They regularly showcase environmental artists in the gallery. Every Memorial Day weekend, the gallery sponsors a show called "Things with Wings," in which the work, according to Judy, "has to have a pair of wings in the painting somewhere. It can be an airplane, a butterfly, a dragonfly. It can be a statue in a park." As part of the exhibition, the Simpsons bring to the gallery not only many of the artists, but also people from Wild Haven, Inc., an organization dedicated to nature education and wildlife rehabilitation, particularly of birds of prey.

In 2006, the winery celebrated its 25th anniversary, a substantial achievement. As they look to the future, the Simpsons have a number of long-range plans. None of them, however, involves becoming a large, automated operation capable of producing tens of thousands of cases. David says, "We have no desire to be big. I'm glad Shelton, Westbend, and RayLen are doing what they're doing. It's good for everyone. But we want to stay small. We do everything literally by hand. We crush by hand. Press by hand. Bottle and label by hand. And that's the way we'd like to keep it." Such a philosophy requires a tremendous time commitment, and the Simpsons admit they can maintain their tiring schedule only because of the help of their son Michael McGee and their nephew Tommy Preston. Judy says, "Without them, we could not do this."

Despite the demands of running the winery, the Simpsons don't regret what they regard as an adventure and "a great learning experience." David insists, "We're having fun. Life's too short not to." He believes in the value of what they're doing. He says with confidence, "The wine is good. The art's good. If you come here and experience this, you may not buy right away, but you'll be back."

GlenMarie Vineyards and Winery

1838 Johnson Road
Burlington, N.C. 27217
Phone: 336-578-3938
Website:
www.glenmariewinery.com
E-mail: glenmariewinery@aol.com
Hours: Thursday–Sunday, noon–6 p.m.

Owners: Glendale and Joyce Marie Dickey
Winemaker: Glendale Dickey
First year as bonded winery: 2005
Tasting fee: Yes
On-line ordering: No
Wine club: No

Wine List
Whites: Chardonnay, Golden Nugget (blend of two French-hybrid grapes), Scuppernong, Summer's Promise (blend of four white wines including Riesling)
Blush: Syrah Carolina Springtime (red and white blend)
Reds: Cabernet Sauvignon, Chambourcin, Dallas Red (French-hybrid blend), Muscadine, Sweet Marie
Fruits: Blackberry, Strawberry

Directions: From Interstate 40/85 East, take Exit 150 and turn left on Jimmy Kerr Road. At the fourth light, turn right on Bason Road. Go approximately 3 miles, turn left on Mebane Rogers Road, go 1.5 miles, and turn right on Johnson Road. The winery is on the left. From Interstate 40/85 West, take Exit 150, turn right on Jimmy Kerr Road, and continue as above.

The Dickeys

Glendale Dickey laughs that when his wife, Joyce Marie, retired and he sold his business, she thought they might take a cruise, "but we built a wine rack instead." When they finished it, there were other tasks to complete in the tasting room that they intended to open in their house's renovated carport. Finally, on March 5, 2005, Glendale's 66th birthday, the husband and wife officially unlocked the door to GlenMarie Vineyards and Winery.

The winery's origins can be traced to a winemaking kit that the couple's son Ivan gave his father in 1999. As his new hobby developed, Glendale made larger and larger batches. Joyce notes wryly, "When you get down to it, 200 gallons is a lot of wine for two people to have." The Dickeys decided to throw a party to see what people thought of the wine, and 150 people came and drank four cases. "We had a good time," Joyce remembers. At a second party, word of mouth resulted in more than 350 people showing up. Encouraged by this interest, the Dickeys decided to look into getting a license.

Glendale admits, "If anybody had told me that I would have a winery, I would have said, 'You've got to be kidding.' " Other people were skeptical as well. Joyce says that when they went to one government office for paperwork, the clerk asked, "Why are you even doing this thing?" For the Dickeys, the logical answer was "We want to."

In establishing GlenMarie, the couple planted two acres of grapes on leased land that had been used in the past for growing tobacco. As someone who grew up on a farm, Glendale enjoys experimenting with different grapes, and the vineyards contain 23 varietals. Glendale ferments each one separately, then blends them into small batch wines. Pointing out that the largest container in the winery is 132 gallons, he notes, "We do everything the big wineries do, but on a smaller scale."

Because the winery is at their home, it has a number of personal touches, such as a fireplace and a couch in the tasting room. There are also reminders of former careers. Joyce directed the Child Development Center at First Presbyterian Church, so GlenMarie is one of the few wineries that has Legos and children's books available. Glendale used to own a gem and rock business, so their son Michael constructed an outdoor fountain using rocks collected from all over the world.

The Dickeys like their size and location, even though visitors sometimes drive past looking for a larger building. Glendale says that although people often think of wineries as huge castles, they shouldn't: "You go back through history, and you're going to see all these little, small wineries." Having the winery at their home means they can attend to it and also take a break when they want. For the Haw River Wine Trail event, Art on the Vine, they had people at GlenMarie until nine at night. Joyce points out that it was nice to just step through the door and be home. Furthermore, Glendale admits that sometimes in the winery, "we'll be in here bottling and sampling this and that and then get the giggles and have to quit and go inside and get something to eat."

GlenMarie doesn't distribute its wines, and the Dickeys attend only a few festivals. Glendale likes the way this makes their product a unique experience: "If you want our wines, you've got to come see us." In 2006, the winery made approximately 1,200 gallons, and the Dickeys don't have plans to become much larger. They would like to make enough to buy some land beside their property before it gets developed and leaves them looking at a row of back doors. Glendale says, "We're going to do just what we're doing for 10 to 15 years." He jokes, however, that there have been some changes. He says of his partnership with his wife, "It was very simple. When we started out, I was going to get to boss for four days, and she would boss for three. Then it became she bossed for four and I would boss for three. Now, she's the boss for seven days, and I'm the boss for zero." When Joyce hears this, she counters, "I boss, but he doesn't listen."

Joyce notes that her husband has said about the winery, "Of the things we've accomplished, except for the children, this is what I'm most proud of." Running GlenMarie is a lot of work. The Dickeys have yet to take a cruise, but Glendale insists, "We have fun making wine. If you can't have fun with it, you don't need to mess with it."

Rock fountain

Grove Winery

7360 Brooks Bridge Road
Gibsonville, N.C. 27249
Phone: 336-584-4060
Website: www.grovewinery.com
E-mail: info@grovewinery.com
Hours: Monday–Saturday, noon–5 p.m.; Sunday, 1–5 p.m.

Owners: Max and Denise Lloyd
Winemaker: Bob Moncsko
First year as bonded winery: 2004
Tasting fee: Yes
On-line ordering: Yes
Wine club: Yes

Wine List
Whites: Chardonnay, Haw River White (white blend), Niagara, Traminette
Reds: Cabernet Sauvignon, Claret (red blend), Merlot, Nebbiolo, Norton, Red Clay Red, Sangiovese, Tempranillo

Directions: From Greensboro, take U.S. 29 North to the Browns Summit exit. Go east on N.C. 150 and stay straight on Osceola-Ossipee Road for approximately 7.5 miles, then take a left on Brooks Bridge Road. The winery is on the right.

Max Lloyd's wine education began after his college education was finished. Upon graduating, he got a job as a computer programmer, and

Max Lloyd

his company sent him to install software in a hospital in Sonoma, California. There, as "a young kid with his first expense account," he toured the small farm wineries of the area. Since it was a simpler time "before the limos," as Max puts it, and since he had his afternoons free, he often helped out in the vineyards. Consequently, Max laughs, "as a redneck guy growing up drinking beer, my first introduction to wine was the great Cabernets and Zinfandels of Sonoma." He went on to learn about Rieslings, Gewürztraminers, and the other wines of the world.

Eventually, Max's career brought him back to the Southeast, where he had grown up. In 1993, he decided to plant a vineyard, Vista Ridge, in southern Virginia near Smith Mountain. He and his family began growing Cabernet Sauvignon and Norton and teaching themselves about viticulture. Max admits, "We probably made every mistake you can make," but he also is quick to point out that "with every field, we got better and better." Eventually, they began to consider going commercial, but they realized that "to make money, we either needed a very large vineyard or our own winery." Consequently, Max began to look for a location in North Carolina.

Max knew that he wanted a site with an elevation of at least 700 feet and an easterly aspect. He also wanted the land to be relatively close to the Virginia vineyard. In 2001, after looking at several properties, he chose 44 acres in the Haw River area. Max insists, "It's a great location" that, in addition to having a slope that provides good drainage, has "beautiful soil" containing key minerals. Max is experimenting with tilling in seashells to enhance the vineyard further.

To establish Grove Winery, which opened in 2004, Max and his partners have planted Nebbiolo, Sangiovese, Chardonnay, Traminette, and Tempranillo on seven acres. However, they know that grape growing is a long-term educational process. No growing year is the same. Max points out, "You have a couple years of drought, and everybody talks about irrigation," and then there will be a summer of constant rain. Consequently, it may be years before they know what grows best on the site. Grove uses grapes from Vista Ridge, which is 65 miles to the north. As it develops its estate vineyard, it also buys from local growers, including, Max notes, "a guy I played football against in high school." For Grove, one key to a quality product is that every vineyard is close enough that the grapes can go from the field to the crush pad in less than 90 minutes.

Max likes Grove's location not only because of the possibilities of its soil and the proximity of other quality vineyards, but also because it's halfway between the Triangle and the Triad, two of the state's metropolitan areas. As a result, the winery gets all kinds of visitors, arriving in all kinds of ways. Max explains, "We've had people on motorcycles. A lot of bikers. We've done tastings for people on horseback. We've had people come by airplane, since there's a landing strip nearby."

No matter how people get there, Max and Grove's tasting-room staff tell them about other wineries, particularly the ones on the Haw River Wine Trail. Max insists that these wineries are "producing some of the best wines in the state." The group has even begun the process of having the region recognized as a distinct American Viticultural Area. In addition to offering informal recommendations and pooling their advertising resources, the five Haw River Wine Trail wineries often hold events together. For Mother's Day, in conjunction with Creek Side Winery, Grove offers four chocolates paired with four wines. For Father's Day, they pair four cheeses with four wines. Max points out, "The good thing about a winery is that it gets people to stop and try local food."

As much as Max admires California wines, Grove looks eastward for its models. He explains, "We definitely want to be European-style. We're not opposed to doing a little blending. We can learn a lot more from the wineries in Italy, Spain, and France, rather than California or Australia. Those are great wines, but they're in a desert." Overall, Grove's governing philosophy is to keep things as simple as possible. Max insists, "We're minimalist in the vineyard and the winery." This philosophy can be seen in the winery's name, which Max chose because he thought it was easy to remember, and its uncluttered labels. It can also be seen in the building itself, which, Max admits, is functional without being romantic.

Eventually, Max would like Grove to have amenities such as a shaded arbor or a picnic area by the pond. He would like to make the tasting room more appealing, and he would also like to grow the winery's production at least to its capacity of 4,200 cases. However, as a winery owner, the CEO of a semiconductor software firm, and a father of three, he finds that he never has enough time. He says, "You never get everything done that needs to be done. You never catch up." Still, he can at least enjoy watching others relax. He says, "My favorite time at the winery is at the end of the day, and maybe a family is having a party. You see them having a good time, and maybe the kids are playing." Max insists, "That makes the work worth it."

Horizon Cellars

466 Vineyard Ridge
Siler City, N.C. 27344
Phone: 919-742-1404
Fax: 919-742-3885
Website: www.horizoncellars.com
E-mail: info@horizoncellars.com
Hours: Monday, Thursday, and Friday,
11 a.m.–5 p.m.;
Saturday, 11 a.m.–6 p.m.;
Sunday, noon–6 p.m.

Owners: Guy and Nicole Loeffler
Winemakers: Chris Pearmund and Guy Loeffler
First year as bonded winery: 2004
Tasting fee: Yes
On-line ordering: Yes
Wine club: Yes

Wine List
Whites: Carolina Comfort, Chardonnay, Viognier
Reds: Cabernet Franc, Cabernet Sauvignon, Chambourcin, Syrah
Desserts: Late Harvest Vidal, Late Harvest Viognier

Directions: From Siler City in Chatham County, drive south on U.S. 421 for 2 miles. Take Exit 168 (South Chatham Extension) and turn right. Go 1 mile to Old U.S. 421, turn left, go 0.75 mile, and turn right on Vineyard Ridge; you will cross railroad tracks and a one-lane bridge. Follow the gravel Vineyard Ridge as it veers left after about 0.5 mile. The winery is on the right at the top of the ridge.

Guy Loeffler

Guy Loeffler is a man with a plan. Literally. When he told his wife, Nicole, that he wanted to start a winery, she said, "I want to see a business plan." Guy found this encouraging, since it wasn't an outright no. He admits, "She's heard a few crazy ideas from me before." Six months later, he gave her three pounds of documents, including a five-year business plan, and after reviewing them, she gave her approval.

Nicole knew that Guy had grown frustrated with his job at Hewlett-Packard. After 20 years in information technology, Guy says he "got tired of the corporate life." One day, he had a particularly bad conference call with his boss. To cool off, he went to lunch. While at a café, he began flipping through a copy of *On The Vine*, a periodical about the state's wine industry. "Wow," he thought, "North Carolina has wineries." The newsletter piqued his interest, and he began visiting vineyards and wineries. Soon, he became interested in establishing his own.

A methodical man with an impressive amount of energy, Guy states matter-of-factly, "I do research." And the more he researched the wine business, the more impressed he was by it. In particular, he was struck by people's willingness to help. At one point, he sent out requests for information to 50 or 60 wineries, and he heard back from two-thirds of them. He was stunned by the level of response: "I wasn't used to this in the corporate world."

As Guy talked to people, someone suggested that he contact Chris Pearmund, a winemaker in Virginia. He did so, and the two discovered they had much in common. In December 2002, Guy visited Chris's winery, Pearmund Cellars, and he remembers that Chris immediately "had me in the bathroom hanging dry wall. You've got to love someone who puts you to work the first time they meet you. . . . He was getting me to take off my rose-colored glasses. It's about the work and doing what needs to be done." As Guy developed his plan, Chris agreed to serve as a consultant. Eventually, he became a partner in the venture.

Guy decided to develop a "destination model" for the winery. He says, "I knew I wanted people driving through my vineyard." Although people encouraged him to move to the Yadkin Valley, he wanted to stay relatively close to the Triangle area, where Nicole works as an attorney, so for months he drove the back roads on nights and weekends, looking for potential vineyard sites. Eventually, he saw an ad in the *Agricultural Review*. After calling, he checked out the property. It had the characteristics that Guy was looking for, including elevation and deep soil, and he bought it in 2003.

Originally, Guy planned to plant 14 acres, but examining Chris's vineyard made him change his mind. Guy notes, "You can grow grapes anywhere in the world, but you can't grow every grape everywhere." He decided to plant some varietals and buy other grapes from local growers. To determine what would work best on his site, he started relatively small. After timbering the property, which was covered with loblolly pines, he put in five acres of Chambourcin, Viognier, and Cabernet Franc.

Once he had begun establishing the vineyard, Guy turned his attention to the winery. He designed the building and helped with much of its construction. He notes of the experience, "I was the general contractor, and my wife says I will never, ever general-contract again. I love her, so I'll listen to her." Guy is proud of the results, however, which include a large, open tasting room and a deck that overlooks the vineyard.

In his plan, Guy envisioned a 5,000-case winery, one that would sell primarily through its tasting room. He says, "I'd love to have that boutique winery that you don't see in the magazines or newspapers, but people are always talking about." In its first year, Horizon Cellars made 500 cases of wine and won several awards. The second year, production was increased to 1,000 cases, and again the wines did well in competitions. They included what Guy believes is "one of the best Viogniers on the East Coast."

Then, just as Guy and Chris were about to gear up production in the third year and find a distributor, the winery's future was put in jeopardy. In 2006, a Maryland company announced that it wanted to establish a quarry adjacent to Horizons Cellars. Since the quarry would operate seven days a week, 24 hours a day, it would have a major impact on the winery. Because of the dust, dirt, noise, and light pollution, Horizon Cellars would no longer be able to host weddings or do outside events. Despite organizing a formal complaint, circulating a petition, and filing a lawsuit, Guy fears that, ultimately, "we don't have what it takes to stop them."

At the same time Guy heard about the proposed quarry, he learned that the railroad company wanted to close the main access to Horizon Cellars, which is a small bridge that crosses a set of tracks. Guy found this particularly upsetting, since he had contacted the company, offered to renovate the bridge at his own expense, and shown a railroad representative around. In trying to do the right thing and make improvements, Guy feels like he drew attention to himself and was penalized.

The threat of the quarry and the potential closing of the winery's main access have significantly changed how Guy does business. Instead of following his five-year plan, he now operates Horizon Cellars in an environment of day-to-day uncertainty. Nevertheless, he refuses to allow an unclear future to paralyze him or to make him second-guess decisions. He believes that "hindsight affects your judgment. It keeps you from moving forward." He also points out that years ago, when he and Nicole discussed whether or not to open a winery, they asked themselves, "What's the worst-case scenario? What would happen if we don't succeed?" They realized, according to Guy, "if we go belly up, we could lose all our money and five or six years of our lives. We might have to go back to living in apartments and driving secondhand cars. And we decided that we could live with that."

As Guy fights to protect his winery, he still manages to focus on the business's pleasures, including the artistic satisfaction of "coaxing wine into the bottle." He says, "This is going to sound sappy, but the best thing about having a winery is that little five-minute block of pleasure or satisfaction that I bring to the customers when they taste the wines. They say, 'Wow, these are really good.' And it's something I've created and made and have brought to them. That's rewarding." Whatever happens with Horizon Cellars, Guy is proud of what he's accomplished. He believes, "I'll either succeed big or fail big. Either way, I have the satisfaction of knowing that I've done the job as best as I can."

Old Stone Vineyard and Winery

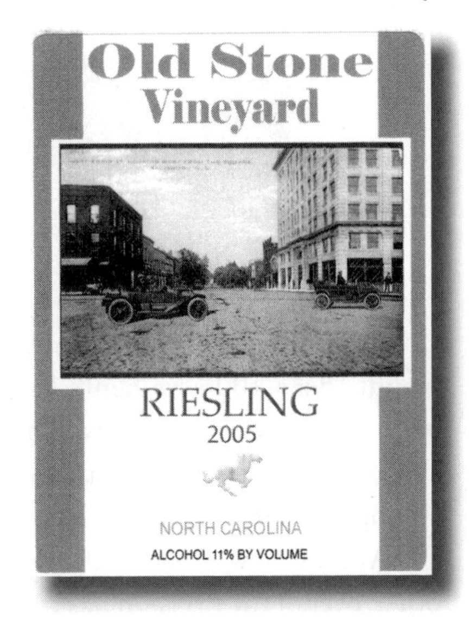

6245 U.S. 52
Salisbury, N.C. 28146
Phone: 704-279-0930
Fax: 704-279-3139
Website: www.osvwinery.com
E-mail: A contact form is on the website.
Hours: Tuesday–Saturday, 11 a.m.–6 p.m.; Sunday, 1–5 p.m.

Owner: Mark Brown
Winemaker: Mark Brown
First year as bonded winery: 2003
Tasting fee: No
On-line ordering: Yes
Wine club: Yes

Wine List
Whites: Carlos (semidry), Carlos Riesling, Carlos Sweet, Chardonnay, Harvest Gold, Riesling
Blush: Wild Horse
Reds: Noble (semidry), Peckerhead Red (Cabernet Sauvignon, Cabernet Franc, and Merlot)
Fruits: Blackberry, Peach
Specialty: Noble Cabernet Sauvignon (dessert)

Directions: From Interstate 85, take Exit 76 and go 5 miles south on U.S. 52. The winery is on the left 1 mile south of the town of Granite Quarry.

In 2001, after more than 15 years working as an animator in the California film industry, Mark Brown felt himself getting "extremely

Mark Brown at Salute!

burned out by being in Los Angeles." He decided to return to Rowan County, where he grew up, and figure out something to do with his grandfather's 100-acre family farm. Having been a winemaking hobbyist when he lived close to Napa Valley, and seeing how the North Carolina industry was starting to take off, he decided to grow grapes and open a winery.

Although Mark finds that he has traded one stressful job for another, overall the decision has turned out to be a good one. He says, "In L.A., I was constantly on concrete or in traffic or in an office with a dark room and a computer for hours and hours. When I moved back to the country, I found myself walking around for almost three months with a smile on my face for no apparent reason, other than the air was somewhat cleaner and the birds were chirping and there was dirt under my feet, and all this was surprisingly new to me. It may sound romantic or sappy, but you really tend to appreciate the land more when you haven't been around it for 10 or 15 years."

After planting 12 acres of vines in 2001, Mark opened his winery in 2003. At first, Old Stone Vineyard and Winery specialized in muscadine wines. Mark feels strongly about the need to promote American grapes, pointing out that in France, Bordeaux wines are made with native grapes, and "we should have the same mind-set." He insists, "When you go to a region, you really should experience what's indicative of that region." Mark acknowledges that muscadine "is not shy. It's a bold wine that's in your face. You're either going to like or hate it, and if you like it, you love it." But he believes that with modern winemaking techniques and a growing acceptance, muscadine "is coming into its own." And he insists that in a blind tasting with a European Riesling, people will choose a white barrel-aged Carlos.

Although he champions muscadine wines, Mark is open-minded and also works with fruit wines and European-style wines. He says, "As a winemaker, you always want a new challenge, a new varietal, something different to play around with." He also wants to make sure that he can offer options to his customers. His blackberry wine is particularly popular. He notes, "Blackberry is completely underestimated. It's a great seller."

Mark believes that his former career as an artist has helped him. Of course, he designs his own wine labels, and winemaking itself is a creative process. However, like computer animation, making wine also requires attention to detail. Mark notes, "It can be very exacting. The technical side can't and shouldn't be ignored."

In only a few years, Old Stone reached its capacity of 3,500 cases. Although Mark would be able to sell more wine if he expanded, he doesn't foresee growing larger. He believes there are advantages to staying small. It allows him to "stay focused and concentrate on the quality of what we're putting out," and he says he "can craft the wines without distribution and production pressure."

Mark named the winery after the area's Old Stone House, which was built in 1766 by his ancestor Michael Bräun. Although the winery may not be around in 300 years, Mark hopes that he's building something to last. Having gone off to the city to "see what that was all about," he finds it rewarding to be involved again in agriculture, where, "literally, what grows is related to what makes you viable and your business viable."

Rock of Ages Winery and Vineyard

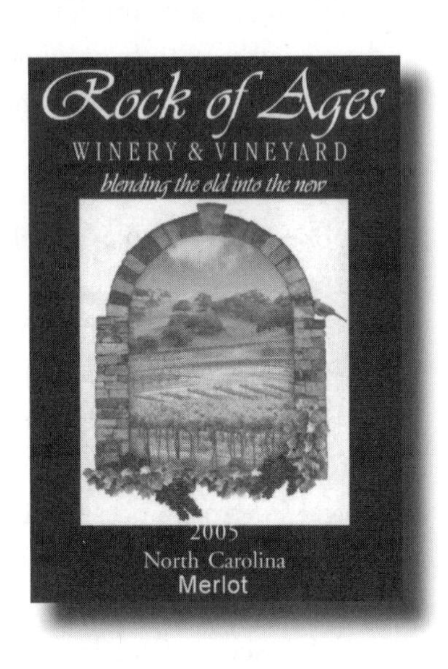

1890 Charlie Long Road
Hurdle Mills, N.C. 27541
Phone: 336-364-7625
Website:
www.rockofageswinery.com
E-mail: info@rockofageswinery.com
Hours: Monday–Thursday, 1–5 p.m.;
Friday and Saturday, 11 a.m.–5 p.m.;
Sunday, 1–6 p.m.

Owners: Kevin and Kimberly Moore
Winemaker: Kevin Moore
First year as bonded winery: 2006
Tasting fee: Yes
On-line ordering: No
Wine club: Pending

Wine List
Whites: Muscadine, Viognier
Reds: Cabernet Sauvignon, Merlot, Syrah

Directions: From Roxboro, take N.C. 49 West off U.S. 501 (Madison Boulevard). Go 8.5 miles and turn left on Charlie Long Road. The winery is on the right after approximately 2 miles. From Durham, take Exit 175 off Interstate 85 onto Guess Road (N.C. 157). Go north for approximately 20.5 miles. Turn left at the stop sign onto Hurdle Mills Road. After 0.25 mile, veer right onto Union Grove Church Road. Go 0.3 mile and turn right on Charlie Long Road. The winery is on the left after 1.3 miles.

Rock of Ages winery
COURTESY OF ROCK OF AGES WINERY AND VINEYARD

In 2001, Kevin Moore went camping with his family. As he sat by the fire with his wife, Kimberly, and his brother, he talked about his restlessness. After a dozen years in the stone industry running his own company, he was ready for a career change, but he wasn't sure in which direction to go. "What," he kept asking, "do I want to do with the second half of my life?"

Intrigued by the state's growing wine industry, Kevin decided to try planting a half-acre of grapes on his family farm. Shortly afterward, he added three more acres, and the following year, he planted over 20 more. As he began taking viticulture and oenology courses at Surry Community College, he knew that he had found the answer to his question. The wine business was interesting, exciting, and challenging. Furthermore, grape growing seemed to offer a way to preserve agricultural land that had been in his family for generations.

As part of his coursework at Surry, Kevin designed a winery. This, however, was not only a classroom assignment. He planned to build his design. And just as his vineyard acreage rapidly expanded, so did his vision of the winery. In the process of its development, the building grew to 28,000 square feet and went from being a $1 million complex to a

$5 million one. Its construction was a complicated undertaking, and Kevin oversaw every aspect. Finally, in the fall of 2006, five years after their campfire discussion, Kevin and Kimberly Moore opened Rock of Ages Winery and Vineyard.

For the winery's design, Kevin says he "wanted something that blends in and fits with the landscape." He also, however, wanted something unique. Because of the number of horse farms in the area, he eventually decided on an exterior that he describes as "a Kentucky horse barn with a taste of Italy." Inside, the winery has a 3,500-square-foot, two-story tasting room with a stone fireplace. As much as possible, Kevin tried to use natural materials, including oak beams and copper ceilings. He has also tried to incorporate items from the farm's heritage, like a planned mural over the tasting counter that will visually portray the land's transition from tobacco to grapes. Throughout, according to Kevin, the design tries to exemplify the winery's motto: "Blending the old into the new." In fact, although Kevin's parents were teetotalers, his grandfather Ernest Moore made wine for his church from the late 1930s to the 1950s, so Kevin sees Rock of Ages as a way to carry on an old tradition in a new way.

The winery can seat 300 people, and with six portable bars, it can easily host large events. An outdoor stage allows concerts, but the grounds are large enough for people to find privacy to picnic. Kevin explains, "We want people to have the feeling of a resort, . . . to enjoy the beauty of it and be able to get away from the rat race." From the winery's upper level, visitors can look over the vineyards, a pond, and the countryside. It is, Kevin has been told, "a million-dollar view." In addition to the tasting room, the winery will have a restaurant and a retail shop that will include Seagrove pottery made especially for Rock of Ages.

The Moores want Rock of Ages to be an asset to the community and a good neighbor, so early in the project's development, Kevin visited people in the area to explain what he was doing. He made it clear that "we were not going to be a bar or a 'Let's go drink to get drunk' place." The winery has a policy of not serving beer or liquor, and it will not host certain types of events, such as class reunions, which tend to be drinking parties. Consequently, Kevin says, "I've not had anyone oppose the winery or think it's a bad thing for the community." Even his mother is excited: "She thinks it's great. She's nervous like me. It's a big adventure."

Kevin has high expectations for the winery. He notes, "We didn't just stumble down the road and hope it came out right." He has a business plan based on economies of scale, which means that within the winery's first three years, he would like to increase the production level to 10,000 cases. He recognizes, however, that this will depend both on the types of wines he can make and on customer demand.

In its first years, the vineyard contains 17 different varietals as Kevin tries to determine what grows best in the area. He notes, "I don't think anybody who plants grapes in a new area knows what's going to be good." It may take five, 10, or 25 years. It may even take the second half of Kevin's life, but he says he's ready to spend the time. He insists, "The definition of a job is something you do for a paycheck. The definition of pleasure is doing something for joy. I've found something that gives me pleasure."

Rock of Ages tasting room
COURTESY OF ROCK OF AGES WINERY AND VINEYARD

SilkHope Winery

SilkHope Winery
CHATHAM COUNTY
Seyval Blanc
2001
ALCOHOL 12% BY VOLUME

2601 Silk Hope Gum Springs Road
Pittsboro, N.C. 27312
Phone: 919-742-4601
Website: www.silkhopewinery.com
E-mail: wally.butler@earthlink.net
Hours: Saturday and Sunday, noon–5 p.m.

Owner: Wally Butler
Winemaker: Wally Butler
First year as bonded winery: 2000
Tasting fee: No
On-line ordering: No
Wine club: No

Wine List
Whites: Vidal Blanc, Viognier
Reds: Chambourcin, Grand Vista, Red Roots

Directions: From Pittsboro, go 4 miles north on N.C. 87, then turn left on Silk Hope Gum Springs Road. The winery is on the left after 2.5 miles, approximately 300 yards past Emmaus Church.

In the 1980s, Wally Butler, a forester, bought several acres of land in Chatham County because he liked its timber prospects. At 700 feet

Wally Butler

in elevation, it also had beautiful views of the surrounding countryside. Wally remembers, "I stood up on the hill and looked at this little church down there in the valley, and I thought, 'Man, that's a sweet place to plant grapes.'" It was an ironic thought since, several years earlier, he had been adamant about the impossibility of growing grapes in the area. In the late 1970s, Wally had appraised timber for a man named David Reed, who was clearing his land to plant vinifera vines. Wally had been skeptical: "I said, 'No, that will never work. You can't grow those kind of grapes around here.'" Reed proved him wrong, and the two men formed a friendship. Later, Wally even bought grapes from him to make wine.

Inspired by Reed's success and the possibilities of his own land, Wally planted a small number of vines in 1985. He dabbled with them for a few years but admits, "I didn't care for them just right." Then he decided to get more serious. He joined the North Carolina Winegrower's Association, sought advice, and eventually planted two vineyards: one for white varietals and one for reds.

As Wally began putting significant effort into grape growing, he also became more serious about his winemaking. He had been a hobbyist for years. "I started making wine because I like to drink wine," he says. After he made the decision to pursue the business commercially, he founded SilkHope Winery.

SilkHope is a small operation. Wally says, "I'm very basic. . . . I don't have any pumps or anything like that." Using a small stainless-steel tank and several barrels of American oak, he produces fewer than 500 cases a year. Everything is done by hand, including putting on the labels. These feature the family crest. Wally says with a smile, "My mother insisted that I put it on."

Although Wally's mother isn't much of a wine drinker, she does like scuppernong and sweet wines, so Wally makes batches of these occasionally. As a winemaker, however, he prefers to work with reds. He admits, "I always wind up, when I'm drinking white, saying, 'You know, this stuff isn't too bad.' . . . Reds, that's my thing."

Wally runs SilkHope from a small metal hangar and a small green sheet-metal building that contains a walk-in cooler for controlled-environment fermenting. Although he acknowledges these no-frills buildings are poorly designed for his purposes, he chose them for a simple reason: affordability. The expense of establishing a winery surprised Wally, who notes that "it's depressing to do taxes." He says, "I thought I realized how much money it would be and how much work it would take, but I didn't."

Wally also has had other difficulties. In 2002, he discovered that Pierce's disease had attacked a large portion of his vineyards. A bacteria that devastates grapevines, Pierce's disease is believed by scientists to be spread by different hosts, including insects called "sharpshooters." It exists only in mild climates and can go undetected for a long time. Wally points out that the vines look good in the early stages of infection, but then, within a season, they can be dead.

The disease reduced SilkHope's crop yield by two-thirds. As a result, the winery's production declined to fewer than 100 cases. Wally notes ruefully, "I at least have the satisfaction of being the first place in Chatham County to be diagnosed with Pierce's disease." For several years, he worked with researchers at the nearby universities to determine what should be done. Eventually, he bulldozed a large space around the vineyards to separate them from the nearby woods. He also replanted much of his vineyards. He now grows six varietals: Symphony, Traminette, Chambourcin, Vidal Blanc, Cabernet Franc, and Norton.

Ironically, the efforts to control Pierce's disease made his vineyards more attractive. Wally notes, "It gives a more spacious look to the whole place and has opened up new views of the horizon." In the past few years, Wally has also improved access for visitors by regrading the driveway and pouring a parking lot. In the near future, he plans on establishing some picnic areas.

Wally is determined to keep SilkHope Winery going and to improve it as much as he can. He hopes that the worst regarding Pierce's disease is over. He says, "I've already had my pride hurt and gotten over that, so now I just have to see what happens." In the future, he is determined not to let the work and expense overwhelm him. He insists, "I'm going to be a little more laid-back and just take it as it comes."

Stonefield Cellars

8220 N.C. 68 North
Stokesdale, N.C. 27357
Phone: 336-644-9908
Website:
www.stonefieldcellars.com
E-mail:
nwurz@stonefieldcellars.com
Hours: Thursday–Saturday,
noon–6 p.m.; Sunday, 1–6 p.m.

Owners: Robert and Natalie Wurz
Winemaker: Robert Wurz
First year as bonded winery: 2006
Tasting fee: Yes
On-line ordering: No
Wine club: Yes

Wine List
Whites: Chardonnay, Chardonnay Doux, Illumination (sweet blend), Niagara, Pinot Gris, Viognier
Blushes: BellaSelena (sweet blend), Rosé
Reds: Beneficence (red blend), Cabernet Franc, Cabernet Sauvignon, Merlot, Sangiovese, Synchronicity (red blend), Syrah, Zinfandel
Dessert: Vin de Narle (blueberry)
Fruits: Peach, Strawberry

Directions: From Interstate 40 west of Greensboro, take Exit 210 and go north on N.C. 68 for 13 miles. The winery is on the right at the intersection with N.C. 65. The entrance is on N.C. 65.

The Wurz family

Robert Wurz was born and raised in Napa Valley. A "cook and chemist at heart," he was curious from a young age about how wine was made. When he was 14, his father brought home a cider press and said, "Let's go get some grapes and start making wine." Robert quickly realized that it wasn't the right kind of press for wine, so the next year, he bought one made from redwood. By the time he graduated from Calistoga High School, he had done science-fair projects on wine chemistry, worked in the area's wineries, cleaned out wine trucks, and made a variety of wines. It wasn't surprising that he continued his studies in college, eventually earning a Ph.D. in wine chemistry from the University of California at Davis. However, just when he expected his professional winemaking career to begin, his life took a different direction.

When Robert graduated from UC-Davis in 1986, the wine industry was "in a terrible slump," and there were no Ph.D.-level jobs. He ended up moving to North Carolina to work as a chemist for Ciba-Geigy (now Syngenta). Although he intended to stay only for a year or so, two things happened. One, he discovered that he liked the area. Two, he met Natalie, the woman who would become his wife.

Almost 10 years into his corporate career, Robert returned to California to attend a wine chemistry symposium. During the trip, he had an epiphany at the beach regarding what he wanted to do with his life. According to Robert, he clearly heard a voice saying, "It's wine, you big fool." When he got back to North Carolina, he uncovered the equipment he hadn't used for years, including the redwood press he had bought as a teenager.

As Robert began working with North Carolina grapes, he discovered that they were different from West Coast ones and required different techniques. He points out that people on the East Coast who make wine "by the book" can be misled, since most texts refer to California grapes. Consequently, their wines often end up chalky, with unbalanced tannins. According to Robert, a winemaker needs to "listen to the grapes" to get a sense of "what they want to be," rather than treating them with a standardized process and template.

After a few years of experimentation, Robert realized that he could make good wine with the available grapes, and he began to consider finding a job as a winemaker. However, friends insisted that he and Natalie should open their own winery and that Guilford County would be an excellent location. So, with the help of friend and major partner George House, they started developing Stonefield Cellars in 2004.

After searching for a site for over two years, the Wurzes finally decided on land in Stokesdale. Although the property has 10 acres that are suitable for planting, they planted only one and a half acres at first, choosing to concentrate on establishing the winery, rather than on extensive vineyards. Robert explains, "I grew up on a farm. I know how to farm, but you can't do everything." For the winery, Robert and Natalie constructed a building with a spacious tasting room and a 4,000-case production capacity. Initially, they envisioned a much larger structure, but they discovered they couldn't realize their plans all at once. As Robert puts it, "There are visions, and there are budgets. It's a compromise between the two."

In developing Stonefield Cellars, the Wurzes have relied on the support of friends and family. Natalie points out, "We've been so fortu-

Stonefield Cellars winery

nate to have a lot of wonderful, wonderful volunteers. They're our lifeblood." They often help in the winery, but Robert points out that there are guidelines: "We learned early on that the people applying the labels can't drink." The Wurzes also use volunteers in blending trials. Robert will make several prototype wines and then pass out samples to 20 or 25 people to get their feedback. After reviewing this input, he makes his final decisions for each particular blend.

Although Robert considers people's tastes when making a wine, he also speaks of the process in artistic terms. A winemaker makes numerous choices to bring out the flavors of a grape. Robert says, "It's like having an artist's palette with many colors." Stonefield Cellars has allowed Natalie to be creative as well. "I'm now able to tap into my talents," she explains. She designed the tasting room and has tried to create a community atmosphere at the winery. Because she believes that "people always seek a sense of fellowship, and we can help provide that," Stonefield Cellars sponsors a number of events. One of her favorites is the Second Sunday Soup and Sing, during which local musicians can come and play. Since Natalie plays the mandolin, guitar, and banjo, she looks forward to Robert working the wine bar, so she can focus on the music.

In the winery's first year, Natalie quit her corporate job to serve as Stonefield Cellars' vice president and director of marketing and sales. It's a role she believes suits her personality and skills. Robert can be himself as well. Although he still works for Syngenta, he has rediscovered his lifelong passion. And despite the difficulties involved in establishing a winery, the Wurzes are having fun. There is in their winemaking and wine selling a sense of play. For example, as Robert experimented with a port-like dessert wine, he and Natalie kept saying as it aged, "Let's go check on that gnarly stuff." When it came time to bottle and name it, they decided on "Vin de Narle."

Natalie insists that people who visit Stonefield Cellars "leave with a smile on their face." This may have something to do with the impressiveness of the winery and the quality of the wine; however, it may also be because the winery owners themselves are smiling and clearly enjoying what they do.

Stony Mountain Vineyards

26370 Mountain Ridge Road
Albemarle, N.C. 28001
Phone: 704-982-0922
Fax: 704-983-2755
Website:
www.stonymountainvineyards.com
E-mail: stonymountain@vnet.net
Hours: Friday and Saturday,
noon–6 p.m.

Owners: Ken, Marie, and Devron Furr
Winemaker: Ken Furr
First year as bonded winery: 2003
Tasting fee: Yes
On-line ordering: No, but call for shipping.
Wine club: Yes

Wine List
Whites: Chardonnay, Seyval Blanc, White Table Wine (Carlos)
Reds: Cabernet Sauvignon, Chambourcin, Merlot, Red Table Wine (Ison), Syrah
Fruits: Blackberry, Strawberry

Directions: From Albemarle, drive east on N.C. 24/27 for 4 miles and turn left at the sign for Stony Mountain. Bear right, then turn right on Mountain Ridge Road and go approximately 1 mile.

In 1995, when Ken Furr retired after 30 years in the United States Marine Corps, he knew he needed a hobby. He explains, "You've got to have a reason to get up in the morning." Having visited California wineries when he was stationed out west, he decided to put in vineyards and try making wine. He planted vinifera vines and began reading every viticulture and oenology book he could find. His hobby quickly grew, and soon Ken found himself giving away a lot of wine to friends, which, he points out, they loved. Eventually, the Furrs decided to establish a winery. In 2003, they opened Stony Mountain Vineyards.

Located in Stanly County near Morrow Mountain State Park, Stony Mountain Vineyards has beautiful views of the nearby Uwharries. The setting, however, comes at a price. Ken acknowledges, "I don't know if you could have a more difficult vineyard site than we have." The terrain is rocky, and the slope makes it difficult, even impossible, to get a tractor into some places. Still, the positive attributes of the site—its elevation, slope, and drainage—make the challenges worth it. Ken also believes that the mineral-rich soil, which has high concentrations of gold and copper, results in high-quality grapes.

When he's working among his four acres of vines, Ken sometimes finds arrowheads and pounding tools chipped out of rock. They are physical reminders that the area has been inhabited for thousands of years. In fact, the Hardaway Archaeological Site, one of the East Coast's

Stony Mountain patio

Ken Furr

oldest sites, is in nearby Badin. Considering this, Ken's family can be considered relative newcomers to the area, since they have lived there for only 250 years.

Ken appreciates the region's history and enjoys sharing it with visitors. He insists that talking to people is one of the highlights of having a winery: "People who like wine are fairly interesting people." However, he admits being surprised by how many visitors seek out his vineyards, since they're relatively isolated, the nearest neighbor being a mile away. Ken laughs, "Wine drinkers will drive 50 miles to go to a winery."

When people do find Stony Mountain Vineyards, "the encouraging thing is that they tend to come back and bring friends," Ken points out. This is understandable, since the 5,000-square-foot building has a spacious, high-ceilinged tasting room, a wall of windows overlooking the mountains, and a comfortable patio. On clear days, visibility is between 15 and 20 miles, and the views encourage people to linger. Many also end up asking for information on booking the space for events such as receptions.

Although the winery grew out of Ken's hobby, all of the Furrs are involved. The family helps staff the tasting room, organize events, distribute the wines, and work in the vineyards. Ken laughs that working with family has been one of the biggest adjustments in retiring to civilian life. For decades, he's had his commands followed, but "I tell my wife and son to do something, and they don't do it. I'm not used to that."

The transition from marine colonel to winemaker may seem unlikely to some people, but Ken feels that his former career serves him well. In the military, he developed organizational and management skills that he uses every day. For example, in the laboratory, he has instituted a simple, comprehensive paperwork system to track each batch. And although winemaking is a creative process, it is also one that requires discipline and attention to details and procedures.

Ken acknowledges that Stony Mountain Vineyards has "just kind of evolved" and continues to be "a work in progress." The Furrs are letting sales determine production and are trying to grow the business out of profits, rather than take on any debt. The winery produces approximately 1,000 cases a year. Ken says, "That's pushing us. We're selling everything we can make." Although they would like to expand, Ken insists that, in general, "our business plan is to remain small. I'm trying not to work myself to death." He believes that if he let it, the winery could grow and become overwhelming.

Ken's hobby has succeeded in fulfilling its function—it gets him out of bed each morning—but he admits, "I don't know whether we'll ever make any money. The saying goes that you're working for your kids and grandkids." Overall, he's pleased. He says of the winery, "We made the right decision. So far, it's been pretty successful. I just wish I'd started 30 years ago."

Uwharrie Vineyards

28030 Austin Road
Albemarle, N.C. 28001
Phone: 704-982-9463 (704-982-WINE)
Website: www.uwharrievineyards.com
E-mail: info@uwharrievineyards.com
Hours: Tuesday–Saturday,
10 a.m.–6 p.m.; Sunday, 1–5 p.m.

Owner: David Braswell
Winemakers: Chad Andrews and David Braswell
First year as bonded winery: 2005
Tasting fee: Yes
On-line ordering: Yes
Wine club: Yes

Wine List
Whites: Chardonnay, Magnolia, Muscat
Blush: White Syrah
Reds: Cabernet Sauvignon, Merlot, Noble
Fruit: Peach

Directions: From the junction of U.S. 52 and N.C. 49 south of Salisbury, drive south on U.S. 52 for 6 miles toward Albemarle. Turn right on Austin Road and go approximately 5 miles. The vineyards are on the left.

In 2000, after a lifetime spent working, David Braswell suddenly found himself with free time when John Deere bought his company. He says, "I had nothing to do but play golf," so he began looking for activities to keep busy. Since he had always been interested in winemaking

Chad Andrews

and often bought books on the subject, he started suggesting to family and friends that maybe he should plant vineyards. The more he discussed the idea with his wife, Anne, whose business sense he respected, the more they believed that it was worth pursuing.

David bought farmland in 2002 and began planting 1,500 vines. He soon bought more acreage. He says, "I got serious pretty quick because I was investing a lot of money." He and Chad Andrews, a fellow Shriner and Mason, laid out the vineyards, put in the irrigation, and designed the winery. Chad explains, "We wanted to do it all ourselves. We wanted to micromanage."

In addition to reading everything they could, David and Chad researched the industry by visiting and volunteering at various vineyards both in North Carolina and on the West Coast. As they examined other people's operations, Chad says that "at some point, we started to figure out what would work best for us." For example, impressed with the way the Callaway Winery in California treats visitors, David decided he wanted to ensure people would have "a great tasting experience" at Uwharrie Vineyards. So, in addition to making sure the interior is spacious and welcoming, he installed an impressive marble counter.

Although David and Chad admire California wine, Chad points out that Uwharrie Vineyards' offerings are not like those of Napa and Sonoma, and for good reason: "We're a different place. The grapes are different. The food is different. You're going to have a different taste." This is one reason why Uwharrie offers muscadine and scuppernong wines. These grapes are unique to the area and give a specific sense of place. David and Chad also believe that their commitment to the technique of lengthy cold stabilization sets the winery apart. Most winemakers allow a wine to heat up to room temperature after the initial fermentation is completed. At Uwharrie Vineyards, wine is kept cold for up to a year. Doing so is worth the additional expense, Chad believes, because it gives the wine "a more enhanced fruit sensation." This also makes the wine age at a slower speed, which "gives a winemaker more time to look and see and manage and figure out what the wine is doing."

David believes that his financial sense has been crucial to the winery's successful development: "I've been in business since I was 24, and I haven't looked back. Banks work with me because I'm a man of my word. When you bring that kind of background, you're bound to succeed." Uwharrie Vineyards carries no debt, and according to David, this is because of sound financial planning: "If you don't have a game plan, you can go broke pretty quick."

Chad also comes to the wine industry from the business world. Before helping to establish Uwharrie, he spent a dozen years in the computer industry. He says, "When you work in business and computer

Uwharrie Vineyards tasting room

networks, you get calls when things go wrong and when they're broke. Here, people call us for positive reasons. It's a lot nicer." In fact, he insists that one of the things he enjoys most about the winery is meeting people. And he particularly likes to encourage people to participate: "I tell people to come in and help work and see how we operate. You can get your hands on a shovel and get into the grapes, or you can clean the tanks and help bottle. It's a great way to show the process to people who are interested, and they enjoy it."

Chad emphasizes that both making wine and tasting wine should be pleasurable. He says, "I enjoy riding on the tractor. I enjoy working, bottling, harvesting. It wears me out, but it's fun." In the winery, he often plays Jimmy Buffett, one of his favorite musicians, and T-shirts in the tasting room carry the slogan, "Serious wine for non-serious people." This atmosphere, Chad believes, makes the winery an appealing place to hold special events such as wedding receptions and car-club gatherings. Yet because of Chad's and David's backgrounds, they also have been careful to design facilities appropriate for business meetings. Uwharrie Vineyards has conference rooms with high-speed Ethernet access and presentation equipment such as digital projectors. It can offer accommodations and catering services for groups of up to 200 people.

Overall, David has found establishing the business gratifying, but there is one bittersweet aspect to the project's success. Anne Braswell didn't get to see it. She passed away in 2003, a month before the winery's scheduled groundbreaking. However, she is honored in the Uwharrie Vineyards logo, which features an angel.

David no longer has to look for ways to fill his time because there is always plenty to do at Uwharrie Vineyards. The 14,000-square-foot winery currently produces 60,000 bottles a year, or approximately 5,000 cases. To reach its production capacity of 150,000 bottles, David and Chad plan to eventually double the vineyards' 35 acres. In the future, they also would like to expand their wine list and increase their distribution. They insist, however, that they intend to make careful, deliberate decisions. David says, "We want to go slow, and we want to be sure we do it well."

The Winery at Iron Gate Farm

2540 Lynch Store Road
Mebane, N.C. 27302
Phone: 919-304-9463
Fax: 919-304-6424
Website: www.irongatevineyards.com
E-mail: irongatefarm@mebtel.net
Hours: Monday–Friday, 10 a.m.–7 p.m.;
Saturday, 10 a.m.–6 p.m.;
Sunday, 1–6 p.m.

Owners: Debbie and Gene Stikeleather
Winemaker: Debbie Stikeleather
First year as bonded winery: 2004
Tasting fee: Yes
On-line ordering: Yes
Wine club: No

Wine List
Whites: Brightleaf White (white blend), Chardonnay, Flue Fire (Niagara and muscadine blend), Sauvignon Blanc
Reds: Cabernet Sauvignon, Chambourcin, Dixie Dawn (Sangiovese), Merlot, Packhouse Red

Directions: Take Exit 153 off Interstate 40/85 east of Burlington and go north on N.C. 119 through Mebane. About 1.5 miles past Mill Creek (approximately 6 miles from the interstate), turn right onto Lynch Store Road. The winery is on the left.

In 1972, Debbie Stikeleather graduated from high school and began her first job. On her way to work, she would pass the farm of Tom and Lucy Lynch. Often, she would see the couple sitting under the trees in front of the house. The image stuck with her, and although over the years Debbie moved around the state because of different jobs, she at times would still find herself driving by the farm.

When the Lynches passed away and their house became vacant, Debbie looked into buying or leasing the property, but she was repeatedly told that it wasn't available. She kept trying. Eventually, in 1998, she managed to get a two-year lease from the owner, who was living in Connecticut. Finally, in 2000, she managed to purchase the 60-acre farm.

Initially, Debbie had no specific plans for the land—which had been unworked for over a decade—except to use it to pasture her husband Gene's 28 Belgian draft horses. Nevertheless, the couple set about improving the property by rebuilding fences, clearing brush, and cleaning the waterways. The Stikeleathers found springs and capped them. They removed enough soil and sediment from the pond to build a small island with it. In an article entitled "Preserving the Land," Debbie writes

Debbie Stikeleather

Iron Gate pond

that "the impact on the property was immediate because it was evident that someone cared for it. It also made a difference in the community because neighbors came over to meet us and to let us know how much it meant to them to see this farm revived."

One day as Debbie was surfing the Internet, she discovered information about the viticulture program at Surry Community College. Although she didn't drink wine, she was curious about whether vineyards might be a good use of the property, and she began researching the industry. She became increasingly enthused about grapes as a crop. After enrolling in the Surry program, she planted three and a half acres of vines in April 2001. Each year, she planted more until the acreage increased to eight. Although at first she planned to sell her fruit to wineries, Debbie says that "we were hauling grapes up the road, and pretty soon we decided that we didn't want to haul grapes up the road." Instead, after Debbie graduated from Surry and did a two-year winemaking internship with Linda King at RagApple Lassie, the Stikeleathers opened Iron Gate in 2004.

The name Iron Gate comes from a previous farm of Gene's in Granville County and from his fencing business. But because Debbie grew up in Caswell County—"the heart of the tobacco region"—the Stikeleathers believe that the winery's story is tied to that of brightleaf tobacco.

Consequently, the area's tobacco heritage is emphasized in the names of the wines, such as Packhouse Red and Flue Fire, and on the winery's labels. For the labels, "we used things that were here. Things that were real," Debbie points out. Iron Gate even shows a video from the Duke Homestead on the history of tobacco. Although Debbie doesn't smoke, she says, "I love to smell tobacco curing in the barn." It's a smell she knows well; the oldest of eight children, Debbie grew up with her siblings "working in tobacco every summer of our lives."

Iron Gate has been well received by the community, and Debbie appreciates its support. She insists, "I cannot run my business without my neighbors." Local schoolteachers and neighbors help out in the tasting room and participate in blending trials. The winery has also established community ties by featuring the wares of local artisans, including honeys, jams, jellies, and the products of Sunshine Lavender Farm and Tranquility Acres goat farm. In addition, Iron Gate has a partnership with No Limits, Inc., an organization for children who are developmentally challenged. No Limits makes wine lamps, corkboards, and other items. Debbie says with pride, "They've been with me since day one." Iron Gate even sponsors the racecar of a local driver and is the official wine of the area's minor-league baseball team, the Burlington Indians.

Ironically, after finally buying the farm that she always admired, Debbie rarely gets to sit on the porch and relax. In Iron Gate's first years, as production grew from 800 cases to 2,000, the Stikeleathers expanded and renovated the winery twice, including building an outdoor bandstand to host regular concerts. And even though Gene now keeps only seven horses on the property and family members help out, "you never have enough time," Debbie says wistfully. Still, it is a commitment she is willing to make because, she insists, the work is not just about making and selling wine. It is also about being a faithful steward of natural resources. Consequently, for Debbie, the success of The Winery at Iron Gate Farm can be seen not only in its awards and the number of bottles it sells, but in the land it allows her to care for and protect.

Wineries of Eastern North Carolina

Wineries of Eastern North Carolina

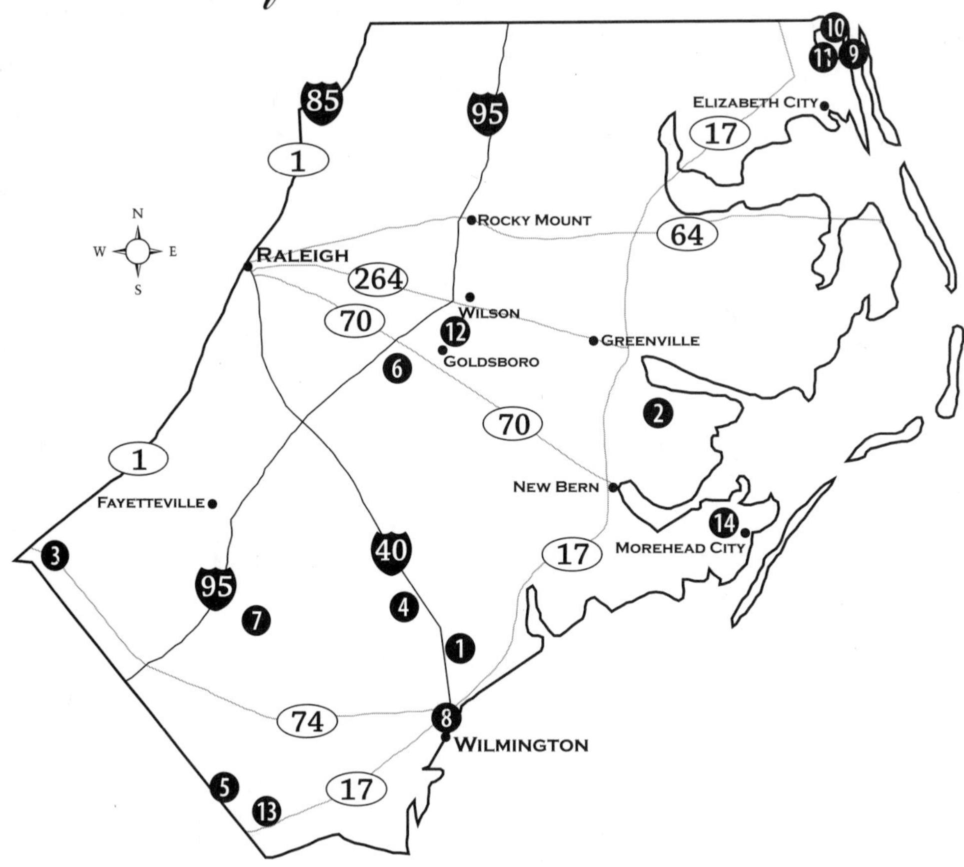

1. Bannerman Vineyard
2. Bennett Vineyards
3. Cypress Bend Vineyards
4. Duplin Winery
5. Grapefull Sisters Vineyard
6. Hinnant Family Vineyards
7. Lu Mil Vineyard
8. Lumina Winery
9. Martin Vineyards
10. Moonrise Bay Vineyard
11. Sanctuary Vineyards
12. A Secret Garden Winery
13. Silver Coast Winery
14. Somerset Cellars

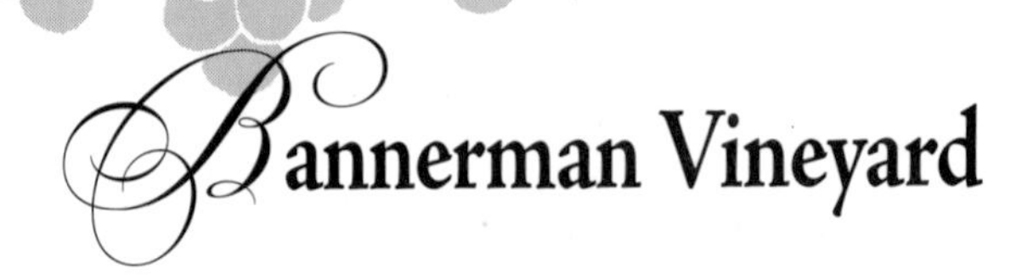

Bannerman Vineyard

2624 Stag Park Road
Burgaw, N.C. 28425
Phone: 910-259-5474
Fax: 910-259-5553
Website:
www.bannermanvineyard.com
E-mail:
admin@BannermanVineyard.com
Hours:
Wednesday–Saturday, noon–4 p.m.;
Sunday, 1–4 p.m.

Owners: Scot and Colleen Bannerman
Winemakers: Colleen and Chris Bannerman
First year as bonded winery: 2005
Tasting fee: No
On-line ordering: Yes
Wine club: No

Wine List
Whites: Marilyn (semidry white table wine), Weeping Willow (Doreen), White Oak Semi-Sweet (Carlos), White Oak Sweet (Carlos)
Blush: Sweet Bay Blush (white and red muscadine blend)
Reds: Red Oak Semi-Sweet (muscadine), Red Oak Sweet (muscadine)

Directions: From Interstate 40 in Pender County, take Exit 398 and turn west on N.C. 53. Go 1 mile, turn left on Stag Park Road, and go 2.5 miles. The winery is on the right.

The Bannerman family has been growing muscadine grapes since 1973, and over the years, their vineyard has built up a loyal clientele.

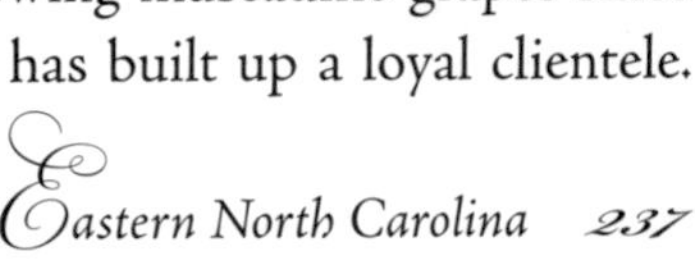

Many of their customers use the grapes to make wine, and others just pick the fruit to eat. Some have been known to bring 50-gallon drums and crush the fruit right at the farm. Often, these enthusiasts swap information and recipes and bring back samples to pass around the next year.

In 2005, longtime customers were offered samples from some new winemakers—the Bannermans themselves. Colleen and her husband, Scot, had been considering starting a winery for a while. The "fresh-pick" business involves year-round expenses but generates income only two months of the year, so they wanted to find a more consistent source of revenue. Inspired by the "big boom" of the state's wine industry, they decided in 2001 that wine could be it.

Colleen admits that they didn't quite know what they were getting into or how involved the regulation process was. The government sent a thick packet for licensing. She says, "I thought that I'd knock it off on a Saturday afternoon," but it took over a year. Mastering the winemaking equipment also proved to be challenging. When the vats arrived, they didn't have instructions: "We called the company in Italy, and of course they didn't understand English." When they finally got the company to send a manual, "it was all in Italian." Colleen laughs, "It's been an ongoing learning experience." Their son Chris agrees, adding, "And it's been fun."

Muscadine grapes

Colleen and Chris Bannerman

Chris has been helping out on the farm all his life. He began a career in restaurant management, but although he was good at it, he says, "One day, I thought it seemed like I never saw the sunlight anymore. I was just stuck inside, counting out drawers. I started talking to Dad, and he suggested I try managing the vineyard." Chris discovered that he enjoys viticulture work, and Colleen and Scot are happy that Bannerman Vineyard can support him. In fact, they're hopeful that their other three sons will someday work full time for the business as well.

There's no question that the muscadine industry is expanding. Colleen notes that people's attitudes toward the grape have changed significantly over the years, and it is now much more accepted. From a business standpoint, Chris points out that muscadine wines offer a significant advantage over European varietals: "Muscadine has the luxury of not having complete and total market saturation." Most retail outlets such as grocery stores have large sections of Merlot and Chardonnay but offer only a few muscadine wines, even though there is a large demographic that enjoys them.

According to Chris, the wines of Bannerman Vineyard sell extremely well: "Almost everyone who tastes them buys some. It's been an overwhelming positive reaction." In fact, "the wines have been so well received, it's pretty much all we can do to keep the shelves stocked." He believes the positive reception is due in part to the Bannermans' focus on quality and consistency. He points out that "people associate sweet wine with low quality, but you can have sweet high-quality wine." His mother agrees: "We have been very, very careful to keep our quality control right."

The vineyard has grown over the decades from three acres to 18, and the winery produces about 1,100 cases a year, but Colleen insists, "We're a mom-and-pop place." Their largest tank is 3,000 liters, they use a single-bottle corker, and the entire family helps out during harvest and other key times of the year.

As for the future, Colleen says, "We're looking forward to seeing the muscadine industry continue to grow in North Carolina, and we all hope that there are prosperous times ahead. We believe there will be. After sampling muscadine wine, you will for sure know that goodness truly does grow in North Carolina."

Bennett Vineyards

6832 Old Sandhill Road
Edward, N.C. 27821
Mailing Address: P.O. Box 150
Edward, N.C. 27821
Phone: 877-762-9463 or
252-322-7154
Fax: 252-322-7154
Website: www.ncwines.com
Hours: Open daily

Owners: Bennett Vineyards, Ltd.
Winemaker: Buddy Harrell
First year as bonded winery: 1993
Tasting fee: No
On-line ordering: No
Wine club: No

Wine List
Whites: Elizabeth II, Mount Vernon White
Blushes: Muscadine Rosé, Plymouth Blush
Reds: Blackbeard's Choice, Charlestown Red, Roanoke Red
Fruits: Blueberry, Strawberry

Directions: From Greenville, take N.C. 33 East to S.R. 1936 and turn right. Drive approximately 0.5 mile, turn right on Bennett Vineyards Road (formerly Old Sand Hill Road), and go approximately 1 mile. The winery is on the right.

Some people consider the wine business romantic, but Buddy Harrell isn't one of them. He knows too much about what can go wrong. Since he co-founded Bennett Vineyards, he has endured several hur-

Grapehouse Country Inn
COURTESY OF BENNETT VINEYARDS

ricanes, a devastating frost, the death of a partner, near-bankruptcies, and other misfortunes. Nevertheless, he has persisted in trying to make the vineyards productive.

In 1990, Robert Godley approached Buddy with an idea. He had family property that he thought would be good for growing grapes, and he knew that Buddy had an old family recipe from his grandfather for making muscadine wine. He suggested they put these two assets together. The men agreed to become partners and formed Bennett Vineyards. The next year, they began planting vines.

Although at first the venture seemed solid, two hurricanes in 1996 damaged much of the vineyards. That same year, Robert died, and Buddy discovered that the title to the land was a tangled matter. As a result, he found himself ineligible for disaster relief funds and unable to borrow money from banks. Finally, in 1998, after twice considering bankruptcy, he decided to take a calculated risk. He let the bank foreclose on the property, then, when the vineyards were sold at public auction, he bought them back. He then had a clear title, but his troubles didn't end. More hurricanes struck, flooding the land, destroying trellis systems, and damaging vines. In 2001, an April freeze ruined 50 to 60 percent of the crop.

Despite all the difficulties, Buddy has not given up, and he remains committed to the vineyards. He believes that he's carrying on an American tradition. In its promotional materials, Bennett Vineyards emphasizes the history of winemaking in the United States and the South. Because muscadine is a native grape, one noted by the first European explorers and settlers, Bennett Vineyards calls itself the "Vintners of America's First Wine." A brochure claims the wines give "a true taste of our American colonial experience." To emphasize this connection, Bennett's wines—for example, Mount Vernon White and Roanoke Red—have been named after colonial places.

The name of the winery also reflects a claim to a heritage. Robert Godley believed that at one time, the land was owned by the Bennetts, one of the area's oldest families. Grapes were even grown here in the 19th century, when the property was part of the Wiley T. Bennett plantation. Behind part of the vineyards is a small graveyard where, according to some, many members of the Bennett family are buried.

In addition to making its own wines, Bennett Vineyards sells fruit to other wineries, including Lumina in Wilmington and Linden Beverage Company in Virginia. The vineyards have some you-pick grapes available, but for the most part, Bennett has concentrated on selling its wines at farmers' markets, festivals, and grocery stores, rather than catering to visitors.

In 2005, the winery did add a new tasting room, and Buddy and

Bennett Vineyards tasting room
COURTESY OF BENNETT VINEYARDS

his wife are in the process of completing a bed-and-breakfast called the Grapehouse Country Inn. Guests are treated to a genuine country breakfast and wine and cheese in the afternoon. Buddy says, "I do the cooking, and my wife makes everything pretty." Two bedrooms are available, and three more are under construction, but Buddy isn't sure when they will be completed because he is so pressed for time. In fact, in 2006, Buddy decided that almost 15 years in the wine industry might be long enough, and that he had devoted ample time and energy to the business. As of this writing, Bennett Vineyards is for sale.

Cypress Bend Vineyards

21904 Riverton Road
Wagram, N.C. 28396
Phone: 910-369-0411
Fax: 910-369-0484
Website:
www.cypressbendvineyards.com
E-mail:
info@cypressbendvineyards.com
Hours: Wednesday–Friday and Sunday, noon–6 p.m.; Saturday, 10 a.m.–6 p.m.

Owners: Dan and Tina Smith
Winemaker: Jim McClanathan
First year as bonded winery: 2005
Tasting fee: Yes
On-line ordering: Via e-mail
Wine club: Yes

Wine List
Whites: Catherine (semisweet muscadine), Chardonnay, Livingston (semidry muscadine), McNeill (sweet muscadine), Riverton Reserve (dry muscadine)
Blush: Roseneath (muscadine blush)
Reds: Campbell (sweet muscadine), Sundown (semisweet muscadine), Syrah
Dessert: Daniel (after-dinner wine)
Specialty: Holly Berry Red (sweet red muscadine)

Directions: From Laurinburg, take U.S. 401 North to Wagram, turn right on Riverton Road, and go approximately 3 miles. The winery is on the left. From Fayetteville, take U.S. 401 South to Wagram, turn left on Riverton Road, and go approximately 3 miles. The winery is on the left. From Pinehurst, take U.S. 15/501 South toward Laurinburg. Turn left on Peach Orchard Road, then turn left on McKay Street and cross U.S. 401 in Wagram to Riverton Road. Go approximately 3 miles. The winery is on the left.

Dan and Tina Smith used to have a "restaurant conundrum." Because he likes sweet wines and she prefers dry ones, they could never agree on a bottle to have at dinner. Consequently, they never shared one. Now that they have established their own winery, one with 11 different offerings, they no longer have that problem. Tina laughs that it also means "I never have to worry about getting a bottle of wine at the store."

The Smiths joke about the benefits of their venture, but they also point out that establishing Cypress Bend Vineyards has meant much more than easy access to wine they each like. It has provided a way to put family farmland back into production, to create something of value they can pass on to their children, and to make a meaningful contribution to the area's economy.

The Smiths' strong commitment to the community is understandable; Dan's family has lived there for two centuries. In 1807, his ancestors Daniel and Catherine White emigrated from Scotland and used Catherine's wedding dowry to buy land along the Lumber River. Portions of that property, which they called Riverton, have been passed down through the generations. Although Dan moved away in 1964, he always knew that one day he would return to his inheritance. For three decades, he pursued various careers in retail and consulting, including

Cypress Bend Vineyards patio

Dan and Tina Smith

serving as the science and technical adviser to Fort Bragg's commanding general. Then, in 1994, Dan came home.

Upon that return, Dan and Tina began asking themselves, "What can we do with the farm? We want it to live. We want it to go on." Because they didn't want to grow the traditional crops of corn, soybeans, and cotton, they looked at alternatives, including grapes. The more they learned about viticulture, the more convinced they became that vineyards were a good idea. Finally, in 2002, they planted several acres of muscadines. The heritage of the crop appealed to them. Muscadines are the state fruit, and Dan says they have "a lot of meaning to us. The house I grew up in has a scuppernong vine, and pictures from 100 years ago show it was there then." The Smiths also appreciate muscadines' health benefits. Tina, who is the president of the state's Muscadine Council, notes that some people call it "the super grape" or "the power grape."

At first, the Smiths intended to grow the crop and sell it to others. But Dan explains, "At acre 20, we decided that a better proposition was to open a winery." Working with an architect, they designed a 4,600-square-foot building with a 10,000-case production capacity. In June 2005, they held a grand-opening party for Cypress Bend Vineyards that hundreds of people attended. Tina fondly remembers the pleasure of "seeing people coming in that first day and seeing the looks on their faces, like, 'Wow, we're in Napa Valley!' . . . We realized that we had accomplished what we set out to accomplish."

The family named the winery after a bend in the Lumber River, which curves past their home. The Smiths are "river people"—Dan has canoed the length of the Lumber from its headwaters to the ocean—and Cypress Bend Vineyards emphasizes this love. The winery sponsors an annual river regatta and displays the winner's trophy, the tasting room features a 1929 canoe as a decoration, and the wine club is called the Paddle Club. The Smiths also had an artist, Skee Johnson, paint a large mural of the river's bend above the tasting-room counter.

When Cypress Bend opened, it offered five wines. Dan and Tina watched, listened, and talked to customers to learn about their tastes. Then they added wines and "filled in the gaps." Now, the winery has nearly a dozen selections, and the Smiths believe they have something for everyone's taste. As a result, "people never walk out of here with one bottle," Tina says. "I've been amazed with how much they buy."

The Smiths insist that the winery's popularity has caught them by surprise. "We totally underestimated the number and size of events that would be wanted," Dan says. This has meant that at times, they are pressed for space. For example, the winery hosts "Jazzy Fridays," Friday-night events that feature a music trio, a dance floor, and tables set up in the barrel room; these often draw crowds of more than 100 people. Consequently, the Smiths would like to add more event space and perhaps even put in a bistro. Ultimately, they would like to make the vineyards a "destination place" where people can spend a considerable period of time or even a day.

Having worked for years as consultants, particularly in electronics and photography, the Smiths appreciate being in the wine business. Dan points out that in the other two industries, customers "tend to be cutthroat and looking for a bargain." At Cypress Bend, however, "our customers are happy when they come in and happier when they leave after having good wine." He also explains, "Sometimes, you can open a business, and people wonder what the purpose is." They don't have that problem. The purpose is obvious. The vineyards have improved the farm and made it beautiful: "Everyone is proud of it. We're proud. The community is proud. We have accomplished a legacy for our family and for their families."

Duplin Winery

505 North Sycamore Street
Rose Hill, N.C. 28458
Phone: 800-774-9634 or
910-289-3888
Fax: 910-289-3094
Website: www.duplinwinery.com
E-mail: info@duplinwinery.com
Hours: Monday–Saturday, 9 a.m.–6 p.m.

Owners: David Fussell and family
Winemaker: Jason Bryan
First year as bonded winery: 1976
Tasting fee: No
On-line ordering: Yes
Wine club: Yes

Wine List
Whites: Magnolia, Midnight Magnolia, Pink Magnolia, Scuppernong
Reds: Bald Head Red, Beaufort Bay Red, Burgundy, Carlos, Carolina Red, Hatteras Red
Specialties: Alcohol-Free Champagne, Alcohol-Free Cider, Alcohol-Free Muscadine, Alcohol-Free Scuppernong, Almondage Champagne, American Champagne, American Port, Raspberry Delight Champagne

Directions: Take Exit 380 off Interstate 40 in Duplin County and follow West Charity Road into Rose Hill. Turn right on U.S. 117 and drive 6 blocks. The winery is on the left.

In 1995, after two decades of being in business, Duplin Winery had its first profitable year. David Fussell, a co-owner and co-founder, credits the Danes. In the mid-1990s, researchers published the Copenhagen

Duplin bottles

City Heart Study, which showed that the mortality risk for those who drink moderate amounts of wine is lower than for those who drink other spirits or are teetotalers. In short, the study said that wine drinkers tend to live longer than other people. Additional studies have suggested that this may be because some wines contain antioxidants. Muscadine grapes in particular have high levels. This fact, David says, got Duplin Winery "out of the red and into the black." Sales took off when "60 Minutes" featured the Copenhagen study in a news report. Now, people write from as far away as China requesting Duplin products. David is excited but cautious about the winery's prospects. He insists, "Man can make his plans, but the final outcome is up to the Lord. The pendulum can swing right back." He speaks from experience. He and Duplin Winery have already gone through dramatic ups and downs.

David traces the winery's origins to the 1960s, when the Department of Agriculture was promoting grapes as a wonder crop and Canandaigua Wines of New York was paying farmers $350 a ton for muscadines. After attending an information meeting sponsored by the state of North Carolina, David's brother, Dan, suggested they try to grow grapes. So, in 1972, in addition to raising hogs and planting tobacco, corn, and sweet potatoes, the brothers put in 10 acres of Carlos vines. Later that year, the crop's price plummeted to $150 a ton. The area's farmers met to discuss what could be done with their 2,492 acres

David Fussell

of grapes, and David and Dan decided to see if opening a winery was a feasible option. They visited two small regional wineries and worked out the cost projections with one of the owners. David recalls, "It was going to cost $76,000, and on the way home, I can remember talking with my brother, and we said, 'Ain't no way. Ain't no way in the world we're going to spend that much money to build a winery.' And that's true, we didn't. We spent a whole lot more."

Eventually, the Fussells founded Duplin Winery, the 26th winery in the state to be bonded since Prohibition. To raise money, they sold stock to 14 local farmers. In the beginning, David explains with a laugh, they needed to figure out how to make wine, since they were "Southern boys" and "wine was not the official drink of the South in the '70s." They read every book they could find, talked to experts at North Carolina State University, and made 30 different test batches in five-gallon carboys. Once they decided on a recipe, they made 3,000 gallons in 1976 for Duplin's first commercial release. At the time, because they had no specialized equipment, they moved the juice in buckets, unloaded the grapes with a front-end loader on a tractor, and crushed them using equipment that Dan built. David remembers when he delivered the winery's first order to Raleigh: "We were still in the hog trade, so I got

The Duplin Winery door

my water hose and cleaned my hog trailer up real good. Got all the manure out of it and put our wine in the hog trailer to carry it to one of these sophisticated distributorships in Raleigh." When he got to the company, everyone came out, shaking their heads. Someone said, "We've seen a lot, but this is the first time that we've seen anybody bring us wine on a hog trailer."

In the next 10 years, Duplin Winery grew rapidly. It sold everything it could make. By 1983, it was producing 200,000 gallons of wine. The rest of the decade, however, was disastrous for the business. Changes in tax laws and new legislation regarding distribution resulted in plummeting sales. Then, according to David, a bad investment in the (now bankrupt) Southland Estate Winery "almost pulled us under." He insists, "I really did not think we would survive." The banks took everything but the winery itself. David had to sell off all the large tanks and "any nice equipment that we could get any money for" so that he could meet payroll and buy grapes. He lost his house and had to get a full-time teaching job. He admits that during those years, he often thought about quitting, but his wife, Ann, would say, "We've invested this much time and effort in it; let's try one more day. Don't throw in the towel today." David notes, "She was actually stronger than me. She was the one that kept it going during those hard times." While he taught, Ann ran the winery.

The Fussells' resilience and commitment sustained Duplin Winery until, as David puts it, "the health issue turned us around." By 2002, sales again had reached impressive levels, and the winery expanded dramatically. It now produces close to 175,000 cases a year and continues to grow.

Not surprisingly, a visit to Duplin Winery is partly an educational seminar on the health benefits of wine. In the tasting room, handouts contain quotations from doctors around the world, and winery staff claim that over 500 studies have findings similar to the Copenhagen one. Suggesting that "if you want to age more gracefully, you'll start taking in natural antioxidants," David points out that "wine is the highest natural product in antioxidants that the Lord has chosen to make." He says, "It's not a cure-all, but it's like a seat belt. If you're in a wreck, you might die, but that seat belt might cut your risks." The winery regularly receives letters testifying to its wines' positive effects on a range of problems including high cholesterol, arthritis, heart disease, obesity, and cancer. In the future, David foresees "a big muscadine industry in the state, with more of it going into health products than is going into wine." Duplin already offers "nutraceutical" products.

In addition to its muscadine wines and products, Duplin Winery has an extensive list that includes vinifera wines such as Chardonnay, Merlot, and Cabernet Sauvignon, fruit wines, alcohol-free wines, sparkling wines, port, and sherry. Many of these can be tried in the large tasting room. Duplin also has a gift shop that includes a selection of wine-related products, a jewelry counter, a glassware section, gourmet food items, and a tasting bar devoted to jams, jellies, and salad dressings.

Since, as David notes, "Rose Hill is not a tourist mecca," the winery offers monthly dinner shows featuring musical acts. It also has a restaurant, The Bistro, which serves lunch and dinner. The winery's theater and dining facilities can be rented for group events. Both of these spaces contain interesting historical items from the state's 200-year-old wine industry. These include old Duplin bottles, advertisements and bottles from other North Carolina wineries, and antique equipment.

The oldest winery in North Carolina, Duplin also has some of the strongest local roots. It still buys grapes from some of the original stock-holding farmers, and it has several local growers under contract. One of the larger employers in the town, Duplin has a payroll of over 20 people, most of whom are named Fussell. In part, this is because the winery is very much a family enterprise. However, it is also true that almost every business in southern Duplin County employs Fussells, since over 50 families by that name live in the area. Each can trace its lineage back to Benjamin Fussell, who moved to Rose Hill from England in 1732.

Besides its deep Southern roots, David's family has strong religious beliefs. In both the gift shop and the meeting room at Duplin Winery, large wooden signs announce, "To God Be the Glory." The bathrooms display the Apostles' Creed. Discussions about alcohol consumption are put in religious terms. One Fussell points out, "The Lord advises everything has to be in moderation." Another family member explains that the Lord has put a natural regulator in your body, so "as soon as you begin to feel the alcohol, you should quit drinking." In fact, the Fussells believe that God has taken a hand in their business. David says, "I feel real good about what God is doing here in the health industry, because we're not doing it. It's a gift."

Because of his religious beliefs, going into the wine business was not an easy decision for David. In addition to financial and agricultural concerns, he had to consider spiritual ones. Although numerous passages in the Bible discuss wine in a positive way, many people of David's faith insist on complete abstinence from alcohol. So before committing to the winery, David prayed. He says that, as he asked the Lord for guidance, "a vision came to go ahead and do this because what [we're] doing is going to help people. Now, that was beyond my comprehension. I said, 'Lord, what do you mean it's going to help people?' And he never revealed that to me." For David, then, the winery is a type of divine mission. He feels that it offers people products that God has put in nature for their benefit. Reflecting on his prayer, David says, "I didn't understand at that time, and I still don't understand the full ramifications of the vision, but I'm beginning to. Now, I can sort of see with this health issue what he had in mind. And I really think we're going to help people."

Grapefull Sisters Vineyard

4903 Ramsey Ford Road
Tabor City, N.C. 28463
Phone: 910-653-2944
Fax: 910-653-2539
Website:
www.grapefullsistersvineyard.com
E-mail:
contact@grapefullsistersvineyard.com
Hours: Wednesday–Saturday, 10 a.m.–6 p.m.

Owners: Sheila Suggs Little and Amy Suggs
Winemaker: Duplin Winery
Tasting fee: Yes
On-line ordering: No
Wine club: Yes

Wine List
Whites: Sister's Folly Carlos, Southern Charm, Waccamaw White (Magnolia)
Blush: Sunset Blush (scuppernong)
Reds: Picnic Red, Red Roof Burgundy (Noble), Tabor's Choice Red, Waccamaw Red (muscadine)
Specialties: Old Timer's Festival (scuppernong dessert), Uncle Pink's Alcohol-Free

Directions: From Tabor City in Columbus County, go 13 miles south on N.C. 904. Turn right on Dulah Road and go 1.2 miles. The vineyard is on the left. Or take S.C. 9 South, go left at Black Bear Golf

Shelia Suggs Little and Amy Suggs

ONTO CAMP SWAMP ROAD, AND CONTINUE TO THE END OF THE ROAD. TURN RIGHT ON DOTHAN, THEN TAKE AN IMMEDIATE LEFT ON RAMSEY FORD. THE VINEYARD IS ON THE RIGHT AFTER 3 MILES.

In 2003, the Suggs sisters inherited 45 acres of land from their parents. Although the property had cotton on it, the sisters wondered if there might be a better use. Sheila Suggs Little remembers, "We were cleaning the ditch bank, trying to keep the place as attractive as possible, and we said, 'If we could just get rid of some of these grapevines . . .' Then we stopped and looked at each other." Her sister, Amy, laughs, "That's the moment we lost our minds."

Since native muscadine vines grew wild on the property, Amy and Sheila became convinced that they could establish a commercial vineyard. They are quick to point out that this is not a new idea: "Our history of this vineyard goes back 90 years. Our uncle Pickney had a muscadine vineyard here, and our father used to work for him for a nickel a day." The more the sisters considered the possibility, the more they liked it. Then, one day, Sheila picked up an issue of *On The Vine*, the state's viticultural newsletter. It had an editorial about the need for

Grapefull Sisters tasting room

North Carolina to find its signature grape. Sheila called the editor and "got up on my high horse," she admits. She felt that the answer was obvious: "Darn it, muscadine is the state grape." After the call, she wrote an article on the issue, did an interview with a reporter, and was inspired to get more involved in the state's wine industry.

The sisters came up with a plan to develop the property in three phases: the planting of a vineyard, the construction of a small inn, and the establishment of a camping area and upscale RV park. Ultimately, they want to create a special destination, one that will be a peaceful oasis in the midst of what they feel is rapid and inevitable change in the area. Amy points out, "A trip to Myrtle Beach used to be a big deal, but the beach is coming here like a runaway train. The development is unbelievable."

Phase one involved putting vines in the ground. This work, Amy laughs, "is not for the dainty. You've got to have a love for the land. You've got to like getting your hands dirty." They began with one acre of vines, and the next year, they planted more. Eventually, they would like to expand the acreage to 10. Grapefull Sisters is not a bonded winery. The sisters cultivate the grapes, and Duplin Winery makes the wine for their label. This arrangement offers the sisters the chance to grow the business in stages. As they proudly point out, it means they are associated with "the oldest, biggest, most successful muscadine winery in the world."

Phase two of the sisters' plan involved establishing Inn d'Vine, which includes both the tasting room and three bedrooms for guests. Because their great-great-uncle had an inn, Sheila and Amy see themselves as continuing another family tradition—that of innkeeper. The sisters designed the building together. Since Sheila lived and worked in Hickory, that meant a lot of time on the phone. Sheila laughs, "We still have the bill for that. It's not easy to do floor plans when you're five hours apart."

There have been other difficulties for the sisters, including financial struggles. Sheila says of the costs, "We had no earthly idea. It was a weekly trip to the bank." Throughout, however, they remained committed to their project and pursued their vision. They thought often of their mother, who would say, "Put feet on your dreams and get moving."

To honor their mother, who was an artist, the sisters exhibit the work of artists from all over the state. The tasting room also serves as a gallery, which, they believe, makes for "a unique gift shop." In the future, they plan to have the vineyard sponsor festivals and heritage events featuring old-time music and crafts. They also would like to open a restaurant, and they are committed to phase three of the property's development, the establishment of a campground on 15 acres of wooded land called Carroll Woods.

The sisters have ambitious plans, but they were raised to believe they can accomplish a great deal if they work hard and take the initiative. Sheila explains, "Mama always told us, 'God's going to open doors for you, but you're going to have to walk through them.'"

Hinnant Family Vineyards

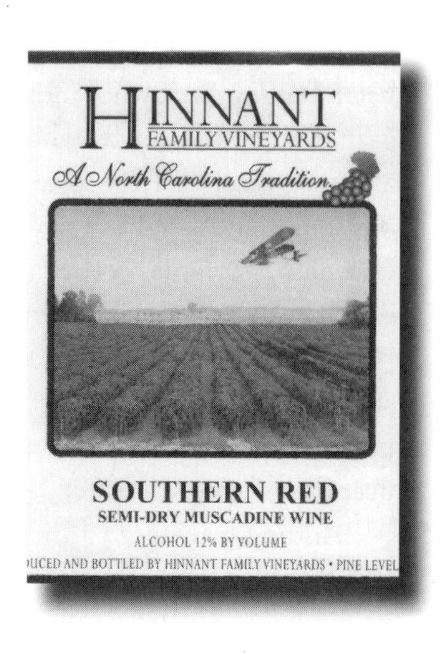

826 Pine Level–Micro Road
Pine Level, N.C. 27568
Phone: 919-965-3350
Fax: 919-965-6103
Website: www.hinnantvineyards.com
E-mail: info@hinnantvineyards.com
Hours: Tuesday–Friday, 11 a.m.–5 p.m.;
Saturday, 10 a.m.–6 p.m.;
Sunday, 1–5 p.m.

Owners: R. Willard Hinnant and
Bob Hinnant
Winemaker: Bob Hinnant
First year as bonded winery: 2002
Tasting fee: Yes
On-line ordering: Yes
Wine club: Yes

Wine List
Whites: Carlos, Carolina Wildflower (white muscadine with honey)
Blush: Muscadine Blush
Reds: Noble, Norton, Scuppernong, Tar Heel Red
Fruits: Peach, Strawberry
Specialty: Holiday Classic

Directions: Take Exit 97 off Interstate 95 in Johnston County and go east on U.S. 70 for approximately 3 miles to the second stoplight. Turn left on Peedin Road and go north for approximately 3 miles. The vineyards are on the right.

Like his father, Willard, Bob Hinnant went into dentistry. Unlike his father, who is still practicing, Bob decided not to pursue it as a lifelong career. He says of the dental laboratory he ran, "It wasn't a dead job; it just wasn't satisfying." So, in 1999 and 2000, he began thinking about opening a winery.

It was an idea that had been in Bob's mind for a long time. He had been making his own wine since he was 18, learning from his father, grandfather, and uncle, who always made some at Christmas to give away as presents. They were, Bob says, excellent teachers; they also had a resource most hobbyists don't—their own vineyards. In 1972, Willard, along with his brother and two sisters, had founded Hinnant Family Vineyards. In the following decades, the vineyards became a popular you-pick operation. In fact, some customers still have a yearly ritual of stopping to ask if the grapes are ready. Bob notes that some of the fresh-pick muscadines "look like plums, they're so big. People just go nuts over them."

Adding a winery to the vineyards seemed like a logical step, and Bob believed that it made good economic sense. Instead of making all its money in six weeks, the business could make money all year long. Nevertheless, Bob had to convince his family that it was a good idea, and this wasn't easy. He says, "My family is very conservative, to say the least." Although his father enjoyed making wine as a hobby, he thought it would be a risky business venture. An example of Willard's cautiousness can be seen in the number of small vats in the winery. Once the family agreed to the project, he insisted wine be made only in small amounts to keep the potential loss to a minimum if a batch went bad and had to be thrown out.

The family's caution was unnecessary. The winery opened in 2002, and Hinnant Family Vineyards' first release won a gold medal in the state's muscadine competition. Since then, the winery has grown by 30 to 35 percent a year. In its first year, Hinnant produced 1,600 cases. Four years later, it was producing 7,500 cases and distributing its wines

Bob Hinnant

in over 600 stores and 200 Food Lion groceries. Managing this expansion has been one of Bob's biggest challenges. "You can never make enough money in this business," Bob points out, "because you're always trying to grow."

The winery's success meant that Bob could sell his dental lab in 2004 and work full time for Hinnant Family Vineyards. By 2006, the winery had outgrown the 5,000-square-foot building that Bob had designed, and more space was needed. At that point, he realized that his father's attitude had changed. When Bob suggested that they add on to the existing winery, Willard, who had always urged caution, said they should construct a whole new building. Doing so would allow them not only to increase production but also to convert the original building into a place more appealing for events and meetings.

Bob points out that constructing the new 6,500-square-foot winery gave him a chance to correct mistakes he made in the first building. For example, he initially didn't realize the importance of drains: "If your floors aren't right, you end up spending hours with squeegees." It also provided him the opportunity to use taller, more cost-effective tanks and gave him more production space. Unlike many wineries that specialize in European-style wines, however, Hinnant doesn't need a large storage area to age wines. Bob insists that muscadine wines are

Hinnant Family Vineyards

"as good at six months as four years." He says, "They're the only wine I know that, if you pushed it, you could harvest in September and bottle by December."

Hinnant Family Vineyards now consists of 75 acres. It grows 10 varieties of muscadines and scuppernongs and sells grapes to a number of wineries throughout the state. In addition to muscadine wines, Hinnant offers strawberry and peach wines, as well as a red Norton, to appeal to customers who prefer a drier wine. In the future, Bob plans to offer a Viognier. He says, "My hopes are our growth continues the way it has been and we reach our target, which is to sell every bit of wine we can." If they succeed in doing that, Hinnant Family Vineyards will have reached a production of 32,000 cases.

Bob notes that he works harder and longer hours than he did in dentistry. He says of a winery, "Everybody thinks it's really romantic, but the work never ends. It can be seven days a week, sunup to sundown." Still, it's a change that he's glad he made: "In dentistry, I spent all day pushing myself around in a chair working on something the size of a pinky nail. Making wine, I'm not confined. That's why I love it."

474 Suggs-Taylor Road
Dublin, N.C. 28332
Phone: 800-545-2293 or
910-866-5819
Fax: 910-862-2799
Website: www.lumilvineyard.com
E-mail: lumilvineyard@intrstar.net
Hours: Monday–Saturday, 10 a.m.–6 p.m.;
Sunday, 1–6 p.m.

Owners: The Taylor family
Tasting fee: No
On-line ordering: No
Wine club: Yes

Wine List
White: Taylor Divine
Blush: Bladen Blush
Reds: Cape Owen Red, Old Cumberland
Specialties: Lucille's Choice (alcohol-free wine), Merry Christmas (seasonal Christmas red wine)

Directions: Take Exit 46A off Interstate 95 and drive 25 miles south to Dublin in Bladen County. Turn left on Fourth Street, go 0.5 mile, and turn right on Suggs-Taylor Road. The vineyard is on the right.

Ron Taylor admits that he's different from most winery owners: "I got into the vineyard business to develop equipment." As the owners of

Ron Taylor

Taylor Manufacturing, a company their father built, Ron and his brother, Oren, wanted to sell machinery. Ron planted a few rows of grapes to have an experimental vineyard on which he could test the prototypes of the Taylor Grapevine Pruner and the Taylor Grape Harvester. Ron discovered, however, that vineyard owners can be hesitant to try out new equipment. He also discovered that growing grapes and turning them into wine can be profitable. Consequently, he decided to found Lu Mil Vineyard.

Although the name Lu Mil honors his mother and father, Lucille and Miller, Ron acknowledges that his mother didn't approve of alcohol: "I can see her balling up her fist whenever anyone mentioned wine." However, when a friend told him, "Ron Taylor, your mother is going to turn over in her grave when she learns that you're making wine," he replied, "I hope not. The farm is beautiful." He also jokes, "Besides, I've got a big picture of my mother by the counter with a blindfold on her, so she can't see what we're doing." The vineyard does offer Lucille's Choice, which is a nonalcoholic wine, and the gift shop provides a variety of nonalcoholic muscadine ciders, slushies, and jellies.

Some people in the community share Lucille's view and have been hesitant to approve of the vineyard. For example, for Lu Mil's grand opening, Ron wanted to do a benefit fundraiser for the Bladen County

Hospital and proposed a wine-and-cheese event. Initially, this idea was rejected. Ron talked to the hospital board members one by one and finally convinced them to approve the event if he agreed to certain compromises, such as referring to "souvenir" glasses instead of wineglasses. The week of the fundraiser, the weather was terrible, but on the scheduled date, "the good Lord parted the skies, the sun was shining, and it was a beautiful day," Ron says. "Everybody who was anybody was here, and we made $18,000 for the hospital." He adds with a grin, "I sold a tremendous amount of wine, and we've been wide open ever since."

Although Ron tells stories with a sense of humor, Lu Mil represents a serious commitment to the community. At one point, Taylor Manufacturing employed hundreds of people; it still has approximately 70 employees. The area needs to find new ventures to diversify its economy, and Ron believes that Lu Mil helps do this. He says, "We're making an investment that we think will be a long-term investment for us and the community." In doing so, "we're going to provide for our families and the families that work for us."

Lu Mil's vineyard consists of 35 acres of grapes. The tasting room originally was located in an old barn built by Ron's father. The building contains a jumble of farm implements and equipment that Ron has worked with throughout his life, and he discovered to his surprise that visitors consider these tools fascinating. In 2006, when Ron built a larger tasting and events facility with air conditioning and modern

Lu Mil truck

amenities, he found that some people still wanted to hold events in the barn because of its "atmosphere."

Ron decided to expand Lu Mil only eight months after opening, in part because he foresees enormous growth ahead for the muscadine grape industry. The vineyard plantings include seven acres of "fresh-pick" grapes. When Ron arrives with these at farmers' markets, he'll find people waiting in line: "It's amazing, the excitement in their faces." People love the taste, and the grape has "tremendous medicinal properties." He also points out that there are still many untapped markets, such as using muscadine byproducts in dog food for people who want "safe, healthy food products for their pets."

Ultimately, Ron wants to turn Lu Mil Vineyard into a destination site. The property, including the vineyard, consists of several hundred acres. It has trails, fishponds, and even a racetrack. It's a place where people "can enjoy nature and have a good time." Each fall, the farm features a corn maze. Ron says, "We're going to keep adding things like this to make it an attraction."

In pursuing this plan, Ron is following the model of his parents. Although they weren't formally educated, "they were brilliant, intelligent, and hardworking people," he says. They also were entrepreneurs continually starting new projects. Ron says of his father, "Whatever you can imagine doing, he did it." He put in the region's first rural telephone system and founded the first seed and hardware store in the area. He was a welder, builder, and inventor. He patented cotton-picking and tobacco equipment and used the property as a "research farm" where the family "was always trying to make a better mousetrap."

Ron learned from his parents the curiosity to experiment and the courage to try new ventures. He also learned values that he emphasizes on the welcome sign of Lu Mil Vineyard: "Religion, family, tradition, honesty, and hard work." Ron believes the vineyard honors their memory. He says, "It's preserving our heritage and preserving the farm and doing what we enjoy doing and seeing what the good Lord wants us to grow."

Lumina Winery

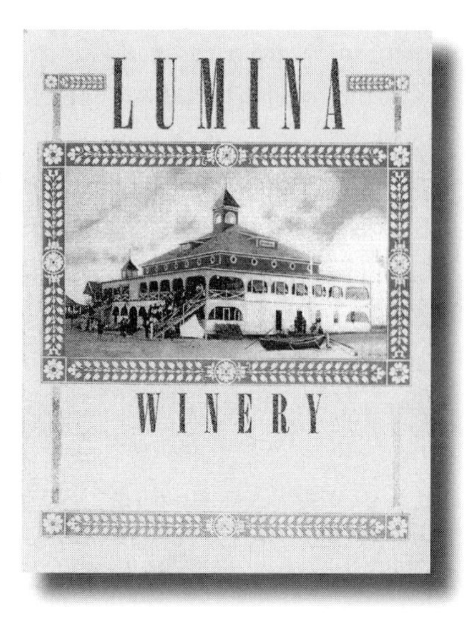

206 South Kerr Avenue, Unit 112-A
Wilmington, N.C. 28403
Phone and fax: 910-793-5299
Website: www.luminawine.com
E-mail: davehursey@juno.com
Hours: Monday–Wednesday,
noon–6 p.m.;
Saturday, 11 a.m.–3 p.m.

Owner: Dave Hursey
Winemaker: Dave Hursey
First year as bonded winery: 2005
Tasting fee: No
On-line ordering: Pending
Wine club: No

Wine List
Whites: Airlie Bianca Pinot Grigio, Green Apple Riesling, Ice Wine, Lune Blanc Chardonnay, Peach-Apricot Chardonnay
Reds: Black Raspberry Merlot, Blackberry Cabernet, Wildberry Shiraz

Directions: Take Interstate 40 East to N.C. 132 (South College Road). Go 1.7 miles and exit onto U.S. 17 South (Market Street), heading toward downtown Wilmington. Go 1 mile, turn left (south) on South Kerr Avenue, and go approximately 0.3 mile. The winery is on the right next to Martin Self Storage.

For 16 years, Dave Hursey worked for the Wilmington police force. During the last four, he was a crime-scene investigator. While investigating a case, he stepped into a hole and badly damaged his knee. When a doctor determined that he could no longer fulfill the physical requirements of his job, Dave was given early retirement.

Ironically, Dave's injury gave him a type of freedom. Although he enjoyed police work, retirement meant that he could finally open a winery, something he had wanted to do for several years. He had been making wine as a hobbyist since 1999, but when he had explored the possibility of going commercial in 2002, the police department had regarded it as a conflict of interest. Now, he could pursue his passion, so he began to develop Lumina Winery.

Dave named the winery after the Lumina Pavilion, a famous local structure that opened on June 3, 1905, on Wrightsville Beach. During its heyday, Dave says, the pavilion "was a big deal." In addition to the Miss North Carolina Pageant, it hosted famous big bands, including those of Louis Armstrong, Tommy Dorsey, Cab Calloway, and Guy Lombardo. In the 1950s, Dave's grandparents bought and ran the pavilion. Dave remembers the sad day in 1973 when his grandfather took him to watch the structure being torn down. To celebrate the memory of the Lumina, Dave started the winery's first official batch of wine on June 3, 2005, exactly 100 years after the pavilion opened.

Unlike the Lumina Pavilion, Lumina Winery is not in a romantic setting. Wilmington considers winemaking to be manufacturing,

Dave Hursey
COURTESY OF LUMINA WINERY

Lumina tasting room
COURTESY OF LUMINA WINERY

so a winery must be located in an industrial zone. Consequently, Dave looked for a suitable location for a long time before he finally settled on a space in a business park next to a self-storage area. Although he knew the 600-square-foot unit was too small, he liked its proximity to the interstate. He explains, "I thought, 'Let's start here, get a foot in the door, and see how it goes.'"

Customers may be surprised by the winery's location and exterior, but when they enter, Dave says, they are impressed with the professional atmosphere and the wine list. At times, Lumina may offer up to 20 selections. Although Dave does buy grapes from local growers such as Bennett Vineyards, Lumina concentrates primarily on kit and concentrate wines. Dave points out, "Anything you try in the tasting room, you can buy and make." The reception of his wines has been good, and local restaurants and outlets like the Wild Wing Café feature them. People are particularly fond of his Green Apple Riesling, and he makes a blueberry-flavored Syrah for the state's blueberry festival that sells "amazingly well."

Eventually, Dave would like to move to a different location, one that is more accessible to customers, more appealing, and more roomy. Because of the city's zoning laws, however, he may have to keep his production facility at the current site and set up a retail store with a tasting counter elsewhere. Whatever he does, Dave says he doesn't intend to get too big. He would like to have Lumina grow to be a "medium-sized" winery—one that sells 1,000 bottles a month, or 1,000 cases a year, but doesn't have more than three employees.

Dave sometimes sees his former colleagues when they come in to buy wine. He points out that his police work helped prepare him for certain aspects of the business. Just like with a crime scene, everything in a winery must be documented. He says, "You have to stay on top of things. There's so many records that have to be kept and forms that have to be sent." There are, however, some big differences as well. He's not dealing with life-and-death situations, people are usually happy to see him, and he spends his time talking about the process of creation rather than destruction. In fact, Dave insists the most rewarding thing about having a winery is "getting to deal with nice people for a change."

Martin Vineyards

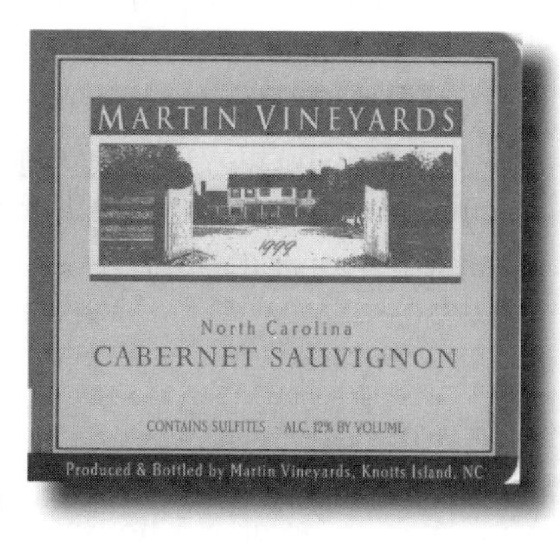

P.O. Box 186
Knotts Island, N.C. 27950
Phone: 252-429-3542 or
252-429-3564
Fax: 252-429-3095
Website: www.martinvineyards.com
E-mail: Lulu1926@aol.com
Hours: Monday–Saturday,
10 a.m.–6 p.m.; Sunday, noon–6 p.m.
Call for winter hours.

Owners: David and Jeannie Martin
Winemaker: David Martin
First year as bonded winery: 1993
Tasting fee: Yes
On-line ordering: Yes
Wine club: No

Wine List
Whites: Chardonnay, Fruitville White, Viognier
Reds: Atlantis Meritage, Cabernet Sauvignon, Merlot, Muscadine
Fruit: Strawberry

Directions: From Virginia Beach, Virginia, drive south on Princess Anne Road to Knotts Island, just across the North Carolina border. Bear left at the Knotts Island Market and go approximately 1 mile to the vineyards, located on the left. From Currituck County, take N.C. 168 to the free Currituck Sound ferry (call 800-BY FERRY for information). After crossing the sound to Knotts Island, follow N.C. 615 North for 2.7 miles to Martin Farm Lane. The entrance to the winery is on the right.

David Martin's career as a farmer began early. Almost as soon as he could walk, he started helping his father, William Martin, on the family's strawberry farm in Virginia Beach. He loved working in the dirt and playing with plants, and when he wandered away from the fields, it wasn't to watch television, but to go into the woods. He says, "I like to watch things grow. I've always been a plant person." Unlike his brothers, who moved away to pursue teaching and coaching careers, David returned home after college to plant the family orchards. He has remained there ever since.

It's hardly surprising that David knows the 88 acres of Martin Vineyards intimately, since he helped plant the trees and vines as a 22-year-old. In the early 1970s, his father decided to move the family from Virginia Beach to Knotts Island. He bought a cattle farm that was slated to become a housing development, but instead of putting buildings on the property, he planted fruit trees. It was an appropriate place for an orchard. Knotts Island has a history of fruit farming that dates to the 1800s; the township is even called "Fruitville." In addition to apples and peaches, the Martins planted strawberries and scupper-

Martin Vineyards entrance
COURTESY OF MARTIN VINEYARDS

Martin Vineyards
COURTESY OF MARTIN VINEYARDS

nong vines. Their you-pick crops attracted a loyal clientele. David says, "People came back every year like clockwork."

In 1987, looking for new agricultural challenges, David decided to experiment with vinifera varietals. He planted several rows of vines and began teaching himself how to make wine. At first, he worked with an old manual press that can still be seen on the winery's porch. He says, "I took a hands-on approach. I learned from the ground up, which is a good way to do it." He is self-taught. In fact, if he had listened to advice, the vineyards wouldn't exist. People at North Carolina State University and Virginia Tech warned him that he wouldn't be able to grow vinifera successfully because it would develop Pierce's disease, which often infects grapevines in mild climates. Although David acknowledges that this can be a problem, he believes he has found ways to combat the disease.

In 1992, David planted more vines, but he soon discovered that he "had too much wine. I couldn't drink it all or give it all away, so we said, 'Well, let's get a wine permit.'" Martin Vineyards became a bonded winery and now has eight acres dedicated to vinifera varietals. Although David says that "we specialize in the Bordeaux reds: Cabernet, Merlot, Cabernet Franc, Petit Verdot, and Malbec," he also makes muscadine and fruit wines that sell out quickly each year. In fact, they are so popular that people reserve bottles months in advance. Jeannie Martin calls the muscadine wine "liquid gold." She says, "I could have thousands of recordings of people saying, 'Oh, my God, it tastes just like the grapes at my grandmother's house.' It's the state taste."

Because making a good wine takes good grapes, David believes that "most of the work is in the fields. If you don't do the work out there, what's done in the winery means nothing." Overall, he calculates that each grape cluster is worked on at least four times in the course of a season, an estimate that doesn't include tucking the vines and trimming them. Then, when it comes time to harvest, a grower needs to know not only when to pick, but how. David explains, "You've got to get the grapes ripe, and uniformly ripe. That means saving only the shoots that are uniform and saving the best clusters. If you go in and pick them all the same day, you're going to have bunches that are ripe, overripe, and underripe." Consequently, he picks three times a year. Insisting that "there's no shortcuts," he points out that "it's total work out here. Seven days a week. You've got to love it, or it will drive you absolutely bonkers." He also notes, "You've got to have a good wife. An understanding wife. You're working here until dark."

According to David, experts who say the coast is a bad place to farm fail to take into account Knotts Island's unique climate. The area is an excellent place for fruit because, he explains, "we don't get a lot of the rainfall that they get just inland from here. The ocean breezes knock it back." The breezes also quickly dry any moisture that does occur, which keeps rot at a minimum. The island's sandy soil provides excellent drainage. David says vines "root like crazy here. Stick a vine cutting in the ground, come back the next year, and it's growing." In fact, the vines can be too vigorous. He constantly needs to cut them back to ensure a quality yield. Even the coast's periodic hurricanes don't damage the vines. They do, however, make for difficult working conditions. David remembers when he was harvesting his Merlot in 1998: "I picked it two days before Hurricane Bonnie. I actually had it out here fermenting. I built walls around it and wrapped it in tarps, in case it got really bad, which it did. Trees were down all over. Right on the coast here, we really take the hit." In spite of Bonnie, the Merlot turned out to be "a great wine."

Because it ripens early, before hurricane season, Merlot usually does well. David also likes his Viognier, which "has turned out to be real nice." He points out, "We had the first Viognier on the market in the state. Now, you see it all over." David has had to experiment to determine what grows best: "When I started here, it was unknown what would do well. It had never been done here." The closest winery was in Williamsburg, Virginia. Now, other people have developed vineyards in the area, including Moonrise Bay Vineyard and Sanctuary Vineyards.

To attract visitors, Martin Vineyards has you-pick orchards and hosts events on major holidays such as Memorial Day and the Fourth of July. The entrance to the property is beautiful. A dirt road bordered by white fences goes through the orchards and vineyards and past the Martin family's 19th-century residence. The winery itself, however, is a working farm, rather than a showcase for visitors. The small tasting room has examples of work by local artists, but most people will probably want to stay outside, where a patio and tables at the water's edge allow them to picnic, look at the bay, or bird-watch. The fruit trees attract so many ospreys and other birds that Jeannie says the orchards can be "like an airport." In fact, when David designed the winery's labels, he included an osprey.

Martin Vineyards' success has a clear cause; it's the effort that David exerts in the fields. He does it because "I love farming. I love producing a good crop. It's hard to do, but when you see the people come out and pick, and taste the wine, that's rewarding."

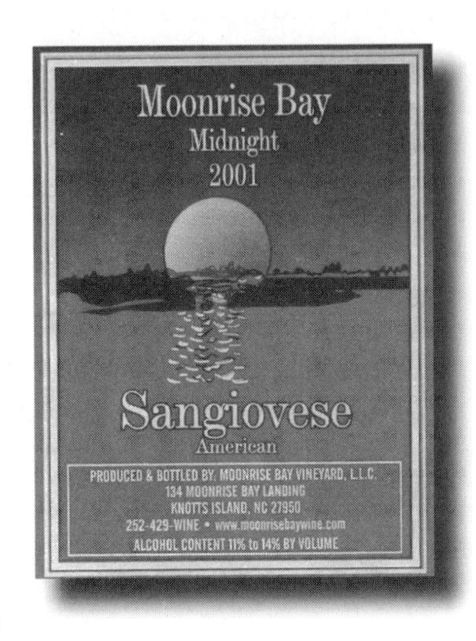

134 Moonrise Bay Landing
Knotts Island, N.C. 27950
Phone: 252-429-9463
Fax: 252-429-3090
Website:
www.moonrisebaywine.com
E-mail: info@moonrisebaywine.com
Hours: Thursday–Sunday, noon–6 p.m.

Owners: Kate and Richard Morris and
Fleet Smith
Winemaker: Richard Morris
First year as bonded winery: 2000
Tasting fee: Yes
On-line ordering: No
Wine club: No

Wine List
Whites: Carlos, Chardonnay, Fumé Blanc, Sauvignon Blanc
Reds: Chambourcin, Nebbiolo, Noble
Fruits: Blackberry, Blueberry, Cherry, Raspberry, Strawberry
Specialty: Magnolia (dessert wine)

Directions: From Virginia Beach, Virginia, drive south on Princess Anne Road to Knotts Island, just across the North Carolina border. Bear left at the Knotts Island Market and go 1 mile. The vineyard is on the left. From Currituck County, take N.C. 168 to the free Currituck Sound ferry (call 800-BY FERRY for information). After crossing the sound to Knotts Island, follow N.C. 615 North for 2.8 miles. The winery entrance is on the right.

Moonrise Bay Vineyard

Moonrise Bay Vineyard had its origin in a walk in San Francisco. That's when Richard "Oakie" Morris, a plastic surgeon with a 20-year practice in Virginia Beach, turned to his longtime office manager and said, "Kate, I don't want to complicate your life, but I love you." Unsure what to say, Kate turned away and asked, "What kind of flowers are those?" "They're cyclamens," Oakie answered. Kate laughs at the memory of that morning: "I thought, 'Surely, he's lost his mind.'" Later, after she was convinced of his seriousness and they, as Oakie puts it, "sorted things out and got our lives in order," the couple bought a house on Knotts Island. They had no intention of starting a winery. They were "just thinking of a place to live away from the world," Oakie says.

Their first year on the island, the Morrises found themselves with an unexpected problem: too many pears. Their tree had produced a bumper crop, and even though Kate loves to cook, bushels of pears still remained after she made pear bread, pear pastries, pear desserts, and other pear products. One day, she came home to discover that Oakie had started fermenting pears in a tub. He had decided to make pear wine. Kate remembers that, during the process, "there were flies everywhere. It was a mess. We had two of us straining it though cheesecloth and

Kate and Richard Morris

pressing it." The couple put the five-gallon batch in unlabeled bottles. As an experiment, they served the wine at a Christmas party. When the guests raved about it, insisting it was the best Chardonnay they'd ever tasted, the Morrises' careers as winemakers began.

Encouraged by the response to their pear wine, and having noticed how well grapes grew at nearby Martin Vineyards, Kate and Oakie decided to plant some vines as a hobby. They bought 1,500 cuttings of Merlot and Cabernet varietals from David Martin. Oakie admits, "I was just going to make a little home-brew. I had no clue how many grapes you'd get off that." He had made "home-brew" before. While studying for his M.D. degree, he often made beer. Although it was popular, Oakie insists that this was no indication of quality because "medical students will drink anything." After his internship, Oakie was drafted. For a while, he continued his hobby even in the service. He fermented batches in a barracks bathtub. He remembers, "When the commanding officer came by, we put up a sign that said the plumbing was out of order. That explained the bloop, bloop, bloop sound." Eventually, Oakie was stationed in Germany, where the local beers were so good and inexpensive there was no reason to make his own. While in Europe, he also fell in love with wine. Because he was posted only five kilometers from France, he often crossed the border to eat and to drink "the wonderful French table wines."

As Oakie grew his first grapes on Knotts Island and planned his retirement, he devoted himself to learning about viticulture and oenology. Kate says that he read "for three years at night in his study. I knew we were in trouble because when he makes his mind up to do something, he is going to do it." He toured vineyards, talked to experts in the state's wine industry, and took courses and seminars at the University of California at Davis. Eventually, the Morrises made the commitment to a full-scale commercial vineyard.

Even with Oakie's research and drive, it was difficult to establish Moonrise Bay Vineyard. Kate remembers, "The first year was hard. I hated it. Oakie was working 14- to 18-hour days and coming home and falling asleep in his soup. . . . Sometimes, it felt like I had died and it wasn't heaven I woke up in." The following years were also stressful, as the vines grew and needed to be trellised. Kate acknowledges, however, that there were also moments of beauty. She remembers how,

Moonrise Bay wine
COURTESY OF MOONRISE BAY VINEYARD

when harvesting the Sauvignon Blanc, the juice ran down her hands, attracting monarchs and swallowtails: "You would pick the grapes, and your arms would be full of butterflies. It was beautiful."

As the vineyard matured, the Morrises discovered that Knotts Island has special agricultural properties. Oakie insists, "If you ask the experts, they say you can't grow grapes here. It's too hot, and [there is] too much disease pressure." However, because of its geography, the island has its own climate. In the summer, it is 10 degrees cooler than places inland, and the constant breezes keep the vines dry and reduce moisture-related problems. Even a heavy dew or rain will quickly evaporate. The tides are wind-driven, and since the nearest opening to the ocean is 50 miles away, the area isn't susceptible to flooding. Hurricanes, the coastal region's main concern, usually arrive too late in the growing season to significantly damage the vines. Consequently, grapes and other fruit crops do very well on the island.

To protect the winery from hurricanes, the Morrises decided to use a Quonset hut that can withstand 180-mile-per-hour winds. Oakie admits, "It looks funny on the outside, but it's nice on the inside." In 2003, the Morrises added a new tasting room complete with stone fireplace and wood-burning bread oven. The room has a romantic ambiance. In fact, when the nighttime weather permits, visitors can watch the moon rise over the bay, a view that inspired both the winery's name and Oakie's design for the label. Moonrise Bay Vineyard even schedules special tastings to coincide with full moons and the lunar calendar. It also hosts events such as candlelight barrel tastings for Valentine's Day, a Fourth of July barbecue, and harvest parties.

The winery is, Oakie points out, "a family operation." The children help in the vineyard, the tasting room, and the barrel room. Kate says proudly, "They know what needs to be done, and they do it." Although the children were initially skeptical about the business—one daughter admits that she thought her mother and Oakie "were crazy" and "wouldn't go through with it"—they now think having a winery is "kind of cool work." Other family members who contribute are Kate's mother, who regularly comes from Virginia Beach to assist in the tasting room, and Kate's brother-in-law, Arthur Trottier, who has taken over the management of the vineyard. Calling Arthur "Oakie's right hand," Kate says, "He truly nurtures the vineyard. He spends many sleepless nights when the weather conditions as well as other factors are affecting the grapes."

Although Moonrise Bay now produces 6,000 cases a year and has a 14-acre vineyard, the Morrises guard against growing too big. They don't want to get to the point where, in Oakie's words, "it becomes a real commercial enterprise, rather than an art form." He explains, "I don't want to be a person in a corporate office. That's not why I got into this." For Oakie, "making wine is a very soulful thing." He values the artistic and aesthetic aspects of the process. For example, he particularly enjoys using tubs instead of tanks because "it's very personal. You taste it. You work with it."

An attempt to find a place away from the world unexpectedly turned the Morrises into winemakers. It's a transformation they appreciate. Kate says, "Sometimes, we're walking in the vineyard in the evening, and it's like a dream. I'm so grateful that we're getting to enjoy it. It's so peaceful." As for Oakie, he admits, "I just love the whole process. Just being involved with it from planting to harvesting, it's all such a neat experience."

Sanctuary Vineyards

6957 Carotake Highway
Jarvisburg, N.C. 27947
Phone: 800-637-2446
Website:
www.sanctuaryvineyards.com
E-mail:
john@sanctuaryvineyards.com
Hours: Open daily;
call for an appointment.

Owners: Tom and Jerry Wright
Winemaker: Richard Morris of
Moonrise Bay Vineyard
Tasting fee: No
On-line ordering: No
Wine club: No

Wine List
White: Chardonnay
Blush: The Lightkeeper (Sangiovese, Chardonnay, and Vidal blend)
Reds: Coastal Collage (red blend), Muscadine, Norton, Sangiovese, Syrah
Fruit: Blackberry

Directions: The vineyards are located in Currituck County off U.S. 158 approximately 11 miles north of the Wright Memorial Bridge, next to the Cotton Gin.

John Wright is passionate about the land he grew up on. His family has farmed it for seven generations, and he would like his descendants to be able to do so as well. He knows, however, that agriculture in the area is endangered. He explains, "We live in an area that's changing rapidly due to development. It's happening almost too fast to imagine." The area is between booming populations at Norfolk and the Kitty Hawk area. As a result, "people see this farmland and are salivating over it." John fears that his may be the last generation in the region to grow crops, a prospect he finds "wrenching." Consequently, he regards Sanctuary Vineyards as having dual missions to grow the best wine grapes possible and to preserve the land so that, in the future, "people can see how it used to be."

The vineyards' name, which came from John's uncle, Jerry Wright, reflects the family's "outlook toward conservation." Each winter, they flood part of the land to make it a sanctuary for migratory birds. With water covering 20 to 30 acres, the farm becomes "basically a big birdbath," one that is "blanketed with thousands and thousands of snow geese." The practice, John explains, "is our way of keeping the farm in balance and being environmentally responsible. You don't have to develop every inch of land, and you don't have to farm every bit of land." The open areas result not only in a sanctuary for birds, but a sanctuary for people as well.

John Wright
COURTESY OF SANCTUARY VINEYARDS

Sanctuary birds
COURTESY OF SANCTUARY VINEYARDS

John admits that grape growing is hard work (although he points out that "my great-grandfather would say we've got it good"). Viticulture on the coast can be especially challenging because the ocean creates a unique climate. "It's not like France or Italy or anywhere else. We've done weather-data comparisons, and nothing compares." There is a lack of humidity and also of cool nights. As a result, "the grapes get really ripe . . . if I don't have hurricanes." Storms are a constant concern, but John insists, "I really enjoy seeing how weather affects this place. The most exciting part of growing fruit out here is playing the stakes. You either really thrive or really struggle. Your grapes are great, or you wake up and find the stakes have been blown over." The trick, he believes, is to remember that "we can't conquer nature, but we can take these things into account."

John planted his first vines in 2001, and Sanctuary Vineyards now grows a variety of vinifera, French-American, and native American grapes on 10 acres. John is still learning which ones will do best in the area, but he knows "thin-skinned varietals need not apply." So far, he has been impressed with Norton because "it's a pleasure to work with" and has a regional character.

Sanctuary Vineyards is not a bonded winery. Oakie Morris, the winemaker and co-owner of nearby Moonrise Bay Vineyard, makes the wine for the Sanctuary label. John explains, "We knew that building a winery for an uncertain crop was not the right move. We were very cautious at first. We're still cautious." The arrangement with Moonrise Bay allows him to take advantage of Oakie's "wealth of knowledge," to learn oenology from him, and to concentrate on growing the grapes. John says, "It's a great business relationship."

Instead of having an official tasting room at the vineyards, Sanctuary sells its wines in the Cotton Gin, a chain of three retail stores owned by the Wright family since the 1970s. These stores specialize in what John calls "coastal country lifestyle" products, and they promote and sell the 1,000 cases of wine Sanctuary has bottled each year. John points out, "We are not a big wine in North Carolina, but out here on the coast, we produce enough." The stores also sell the wines of Moonrise Bay Vineyard and Martin Vineyards. In fact, the three businesses are working together to form an American Viticultural Area.

John believes an AVA designation might be another tool he could use to promote land preservation. Although the farm still grows corn and soybeans, John feels that vineyards may be the property's future. He says, "I wish other people would grow grapes, but you can't tell people what to do, and I can understand why someone would sell the land for millions of dollars and just buy wine." Nevertheless, he wishes people would remember that "every acre that falls to a putting green or parking lot, you can't get that back."

A Secret Garden Winery

1018 Airport Road
Pikeville, N.C. 27863
Phone: 919-734-0260
Website:
www.asecretgardenwinery.com
E-mail: lwallhall@hotmail.com
Hours: Thursday–Saturday,
9 a.m.–6 p.m.; Sunday, 1–6 p.m.

Owners: Linda and Gerald Hall
Winemaker: Linda Hall
First year as bonded winery: 2003
Tasting fee: No
On-line ordering: No
Wine club: No

Wine List
Whites: Carlos varieties
Reds: Noble varieties
Fruits: Blueberry, Peach, Strawberry

Directions: From U.S. 70 in Goldsboro, take the U.S. 117 North/William Street exit to Airport Road. Bear right on Airport Road. The winery is on the right after 2 miles. (Note that there is a new U.S. 117 and an old U.S. 117. These directions are for the old U.S. 117.)

Linda Hall began making wine in 1992, as she puts it, "just to see if I could do it." Winemaking, however, has a long tradition in her farming family. She remembers, "Mama always made a little bit of wine just

A Secret Garden's entrance

for medicinal purposes, and we would always go pick the fruit for her." Family and friends who liked what Linda was doing encouraged her to consider pursuing her hobby more seriously. And in 2002, she decided she would. After 25 years of working in the welding and steel business started by her father and continued by her husband, she wanted to change careers. She taught her daughter-in-law how to do her job and told the family, "It's time to do something more fun."

After taking a short course at Virginia Tech and visiting various wineries around the area, she planted 100 muscadine vines on the farm. The property has been in her family for four generations, and she was born in the house across the road from the winery. These deep Southern roots and her commitment to sustainable methods that don't require the use of chemicals or pesticides made muscadine grapes a natural choice. Two years later, in 2004, Linda opened A Secret Garden. Unfortunately, because her mother suffered a serious illness, she had to temporarily close soon afterward. Although that "kind of put a setback on everything," Linda believes in retrospect that it had a positive effect in forcing her to delay the release of her wines. She explains that one key to making her wines is patience: "You've got to wait at least two years, and three is probably better."

The wines take so long because Linda refuses to engage in the usual practice of killing the native yeasts and controlling fermentation with chemicals. Although this allows a winemaker to exert more control over the results and ensure uniform products, Linda chooses to let fermentation occur naturally and then wait for the process to end. As a result, it can take much longer for her wines to be available for sale.

Because of Linda's winemaking practice, her wines are different each year. She also needs to make sure her customers know how to take care of them. At times, fermentation can continue after a wine has been bottled. Linda laughs, "You might call it bubbly." If the wine isn't kept cool, the fermentation can pop the corks. Consequently, the winery's small tasting room has an announcement that explains, "These are 'living' wines" that must be properly stored. Linda notes that a few people have come back with popped corks, but she says, "They aren't mad. All they want is more wine."

Although Linda sometimes gets help from her husband or her granddaughters, she does most of the winery and vineyard tasks herself. This is the way she prefers it. She says, "I don't want 15 employees. I don't want three." She laughs that running a larger business would be more stressful, and "I'm trying to eliminate stress from my life." At times, however, that's impossible. She admits, "There's been so many times I've said, 'Why did I do this? Why did I do this?'" For example, she remembers when she was painting the ceiling beams purple while finishing the interior of the winery: "I dropped the bucket. Purple paint went all over. When the inspector came in, he said, 'Is this a part of your decoration?'" She also didn't enjoy doing the floor. She warns, "Don't let anyone tell you that putting down a tile floor is a fun weekend project. There's nothing fun about it."

A Secret Garden is a small operation. In 2006, Linda made just 100 gallons of blueberry wine, 50 gallons of peach, and approximately 1,000 gallons of grape. She doesn't distribute her wines yet or attend many festivals. Consequently, she's surprised by the number of tourists who have discovered her place. She says, "I thought it would be this local little winery for local people," but she gets visitors from all over the country, and from other countries as well. She also has fans. She admits, "I just chuckle sometimes when people come in and ask for my autograph. It's wild. I just make wine. That's it."

Although someday Linda would like to expand her operations and have a larger storage space and an outdoor pavilion for events, she insists that she has no plans to grow very big. "If people find me, okay. If they don't, that's okay, too." She likes having "a homey winery where people feel comfortable." On A Secret Garden's website and on each label is a poem of Linda's that talks about the need to find a "quiet place." Linda believes, "Life began in a garden, and you can get so much peace and contentment in a garden." She points out that "everybody's got their own place where they like to go to have peace and serenity." Some go to the mountains, some to the beaches, and some to the forests. Linda hopes that, for some, that peaceful place will be her winery.

Silver Coast Winery

6608 Barbeque Road
Ocean Isle Beach, N.C. 28470
Phone: 910-287-2800
Fax: 910-457-0608
Website:
www.silvercoastwinery.com
E-mail: info@silvercoastwinery.com
Hours: Monday–Saturday,
11 a.m.–6 p.m.; Sunday, noon–5 p.m.
Winter hours (November through March)
are Thursday–Sunday, noon–5 p.m.

Owners: Maryann and John Azzato
Winemaker: Dana Keeler
First year as bonded winery: 2002
Tasting fee: Yes
On-line ordering: Yes
Wine club: Yes

Wine List
Whites: Chardonnay, Seyval Blanc, Viognier
Blushes: Rosé, White Merlot
Reds: Barbera, Cabernet Sauvignon, Merlot, Sangiovese, Tesouro, Touriga (Cape Fear Blood Wine)
Specialty: Holiday Red Table Wine

Directions: Take U.S. 17 to N.C. 904 in Brunswick County. Drive 2 miles west on N.C. 904 to Russtown Road, turn right, go 1.5 miles to Barbeque Road, and turn right again. The winery is at the end of the road.

Maryann Azzato

On May 17, 2002, as Maryann Azzato's oldest daughter watched a crowd of people tasting wine, looking at art, and listening to music, she leaned over and said, "I'm proud of you, Mom." She had reason to be. In a short period of time, her mother had conceptualized, built, and opened an impressive winery.

Maryann's achievement in establishing Silver Coast Winery was even more notable since she was new to the industry. In the 1990s, she worked as a trader in the financial markets, but she wanted to find a different career because, she says, "the market scared me" and because she didn't enjoy trading. She believes that "in order to have a fulfilling life, you have to like your work. If you don't like your work, there's no point; you've got to find another job."

At first, Maryann considered a mail-order wine business. She had been interested in wine for a long time. Her father made a batch every year with friends, which, she says, "was something that was always fascinating to me." She also collected bottles and labels. After researching the idea, however, she decided it wasn't feasible. Then, as she considered other possibilities, she received one of those phone calls that changes a person's life. A friend told her about a Massachusetts winery that was selling its assets. Suddenly, Maryann had a chance to buy equipment with which she could open a winery. After the call, "my husband looked at me, and I looked at him," she says. They knew it was an enormous

Entrance to Silver Coast Winery

commitment, and they decided to make it.

Although Maryann says she never hesitates to "take a little bit of a gamble," she also does her research. After analyzing the region's demographics, the Azzatos bought property near Ocean Isle Beach. This meant Maryann would have to commute 45 minutes from their home, but it placed the winery within a 100-mile radius of 15 million annual visitors. Besides attracting people from Wilmington, Silver Coast Winery would have the potential to draw visitors from Myrtle Beach and other parts of South Carolina.

The winery's grand opening was the first of many parties. Silver Coast hosts monthly events including the Purple Feet Harvest Festival and an Octoberfest. Its large back patio, designed for groups, has picnic and bistro tables, sun umbrellas, a horseshoe pit, and a stage. In fact, the property has a tradition of good times. For years, it was the site of a "barbecue barn" where people ate and danced. Almost every day, visitors to Silver Coast's tasting room say, "We used to come in when it was Sim's Barbecue." They reminisce about the pickers who played and the clogging they did. Although Maryann wanted to preserve parts of the old building, the wood was too decayed. She did manage to keep the barn's stone fireplace, which now anchors what she calls the winery's "winter room."

The winery's other areas include a tasting bar, a country-store gift shop, and an enormous barrel room inspired by the cave at Shelton Vineyards. Maryann says, "When I was working on the design of the barrel room, I told my husband that I was going to put a waterfall in, and he told me, 'Maryann, if you're going to put a waterfall, put a waterfall.'" She took his advice. The waterfall takes up one wall and creates, she believes, "a wonderful, soothing feeling." When the winery opened, people immediately asked to book the room for parties, wedding receptions, and meetings. As a result, it has "taken on a different character than originally anticipated," Maryann says. Rather than simply being used for storage, it has become a public space.

Silver Coast also has a high-ceilinged art gallery that displays the work of local artists. Maryann convinced one of her best friends from high school, Justine Ferreri, who owned an art gallery, to become the winery's curator and to choose all the work. In fact, Silver Coast showcases art not only on its walls, but also on its bottles. For the labels, Maryann decided to sponsor a contest. When she took out ads in the local newspaper, she expected to get approximately 60 entries, but she didn't anticipate the way the word would spread. Retired grandparents told their children. Vacationers took the ads home with them. By the deadline, Maryann had received more than 380 entries from all over the nation. She laughs, "My children didn't get Christmas presents," since the contest took up so much time. Although it was a difficult decision because "there were so many wonderful labels," she managed to narrow it down to 10 artists. The winners were exhibited at Justine's gallery, and their work appeared on the initial Silver Coast offerings. Maryann intended to use new designs every year, but she discovered that she liked the labels too much to change them so frequently.

Silver Coast grows several acres of muscadine vines, but since the area is unsuitable for vinifera, it buys the majority of these grapes from regional farmers. The winery produces 10,000 cases a year. Maryann doesn't expect to expand beyond that because, she notes wryly, "I still have a family, and I like them." In fact, the entire family has been involved in the winery since the beginning. Maryann remembers the day the tanks were delivered and she and her son Gabriel, who was six at the time, cleaned them. To get rid of a particularly tough patch of tartrate, she mixed a baking-soda paste and told him, "Okay, Gabriel, now we have to use some elbow grease." He picked up the paste and asked, "Mom, is this the elbow grease?" Maryann says, "It was so precious. He was so sincere. I had to spend the next 10 minutes explaining what elbow grease was."

Maryann feels good about what she has accomplished at Silver Coast. She likes the winery's physical elements, such as the ceiling lights from a renovated Baptist church, but she insists that what gives her the most satisfaction is "the reception of our customers." She says, "It was always my concept that in southeastern North Carolina, this would be considered 'our winery' by all the people who live here." She envisioned people asking, "Have you seen our winery?" This, she notes with pride, "seems to be happening." Guy Ferreri, Justine's husband, suggests one reason why. He says, "It's amazing to come down that dirt road. You don't know what you're going to see, and it's like the curtain comes up. It's a wonderful place."

Somerset Cellars

3906 East Arendell Street
Morehead City, N.C. 28557
Phone: 252-727-4800
Website: www.somersetcellars.com
E-mail: sales@somersetcellars.com
Hours: By appointment

Owners: Susan and Eric Luhmann
Winemakers: Eric and Susan Luhmann
First year as bonded winery: 2006
Tasting fee: No
On-line ordering: Yes
Wine club: Pending

Wine List
Whites: Chiaretto (white Zinfandel), La Savana Rosso Vino da Travola (Chianti), La Savana Vino Biano (Pinot Grigio), La Savanna Tre Vini Bianchi (white blend), Nektar von den Gottern (Riesling), Premi di Sabana Vino Biano (Grillo)
Reds: La Savana Audace Rossa (Petite Sirah and Zinfandel), La Savana Vino Ricca Rossa (Nebbiolo), La Savane Vin Classique Rogue (Cabernet), La Savane Vin Noir (Pinot Noir), Le Petite Oiseau Noir (Merlot), Sabana Mezclo Vino Tinto (Cabernet and Carmenère), Sabano Vino Tino Rico (Malbec), Vino Tinto de Sabana (Merlot)

Directions: The winery is in the back of the Parkway TV building on Arendell Street (N.C. 24) in Morehead City.

Eric Luhmann likes things clean. He says, "Walk through my house, you'll see. It's spotless." He acknowledges this desire may be because "I'm compulsive about everything I do," but he also believes it makes him a

Somerset Cellars tasting room
COURTESY OF SOMERSET CELLARS

good winemaker. He points out that failures in winemaking usually "are because of human errors, and that's due to a lack of cleanliness. It is the biggest key." Consequently, at Somerset Cellars, "everything is sanitized six times before the wine touches it."

Eric has been making wine for almost 20 years. He began as a hobbyist while living on Long Island. He remembers working with 55-gallon drums and going to get grapes from "an old Italian guy sitting in a recliner and chewing on a cigar. He would tell you, 'Get five cases of that, five cases of that, 10 cases of that, and 15 cases of that, and blend them up.' If you had any questions, you went back and asked him." Eric educated himself about winemaking by reading "everything I could get my hands on," talking to people, and hanging out with other winemakers in an informal club: "We'd go around to restaurants and share bottles of wine and critique them."

For a long time, Eric's friends told him his wine was good enough to be sold commercially. He insists, "My friends are real friends. They'll tell me if it's no good, and they'll spit it out. They're honest." However, Eric kept his winemaking a hobby as he put in 20-hour workdays pursuing careers in the tire and restaurant industries. Then, several years ago, Eric's leg was crushed in a freak accident, and he found himself unable to walk. He could no longer work the same hours, but he continued to make wine—"a lot of it," he laughs. In fact, "it got a little odiferous in the house. We got a bigger house, and it was still odiferous."

Because of his injury, Eric had a great deal of time to think about the wine industry. "I sat back, and I looked at this for years. I looked at every variable that was there, and the biggest variable was the production of the grapes." Eric decided that it wouldn't make business sense to try to develop a vineyard and struggle with the state's unpredictable climate, Pierce's disease, Japanese beetles, and other agricultural challenges. And he admits, "I'm not a farmer. If you give me a Ferrari and tell me that it's not right, I can make it right for you, but I'm not a farmer." Furthermore, even if he did want to grow grapes, real estate in Carteret County is expensive, and buying farmland would be cost-prohibitive. Consequently, when Eric opened Somerset Cellars in 2006, he did so with a winery model based on buying grapes from others.

Eric imports fruit from a variety of countries, including Italy, Germany, Argentina, Australia, Chile, and France, and it's computer technology that makes this feasible. He laughs, "Thank God for the Internet. We've built this company on it. I can look for grapes at three in the morning, and my spelling doesn't look as bad in Italy."

In addition to making crops more accessible worldwide, computers have affected other aspects of the wine industry. For example, they can dramatically reduce the time it takes a label to be approved. Eric explains, "It takes 45 days when you mail it to get into the hands of an agent. Nothing less. Anything wrong on that label, and it gets mailed back, and then it takes another 45 days after you've redone it because it goes to the back of the line." On-line applications are different. According to Eric, "You can have an answer in two days, and 99 percent of the time it's approved because the system is almost foolproof." If you have made a mistake, it goes to the top of the pile rather than the bottom when you resubmit the application. This reduced time in receiving government approval is crucial to Somerset Cellars, which is building its business on private labels for restaurants and special events such as weddings. Eric says that with the typical customer, ideas for a label will be passed back and forth several times. His wife, Susan, an artist, often helps with the design. Consequently, "there are four computers in my house. They're all burning up." Once the customer likes the proposed label, "even as we're talking on the phone, I'll be sending it to the agency for approval." It's an efficient way to operate, which is important to Eric, who emphasizes, "I hate inefficiency."

Eric was also efficient in planning the physical space of his winery. Somerset Cellars consists of 1,000 square feet, half of the space dedicated to equipment and half to a tasting room. Not surprisingly, Eric specializes in small batches. He doesn't filter his wines, a process he says is "unnatural" and takes away the flavor. He also keeps the sodium and sulfite levels as low as possible. As a result, "in 20 years of making wine, I've yet to have someone tell me that they get a headache drinking my wine."

When Somerset Cellars opened, Eric offered 14 different wines to find out what people liked. In the future, he probably will reduce these offerings, but he recognizes the need to be open-minded. For example, he didn't plan on making a White Zinfandel, but a friend pleaded with him to do so. Subsequently, when Eric brought it to the North Carolina Seafood Festival, "people went bonkers over it," and it was his bestseller.

The winery is growing faster than Eric expected, and although he wants it to develop, he doesn't want "the grand scale with 10,000-gallon tanks and five hoses." He sees Somerset Cellars as producing under 5,000 cases: "I want it to be as big as I can physically handle and still enjoy it. I do it because I love it. I don't have to do it. Everything's paid for. I have no debt."

Eric has four kids, and he might like to have them join the winery someday, but that's in the distant future. He says, "If they're interested in the business after college and after working for someone else for a while, maybe they'll come here." If they do so, however, they'll have to earn it. Eric laughs, "No nepotism." He can, however, envision a scenario in which his children run Somerset Cellars. He tells them, "I'll be here in the country for six months making wine. The other six months, I'll be traveling and finding grapes."

Eric loves to travel, but he has no desire to leave the area permanently. As someone who grew up in the Northeast and has been all over the world, he says, "I know how good it is down here. It's so peaceful." The area has "boating, the coastal waterway, fresh produce, and now," Eric laughs, "a winery conveniently located in Carteret County. It's paradise."

Appendix 1
New Wineries

The following wineries plan to open in 2007.

Allison Oaks Vineyards

2323 Old U.S. 421 East
Yadkinville, N.C. 27055
Phone: 336-414-6789 or 336-677-2659
Fax: 336-677-2192
Website: www.allisonoaksvineyards.com
E-mail: info@allisonoaksvineyards.com
Owners: Gene and Pam Renegar
Wine List: Cabernet Sauvignon, Chardonnay, Merlot, Orchard White, Proprietor's Blend

Lac Belle Amie Winery and Vineyard

195 Vineyard Drive
Elizabethtown, N.C. 28337
Phone: 910-645-6450
Website: www.LaBelleAmie.com
E-mail: info@LaBelleAmie.com
Owner: Vicki Weigle
Winemaker: Vicki Weigle
Wine List: Vinifera and muscadine wines

Appendix 2
Wine Trails

The Yadkin Valley appellation has almost two dozen wineries, all close enough together that several can be visited in a single afternoon or day. People can easily put together their own itineraries depending on the amount of time they have to spend and their tastes. There are also organizations that offer suggestions and scheduled tours. These include Yadkin Valley Wine Tours (www.yadkinwinetours.com; 336-793-4488) and the Yadkin Valley Wine Trail (http://www.allamericanwineries.com/nc/yvwt/), run by Bob Hodges of All American Wineries.

There are two formal wine trails or groups of wineries that market themselves together:

The Wineries of Swan Creek:
Buck Shoals Vineyard, Laurel Gray Vineyards, Raffaldini Vineyards, and Windy Gap Vineyards

The Haw River Wine Trail:
Benjamin Vineyards and Winery, Creek Side Winery, GlenMarie Vineyards and Winery, Grove Winery, and The Winery at Iron Gate Farm

In several places throughout the state, wineries that are clustered together are exploring the feasibility of applying for an American Viticultural Area designation. These include

The Knotts Island area:
Martin Vineyards, Moonrise Bay Vineyard, and Sanctuary Vineyards

The Uwharrie area:
Stony Mountain Vineyards and Uwharrie Vineyards

The Green Creek area:
Green Creek Winery and Rockhouse Vineyards

Appendix 3
Wine Festivals

Numerous wine festivals and events featuring wine are held throughout the state. Although the dates may vary, some of the major ones are as follows:

April
Beaufort Wine and Food Festival, Beaufort
Blue Ridge Wine Festival, Blowing Rock
Great Grapes Wine, Arts & Food Festival, Cary
Taste Carolina Wine Festival, Greensboro

May
Salute! The North Carolina Wine Celebration, Winston-Salem
Shine to Wine Festival, North Wilkesboro
Yadkin Valley Wine Festival, Elkin

June
Festival of the Vino, Chapel Hill
WSJS North Carolina Wine Festival, Tanglewood Park, Clemmons

July

River House Wine Festival, River House Inn, Grassy Creek

August

Vino Extravaganza, Pinehurst

September

North Carolina Muscadine Harvest Festival, Kenansville
Tar River Wine Festival, Rocky Mount

October

Foothills Wine, Art, and Music Festival, Wilkesboro
Great Grapes Wine and Music Festival, Charlotte
North Carolina Seafood Festival, Morehead City
Yadkinville Grape Festival, Yadkinville

November

Fall Art and Wine Festival, Wilmington
Southern Christmas Show, Charlotte

Index